Ehrenfried Pfeiffer (1899-1961)
A MODERN QUEST FOR THE SPIRIT

Ehrenfried Pfeiffer (1899 – 1961)

A MODERN QUEST FOR THE SPIRIT

Translated from the German by Henry Goulden

Pfeiffer's autobiographical memoirs; articles on etheric research and nutrition, the etherization of the blood, the function of the heart.

Compiled and Introduced by Thomas Meyer

Supplements by Lexie Ahrens and Paul Scharff, M.D.

A MODERN QUEST FOR THE SPIRIT
Ehrenfried Pfeiffer (1899-1961)

Pfeiffer's autobiographical memoirs on etheric research and nutrition, the etherization of the blood, the function of the heart, letters and memoirs from his estate.With contributions by Lexie Ahrens and Paul Scharff, M.D.

Originally published by
Thomas Meyer

Under the title:
EIN LEBEN FÜR DEN GEIST

English translation from the German by Henry Goulden

ISBN: 978-1-957569-38-3

MERCURY PRESS
an imprint of SteinerBooks
834 Main Street, PO Box 358
Spencertown, New York 12165
www.steinerbooks.org

Printed in the United States of America
by Integrated Books International

Contents

Translator's Preface
Introduction by Thomas Meyer ... 1
Editorial Preliminary Remarks ... 22

PART I: THE MEMOIRS OF EHRENFRIED PFEIFFER
Fragments of a Biography ... 29
A Soliloquy (1948) ... 121
The Heart as a Spiritual Organ of Perception (1950) ... 129
"This is a Problem of Nutrition" (1956) ... 145
The True Basis of Nutrition (1958) ... 147
On Experiencing the Christ (1959). ... 172
The Johannine Brotherhood (1959) ... 179

PART II: FROM PFEIFFER'S LETTERS
"Do We Pose the Right (…) Questions?" (To Ita Wegman, 1924) ... 185
Christian Rosenkreutz and the Spiritual Function of the Heart (To Gwenda Ormiston, 1950) ... 189
The Rosicrucian Background of Edith Maryon (to Lexie Ahrens, 1950) ... 191
R. Swinburne Clymer (to Lexie Ahrens, 1960) ... 193
In the Temple of Hatshepsut (to Lexie Ahrens, 1960) ... 199
Music — The Unfulfilled Aspiration (to Lisa von Herwarth, 1959) ... 201

PART III: PERSONAL MEMORIES OF PFEIFFER
Personal Memories of Ehrenfried Pfeiffer (by Lexie Ahrens) ... 205
Ehrenfried Pfeiffer and the Future (by Paul W. Scharff, M.D.) ... 211

Pfeiffer's Crystallization Work and its Role in the Origin of the Book *Fundamentals of Therapy: An Extension of the Art of Healing through Spiritual Knowledge* (by Paul W. Scharff, M.D) 217
A Conversation with Pfeiffer about the Night of the Fire (by Paul W. Scharff, M.D.). 219
The Background to the Plot for Poisoning Rudolf Steiner 225

APPENDIX

Sir Albert Howard's Deed for Science 229

References 239

Bibliography 271

Name Index 277

Translator's Preface

Pfeiffer's Autobiography was written in English, albeit "English" learnt for the most part in the U.S.A. It should be borne in mind that his mother tongue was German, so that when lost for words he uses German expressions, where we show the English between square brackets.

In translating the rest of the book, wherever possible the English originals of the various letters, articles, etc. have been used.

Thanks are due to those friends who assisted in translating difficult passages!

I am especially grateful for the professional assistance given by Dr. Desmond J. Cumberland in the preparation of this book for publication.

Henry Goulden
May 2009

Introduction

Ehrenfried Pfeiffer and the Appropriate Unfolding of Spiritual-Scientific Impulses in the Third Millennium

by Thomas Meyer

"In spiritual life there is not failure, but lack of success and postponement." [1]

1. In the Sign of the Light Epoch

Ehrenfried Pfeiffer was born on the same day that Kali Yuga—the five-thousand-year-long epoch of spiritual darkness—came to an end: on February 19, 1899.[2] More significantly: on the same day that the *New* Epoch began. Thus, as borne out by his entire life's work, he belongs with unexcelled precision to the very first pioneers of this new epoch which will prevail once again for thousands of years, overcoming all materialism, all delusions of power.

To the impulses of this Light Epoch, complementing and furthering natural science, belongs the Spiritual-Scientific approach to the world as inaugurated by Rudolf Steiner; a spiritual science that does not lead into abstract heights but reveals the spiritual foundation of the most material processes. For example, in accordance with this demand of the New Epoch, Rudolf Steiner established the fundamentals of a new agriculture, promoted the recognition and scientific support for the etheric formative forces active in all life and sketched a technology of the future based on the energy of the ether: three research projects in which Ehrenfried Pfeiffer, as well, was closely involved. Thus Pfeiffer with his friend Guenther Wachsmuth, created "Preparation 500," the first biodynamic manure preparation developed according to Steiner's indications. He

1. Ehrenfried Pfeiffer on December 12, 1948.

2.. Nicolaus Copernicus' birthday falls on February 19, 1473.

conducted experiments to demonstrate the existence of a life force while developing the method of "sensitive crystallization."[3] Throughout his life he was occupied with the possibility of developing a new technology based on the selfless management of etheric energy. However, in this respect he was warned by Rudolf Steiner to keep silent regarding the outcome of certain experiments: only when the threefolding of the social organism has been realized to a certain extent can implementation begin; until then, the danger of misuse would be far too great. In the stage model of the "Strader Apparatus" Steiner had given indications for the technical control of the "resonance of oscillations," with which the American John Worrell Keely (1837-1898) had already been successfully engaged; but to this day the essential key remains hidden or lost. Today many people are again in search of this key. A recent publication by Theo Paijmans about Keely contains a survey of investigations in this respect, including explicit reference to the indications of Steiner and the work of Pfeiffer.[4]

Meanwhile the crystallization method developed by Pfeiffer has been recognized and applied not only for the diagnosis of cancer and other disease, but also for the determination of food quality.[5]

Apparently the weakest continuation of his efforts has been accorded to his endeavors for a renewal of agriculture, although Pfeiffer did pioneering work in this area also: for example, he developed a compost starter and cultivated a new heat-resistant strain of wheat with increased protein content.[5]

Overall, Pfeiffer's work received the best response and publicity in America, where after his final immigration in 1940 he forged

---

3. See Bibliography: 1 and 2.

4. Theo Paijmans, *Free Energy Pioneer: John Worrell Keely*, IllumiNet Press, Lilburn, GA, USA, 1998, p. 320 and 448. See references 1 and 2.

5. See, for example, the work of Dr. Ursula Balzer-Graf at the *Forschungsinstitut für Vitalqualität* [Research Institute for Vital Quality] in Wetzikon (formerly in Frick), Switzerland. Website at: http://www.fiv.ch/.

numerous links with public research institutes and held occasional teaching positions at universities. In connection with early cancer diagnosis, Hahnemann Hospital in Philadelphia bestowed on him an honorary M.D.—in the same city where Keely developed his machines. And shortly before his death, the government of Korea approached him with an unusual manure project, described by Paul Scharff (p. 211).

2. The Hidden *Leitmotif*

No light will be thrown here on the details of Pfeiffer's life. Much can already be found in the portrayal by Alla Selawry,[6] much that is new in the contents of this volume; for example, that the very first lecture by Rudolf Steiner that the young Pfeiffer heard dealt with the ear and musical experience. The *musical* theme can in fact be regarded as the hidden leitmotif in Pfeiffer's life. To be sure, on the advice of Rudolf Steiner he officially studied chemistry in Basel. But from the Spiritually-Scientific point of view, the chemical ether also manifests as *sound ether,* thus revealing a secret affinity between the structure of matter and the human experience of sound. Pfeiffer not only possessed "absolute pitch," which alone is no proof of profound musicality, but he was also truly musical and had significant thoughts concerning music. One may read in these autobiographical sketches what he had to say on the subject of harmony and dissonance (respectively, disharmony) (see p.57), or what he wrote to Lisa von Herwarth in 1959. (see p.201f.)

This deep-seated musicality helps us understand Pfeiffer's love of peace and his need for harmony with man and the world. He yearned for a new "heart-thinking;" and not coincidentally the human heart in its physical and etheric aspects stood at the center

---

6. *Ehrenfried Pfeiffer: Pioneer of Spiritual Research and Practice*, by Alla Selawry, Translated by Joe Reuter and edited by Gerald Karnow, M.D., Mercury Press, Spring Valley, New York, 1992. Originally published as *Ehrenfried Pfeiffer - Pionier Spiritueller Forschung und Praxis, Begegnungen und Briefwechsel – Ein Beitrag zu seiner Biographie*, Philosophisch-Anthroposophischer Verlag Am Goetheanum, Dornach/Switzerland, 1987. See reference 2.

of his research for many years, reinforced by goal-directed meditations as well as a series of artistic sketches. His three "Heart Lectures" from the year 1950 bear witness to this research. As opposed to such "heart thinking," however, almost the whole of mankind today is dominated by "kidney-thinking." (See p.137) This alone can only produce destructive effects, which in today's worldwide science and politics are at work in the worst manner.

3. Relationship to Rudolf Steiner and His Other Students

Pfeiffer's relationship to Steiner had a unique dual nature. In his twenty-first year, the thirty-eight-years younger man wins a fatherly friend and counsellor; Steiner calls him familiarly by his Christian name, though he did so very rarely. Pfeiffer grasps the superhuman greatness of the spiritual researcher and at the same time is wonderfully sensitive to his human needs and vulnerability. During a lecture to workers on a very hot day, he takes care that his spiritul teacher has something to drink, like his listeners. Along with others, he acts as a youthful bodyguard on journeys. And on the night of the fire 1923/24, he helps Rudolf Steiner through the crisis (see also p.221).

The young pupil also transfers his great respect for the spiritual researcher and devoted love for the human being Rudolf Steiner to Marie Steiner, and after the death of the teacher stands faithfully at her side as a chivalrous protector. This loyalty even induces him in the year 1935 to sign the fatal, influential and manipulative "Memorandum,"[7] which prepared for the exclusion of Ita Wegman and Elisabeth Vreede from the Steering Committee of the General Anthroposophical Society, as well as the loss of numerous capable and in many cases leading members. This step prevented Pfeiffer from making or maintaining closer connections with similarly gifted and aspiring students of Rudolf Steiner such

---

7. *Denkschrift über die Angelegenheiten der Anthroposophischen Gesellschaft in den Jahren 1925 bis 1935* [Memorandum concerning the affairs of the Anthroposophical Society in the Years 1925 until 1935], Manuskriptdruck [Printed copy] Dornach 1935. See reference 3.

as Wegman, Vreede, George Adams, W. J. Stein and Ludwig Polzer-Hoditz: objectively a disadvantage. This contributed to the relative isolation from such congenial colleagues in which he had to carry on his work in the second half of his life, though fortunately with the help of a circle of loyal independent coworkers. D. N. Dunlop, for example, who had seen the Keely Engine with his own eyes at the end of the 19th century, would no doubt have bestowed his warmest support on this brilliant student of Rudolf Steiner's.

The most positive fruit of his loyalty to Marie Steiner consisted of Pfeiffer's impetus, on Rudolf Steiner's 100th birthday, toward a publication of the Centenary Edition of his complete works. If this project is now largely accomplished, that is chiefly thanks to Pfeiffer's energetic initiative, as can be inferred from his correspondence on the subject with Marie Steiner.[8]

Deep was the friendship which united Pfeiffer with Guenther Wachsmuth; equally deep his bonds with Ernst Lehrs and with Maria Roeschl, with whom he recalled sharing a spiritual experience in ancient Egypt (see letter to Lexie Ahrens, p. 205) And in America, Lexie Ahrens and Gwenda Ormiston belonged to his most intimate friends, as witnessed by a rich correspondence. But Pfeiffer also had friendly associations with his closest coworkers, such as Frieda Bessenich, Lisa von Herwarth, Erika Riese, Erika Sabarth, Alla Selawry and others, and with the physician Paul Scharff.

Pfeiffer's love of peace and objectivity fundamentally excluded any kind of partisanship. It did not correspond to his nature. And even if he once wrote, "*Alexander war nun mal nicht mein Fall*" [Alexander does not appeal to me] (to Lisa von Herwarth), he proved how deeply he could also acknowledge Dr. Wegman. Indeed it is noteworthy that Rudolf Steiner included him as a chemist in the preparation of the book *Grundlegendes für eine Erweiterung der Heilkunst* [Fundamentals for an Extension of the Art

---

8. Marie Steiner, *Briefe und Dokumente* [Letters and Documents], Dornach 1981. See reference 4.

of Healing][9], which he co-wrote with Ita Wegman (currently available as *Fundamentals of Therapy* from Mercury Press). Perhaps he did so also in the quiet hope that this young esoteric student, who only revealed his inmost being gradually and with difficulty, might not merely pass by certain other students silently and unnoticed. In order to reveal *this* little-known Wegman-thread in the tangle of Pfeiffer's human connections, quite a voluminous letter by him to Ita Wegman has been included. Extracts from another letter show how very close Pfeiffer was to the sculptress Edith Maryon.

Also in this realm of human relationships, Pfeiffer's life is clearly inclined to harmony with *all* of Steiner's students, even though this might only find fulfilment at a later time.

4. Swinburne Clymer—an American "Hilarius"

The most unusual and in some respects enigmatic friendship Pfeiffer made in the U.S.A. was with the doctor and occultist Reuben Swinburne Clymer (1878-1966). Since this connection has remained practically unknown until now, some light should be thrown on it. Since 1905, Dr.Clymer had been the Supreme Grand Master of the *Fraternitas Rosæ Crucis,* which was founded in the year 1614. The headquarters of this Order are located at Beverly Hall (Quakertown, Pennsylvania) near Philadelphia, as part of a spacious estate, where picturesque ponds are found, along with a small pyramid.

When and where Pfeiffer met Clymer is uncertain; but it may have been in the 'forties, possibly soon after his move to the U.S.A. In the *Heart Lectures* Pfeiffer speaks of a meeting with a "publicly unknown leading occultist" who made ominous statements in connection with occult opposition to the activity of Rudolf Steiner (p.130). This meeting must have taken place at the time of Pfeiffer's first American journey in 1934. Although this occultist, described by Pfeiffer as "grey," was likewise a doctor, this does not identify him with Clymer, who as the author of many books was not unknown. Also, other qualities of Clymer speak

9. G.A. 27. See reference 5.

against such an identification. It is possible, however, that both occultists stood in a more or less distant connection to one another.

Of Pfeiffer's relations with Clymer we only know something from the letters he wrote to Lexie Ahrens (p.195), as well as the memories of Paul Scharff (p.214). Pfeiffer constantly visited Beverly Hall—for recuperation, but also for intensive meditative work, Rosicrucian studies and conversations with Dr. Clymer. These visits were almost without exception kept hidden from his Anthroposphical friends and coworkers. Pfeiffer discovered the Templar background of Clymer and found him to have been one of the Templars who were tortured. Clymer confirmed Pfeiffer's discovery. This shows that Clymer had spiritual experiences of his own, but on the other hand was a faithful guardian of ancient occult traditions. These two elements make him appear comparable to the noble figure of "Hilarius", who, in Rudolf Steiner's fourth Mystery Play (*The Soul's Awakening*), is the Grand Master of a modern Rosicrucian order while having been Grand Master of the order of the Templars during his mediaeval incarnation (as presented in the second drama, "*The Soul's Probation*"). Besides, in the course of the fourth drama, the Egyptian incarnation of Hilarius is revealed, in which he had likewise been involved in the Mysteries and functioned as "Keeper of the Word." Although Hilarius distinguishes himself by an admirable acceptance of fate and unlimited spiritual faith, his spiritual experiences are often clouded by delusions, i.e. misjudgments no doubt because of too one-sided an emphasis on past occult traditions. This is shown most impressively when he dwells in the realm of Ahriman without recognizing the lord of that kingdom (Drama III, Scene 8). So it is also with the representatives of those occult streams of the West, well-intentioned in a certain sense, with whom Pfeiffer came in contact through Clymer:[10] A certain blind spot prevented them from advancing with the times. For example, in the Rosicrucian movement which Clymer repre-

---

10. We are here disregarding those lodges that in the service of Anglo-Americanism clearly pursue aims of power politics and partly work with dangerous occult means from grey to black ceremonial magic.

sented, Christian Rosenkreutz is valued purely as a mythical figure and not taken to be a real individuality. Yet just as Hilarius formed a bond with the esoteric students, so Clymer, through his friendship with Pfeiffer, joined the sphere of the most modern spiritual research, though with great reservations. In this sense, the friendship of Clymer and Pfeiffer (here representing "Strader") is fraught with great future significance: it demonstrates how the Spiritual-Scientific movement of Steiner can and should join with reputable representatives of other occult streams in a fruitful union. These parallels to the themes in Steiner's mystery dramas seem justified, for Pfeiffer had a profound knowledge of the dramas and valued them highly.[11] He had seen all the plays in Dornach with his own eyes and called the dramatic tetralogy the "Book of Life," in deliberate contrast to the Egyptian "Book of the Dead".

The Chapel at Beverly Hall displays a colored glass panel which Dr. Clymer himself brought over from Europe; supposedly it was once in the possession of Jacques de Molay, the last Grand Master of the Templar order, who together with Guy de Normandie was burnt at the stake in Paris in March of 1314. This is not to claim that Pfeiffer considered Clymer a reincarnation of de Molay.

Besides questions about occult streams, Pfeiffer and Clymer must also have discussed many other topics of occult life and development. A later Supreme Grand Master of the order, G. E. Poesnecker[12], affirmed to this writer that a number of Pfeiffer's letters to Clymer are archived in Beverly Hall. The problem of the new technology based on the use of "harmonization of oscillations," amongst others, is dealt with. It is quite obvious that the two friends would have discussed this question, which closely con-

11. See his comments *On Rudolf Steiner's Mystery Dramas*, four lectures by Ehrenfried Pfeiffer, Nov/Dec 1948, Mercury Press, Spring Valley, New York, 1988. See reference 6.

12. Dr. G. E. Poesnecker was Supreme Grand Master from 1983-2003. Dr. William G. Kracht is the current Supreme Grand Master, since 2003.

cerns the mechanical occultism[13] cultivated in the West. Unfortunately an examination of Pfeiffer's letters was denied.[14] In the correspondence of Pfeiffer available to this writer, none with Clymer was discovered. After Pfeiffer's death on November 30, 1961, Clymer wrote an encoded tribute entitled "*Graal L*", [15] reading, in part:

"*Graal L was of two positive natures.* With him there was no middle ground. To his search for the basic mysteries of life he gave *every thought* during the hours when he was so engaged. The search WAS LIFE ITSELF TO HIM. It possessed him mentally. But the precious hours outside his laboratory found him engaged in duties as a citizen, a husband and father, offering his personal *Spiritual* devotions and serving as Monitor and guide to the select group over which he presided at call.

"On the opposite side of his nature, in his *Spiritual* search for reality, he was equally positive, PERMITTING NOTHING OTHER THAN AN EMERGENCY *to in any way interfere.* HE CONCENTRATED INTENSELY and during his period of *devotion* NOTHING EXISTED IN MIND AND EMOTION OTHER THAN THE DESIRE TO ACHIEVE THE ULTIMATE. It is not to be wondered at that he was as successful in his *Spiritual* efforts as he was in his search for the basis, the secret, of life. He succeeded within a very short time in reaching the VERY HEART of the CENTER IN THE TEMPLE WHERE HE FOUND THE INEFFABLE LIGHT BRIGHTLY BURNING ON THE ALTAR

---

13. Cf. R. Steiner's remarks of December 1, 1918, G.A. 186, *The Challenge of the Times*, reference 7. See also *Der Strader-Apparat, Modell—Skizzen – Berichte* [The Strader Apparatus, Model—sketches—reports], in *Beiträge zur Rudolf Steiner Gesamtausgabe* [Supplements to the Collected Edition of Rudolf Steiner], Dornach, Nr. 107, Michaeli [Michaelmas] 1991. See reference 8.

14. According to Dr. Poesnecker, the writer could possibly have gained access to the letters by joining the order.

15. p.121f. in *The Great Work –The Council of Three*. Quakertown, PA: Philosophical Publishing Co. Orders from megbevhall@comcast.net. See reference 9.

AND, BIBLICALLY SPEAKING, FOUND GOD IN THE LIGHT AS HAD JOHN. He did more, *much more*, than any other Initiate had accomplished within the last hundred years. He *found the* CENTER OF LIGHT SO COMPLETELY REVEALED THAT HE WAS ABLE TO ILLUSTRATE THAT WHICH, ordinarily speaking, CANNOT BE ILLUSTRATED.

"Such was *Graal L*, one of the gods, a Son of God.

"Although positive in all things, his nature was kind, sympathetic, and most forgiving to those *not* on the *Path*. In those on the *Path* he would brook no weakness, no excuse, no infringement on the right, no immorality or irresponsibility. He not only expected, but he demanded obedience of those who had entered the *Path*. HE LIVED HIS PHILOSOPHY, FAITHFUL IN THE PRACTICE OF HIS DEVOTIONS. He was SELECTIVE BY NATURE. Many recognized his greatness, while not knowing why, even though he was most modest in all things except when TEACHING THE LAW. Those who admired him as an *examplar* and sought to become one of the group of Unknowns who met on call or by request, usually were refused because he immediately recognized weaknesses in them which he knew they would not overcome because of their lack of DESIRE AND WILL, too ready to find excuses for not doing what they must in order to succeed in the *Great Work*. He was fully aware that they would be a hindrance to others on the *Path*. In his *Spiritual* nature he was like *John*, in his practice the opposite. Whereas *John practiced and preached, Graal L* practiced and mostly observed the Law of *Silence*. Their *Paths* led in opposite directions though their aims were the same." —This passage shows just as clearly the deep respect Clymer had for his friend as it reveals his misjudgment of the significance of *Rudolf Steiner*. Towards the end of this tribute, Clymer writes: "…Having a premonition that his transition would soon take place, he spoke of the work he was trying to do for humanity in the material realm, … he said that he would do all he could to wisely direct those who were so closely associated with him in the little group and felt confident they would continue to be guided in the way he had led them until one by one they entered the *Path*. —This was *Graal L* the

Initiate, *Brother in the Light*, whose heart was as big as heaven itself. Knowing him as *we* did, and others could only guess—and of his preparation for a return incarnation, we are as certain as life itself that he will be one of the LEADERS OF MEN by the time the old age reaches its climax."

The twenty-one-year-older Clymer outlived Pfeiffer by five years. Pfeiffer's ashes do not lie in Spring Valley, the place where most of his Anthroposophical activity took place in the U.S.A.; his widow buried them in Chester, near New York, where Adelheid Pfeiffer, who had for decades selflessly and actively supported and accompanied his life and work, had been the chief manager of their farm.

5. The "Spirit of Purity" and the Capacity for Imagination

As Clymer also strongly experienced, Pfeiffer's life was a path of the strictest esoteric discipleship. On such a path, the true significance of moral qualities for inner development, as well as the difference between mere intellect and living spirituality, become more concrete with every step. However, this must never deteriorate into a barren black and white. For example, in connection with what may be called an inner purity of striving, Pfeiffer, with total strictness towards himself and others, had a wonderful, differentiated attitude. Thus, he wrote on December 16, 1950, in a letter to Gwenda Ormiston: "Now I must say something very strange: one can be a sinner and still bear holiness in one's heart. …No matter how impure and sinful and erring we are, if we bear the spirit of purity in us we can remain pure. No matter how much we are drawn to emotions and 'physical things,' with the spirit of purity we can make them a holy sacrament, as long as we don't lose ourselves but elevate our heart to the realm of the spirit. What we make with it counts. If we get inwardly richer, deeper, freer: we can always stand before the altar with pure hearts." In other words: as long as the star of the higher, true self has been *seen* and its light *experienced* in the everyday self, then "purity" is still possible even in the greatest darkness of the soul. No abstract either/or; no fruitless dualism between "good" and "evil"; no judgment or self-condemnation lead forward on the path of inner development; but solely and alone the will to hold fast to the “spirit of purity” under whatever circumstances. This, too, requires courage and fearlessness. The same teaching is presented by the central figure of Steiner’s mystery dramas, Johannes Thomasius, who in the course of his development learns to distinguish between his true Self and his everyday self which is still far from bearing likeness to it.

This observation by Pfeiffer shows how well he had succeeded in cultivating true objectivity not only in the realms of nature and the spirit, but in that of the soul, also.

The intellect itself must be managed in a similarly differentiated way. Although it must be the basis of every healthy beginning of spiritual activity, nor may be dispensed with even *after* the start—it yet must allow other soul forces to work alongside it.

Pfeiffer, already protected from one-sided use of the intellect by his profound musicality, took further pains not to fall into one-sided intellectuality in his lectures by means of painting. Thus he wrote on December 8, 1950, again to Gwenda Ormiston: “Painting—in a rather unconventional way, not modern, not typically Anthroposophic, but certainly not academic— is a recreation to me, when the brain is overworked—a kind of spiritual relaxation, and many problems which cannot be solved by mere thinking find answer through the imaginative medium of painting. Many of my lectures have been prepared this way—the subject stands before the mental eye as a picture—while painting, color and form blend together and thought is born. This helps never to become abstract, but to remain in the ever-living flow of the ether. In fact, only then I can ‘think’ if it is preceded by this imaginative activity.”

Pfeiffer also found a certain unsurmounted intellectualism amongst one or another of his fellow Anthroposophists. After a last visit to Dornach, he wrote (in German) to Lisa von Herwarth on January 13, 1959: “The natural science discussions…have unfortunately much disillusioned me. There is endless theory and dilettantism behind them.” To the same addressee on February 23, 1958, he declared, “… that our anthrop. natural scientists… for example,

Schiller, instead of imagination develop scruples."[16] He even felt impelled to raise a serious objection to a work which his coworker Selawry published (with her brother)[17], although he acknowledged its worth and significance for the outer world: "I cannot help feeling a certain pain. The crystallization work should awaken imagination. This work does not do that." (To Lisa von Herwarth on January 15, 1957.) Also in his "Soliloquy" (p.121), Pfeiffer notably deplored the tendency to supply external "proofs" instead of "awakening the imagination" where extrasensory etheric force is concerned.

In Pfeiffer's mind, impurity of striving and an unwillingness to awaken the capacity for imagination alongside the intellect could well be regarded as the two greatest obstacles on an individual's spiritual path. And if many individuals do not overcome these obstacles, then the whole Spiritual-Scientific movement is threatened with the danger of becoming contaminated and intellectualized.

6. Witness of Dark Opposition

Through his destiny as through his inner wakefulness, fearlessness and the purity of his spiritual striving, Pfeiffer was as though predestined to look especially deeply into the opposition against Rudolf Steiner's Spiritual Science. At barely twenty-four years of age, he was an eyewitness to the worst external attack against Ru-

---

16. For Paul Eugen Schiller, see Christoph O. Podak, "Towards a History and Sociology of the Anthroposophical Research Institutes in the 1920s." Translated from the original German by Paul Carline, Archetype: Newsletter Articles Supplement, Science Group of the Anthroposophical Society in Great Britain, London, Issue No. 5, September 1999, pp. 48-60; The Schiller File: Paul Eugen Schiller, Supplement to the Collected Edition of Rudolf Steiner Beiträge Nr. 122, Scientific Research Suggested by Dr. Rudolf Steiner, Translated by Henry Goulden, Henry Goulden Books, Delabole, Cornwall, 2007, pp. 113-127. See reference 10.
17. Selawry, Alla and Oleg, Kupferchlorid-Kristallisation in Naturwissenschaft und Medizin [Copper Chloride Crystallization in Natural Science and Medicine], Stuttgart 1957. See reference 11.

dolf Steiner's activity, the burning of the first Goetheanum, on New Year's Eve, 1922/23, and, as was already mentioned, it fell to him on the night of the fire to help Rudolf Steiner over the most critical moments in his spiritual career, as also emerges from Paul Scharff's report on p.219. It is also clear from a few important remarks stated in Pfeiffer's recollections (p.92), that the process of the burning was watched and the firefighting deliberately hindered in an occult manner.

And once again, it is to Pfeiffer that we owe one of the most important disclosures concerning the background to the poison plot on Steiner one year after the fire. His remarks, made to a small circle during his last stay in Dornach, have more the character of a legacy. What Pfeiffer communicated has much more weight than any previously accepted explanation of the events of the afternoon of January 1, 1924. Since in connection with this New Year's attack on Steiner a widely accepted "fable convenue" sets the tone in certain anthroposophical circles even today, we have decided to publish the authentic record of a witness, anonymously, however, for the person's protection, of these communications by Pfeiffer (p.225).

About ten years after Rudolf Steiner's death, certain facts were once more revealed to Pfeiffer in the U.S.A. that are connected with Steiner's illness and premature death. They concern the grey-to-black magical opposition of certain Western occultists to Steiner's revelations about the future function of the heart (p.129).

This varied evidence by Pfeiffer for the direct attacks against Spiritual Science and the person of Rudolf Steiner may incite every reader of the corresponding reports to greater vigilance concerning this kind of hostility. It is also important today, as the completely unfounded accusations of racism bear witness which in recent years have again and again been maliciously directed at anthroposophy in public.

7. Sentinel Regarding Indirect Opposition

Just as Pfeiffer had to experience painfully how in the field of crystallization "departures were made from the original spiritual impulse," so other fields of work which Rudolf Steiner left for humanity to develop after the end of Kali Yuga often were also radically "departed from." A deviation from the original goals and impulses – not to be confused with a *shift* in certain goals when circumstances and changes in the human environment prompted a modification – is always the opening for a second, indirect kind of opposition: for "coworkers" who fail to harbor the core impulse, but only wish to grasp for certain fruits to be distributed *in their manner*. Pfeiffer can also open our eyes to this kind of *self-created* menace against pure Spiritual-Scientific substance, or to the danger of its seizure by another spiritual stream: and this is of especially pressing concern today. In his lectures, *The Spiritual Leadership of Mankind* from the year 1947,[18] Pfeiffer describes a conversation with the abbot of a Catholic monastery. "We discussed educational topics. The next morning I went in to see him and saw all the published books of Rudolf Steiner on his desk. I asked, 'How did you come to these works?' He said, 'That man had very good ideas. His only fault was that he spoke of reincarnation two hundred years too early. We have to prepare the people for another two hundred years, and then we, too, will speak of reincarnation.'" One should not pass over such a remark too hastily. It shows quite clearly that the fight over the central substance of Spiritual Science – which includes reincarnation also – with this kind of adversary consists not of their rejecting it, but much rather of seizing it for themselves and then doling it out to humanity under *their* direction.[19] This can mean under some circumstances, as in the above

18. *The Spiritual Leadership of Mankind*: Notes from lectures given in 1947, Mercury Press, Spring Valley, NY, 1985. See Lecture V, "Rudolf Steiner", August 17, 1947, p. 63, at reference 12.
19. A further actual example of this tendency to take over is to be found in the Russian edition of Valentin Tomberg's work on the Tarot, whose translation bears a foreword by the former chairman of Roman religious doctrine, Cardinal Ratzinger, now Pope Benedict XVI.

example, that spiritually researched scientific facts are first concealed, then given to humanity at a later point in time by another hand, detached from the intentions and name of Rudolf Steiner. He had such prospects in view when he emphasized that his work should never become separated from his name.[20]

In the same lecture quoted above, Pfeiffer mentions a further example which can likewise throw light on this conflict of the spirit. "Another time I had a discussion with a leading Jesuit in the country. He was interested in biodynamic agriculture and said it would provide the only suitable environment for the social order of the future[21]. I said: 'Are you clear that this originates with Rudolf Steiner, whom the Catholic church attacks?' He replied: 'Oh, yes, we are fully aware of that.' I continued, 'He also taught reincarnation.' He said: 'There is nothing in the Bible to contradict the teaching of reincarnation.' I cannot go further into the question here, but would only say: if *we* do not take the teaching seriously—others will."

Thus it is not simply a matter of whether one finds agreement with anthroposophical ideas here or there, but *in what sense* this assent takes place. The future social order in the sense of Jesuitism would of course be quite different from that of Steiner's; for example, it would never allow the development of a truly free spiritual life. This is completely obvious, for it follows directly from the basic principles of Jesuitism that all spiritual life must bear the stamp of Rome. Pfeiffer's here briefly-sketched conversations deserve genuine attention, particularly today, when certain circles

---

20. See for example the lecture of October 25, 1915. GA 254: *The Occult Movement in the Nineteenth Century*, Rudolf Steiner Press, 1973, Lecture Ten at reference 13.

21. Certain current efforts to establish the "Civil Society" and threefolding of the social order, including the bio-dynamic method of working the economy in the Philippines, should be seen in the light of this conversation. See webpages: http://www.cadi.ph/civil_society.htm and http://www.globenet3.org/threefold.shtml.

place great value on worldwide recognition, no matter how superficial,[22] of anthroposophical content.

Thus Pfeiffer's activity can result not only in impulses for positive collaboration with genuine, i.e. knowledge-, not power-aspiring representatives of other spiritual streams (such as Swinburne Clymer), but also in criteria for dealing with the second, indirect type of opposition. Knowledge of these criteria would be particularly important at the present time; for while no clear-headed student of Spiritual Science will believe that he could or should work together with a direct adversary, cooperation with indirect adversaries is often engaged in within the Anthroposophical Society. But this leads quite unavoidably to a diluted substance of Anthroposophic Spiritual Science.[23]

In regard to this danger of dilution, Pfeiffer in no way held it to be guaranteed that pure anthroposophical work and research should or must forever be carried out exclusively through the channel of the Anthroposophical Society.

He once reminded Gwenda Ormiston of certain words of Rudolf Steiner (from the year 1919): "It could happen that one day anthroposophy would have to free itself from the Anthroposophical Society. This should not happen, but the possibility will arise." Insofar as Steiner's impulses and views have recently been criticized or distorted even by leading representatives of the Anthroposophical Society itself,[24] one must say today: what was for Steiner

---

22. One thinks of the questionable, because remaining mostly superficial recognition of the work of Rudolf Steiner here and there through the combining of that which many people see as significant contained in the works of Joseph Beuys.

23. It is obvious that a consistent rejection without compromise of cooperation with indirect adversaries must not lead to intolerance towards them. One must make a distinction: tolerance belongs to the realm of social intercourse between people; in the area of Truth, this noble virtue has no place.

24. We cite here as typical examples 1. The claim made by the council of the Dutch National Society in February 1996 that Steiner held racist views – an imputation which remains unchallenged by the General Anthroposo-

a mere possibility has meanwhile become a necessity: anthroposophical spiritual-scientific work must *also* be undertaken and encouraged quite independently of the above-named Society. But every spiritual-scientific work, even if conducted independently of the Society, must also sooner or later face the danger of dilution, and the criterion of purity as set by Pfeiffer can in no way be dispensed with.

8. Closing Chord

Ehrenfried Pfeiffer distinguished himself by a surprising youthfulness and capacity for learning even in his last years. "It is gratifying to me," he writes to Lisa von Herwarth in the year of his death, on Feb. 6, 1961, "that this nearly sixty-two-year-old brain is still capable of new ideas and can also carry them out. I care a great deal about the practical side and the carrying out. For that is how I have won my position here and in the outside world. Healthwise it could go better. The spirit and the soul remain fresh and young, but the body lags somewhat. But still I am ever astonished when I see my contemporaries – *how old* they are. I definitely do not feel like that yet."

And in connection with the Anthroposophical Society in America, he remarks in the same letter: "The Anthrop. Society here gives me great concern – it becomes weaker and weaker and less active, loses itself. And yet Rudolf Steiner's books are bought as never before – but the readers are not drawn to the Society. When I hold public lectures, these are always well attended, by the hundreds. In the N.Y. branch: poorly, although my lectures are the

---

phical Society (GAS) [1999]. 2. The introduction to the English edition of the *Zeitgeschichtlichen Betrachtungen* [Historical Comments.] *The Karma of Untruthfulness*, Vol. II; Rudolf Steiner Press, 1992, webpage: http://wn.rsarchive.org/Lectures/KarmUntru2/KarUn2_intro.html] suggests that Steiner was emotionally biased, thus considerably compromising his Spiritual-Scientific authority, was published in the *Nachrichtenblatt für Mitglieder* [Newssheet for Members] on March 15, 1992, and is still sanctioned by the *Vorstand* [The Executive Council] of the GAS. See references 14 and 15, respectively.

best attended ones. To the class readings only 15 to 18 come, out of 200 members in N.Y. But what disturbs me more is the inferiority of the Anthroposophical public."

*

Pfeiffer looks back on his last years with increasing satisfaction. In July 1958 he composed a many-sided hymn of thankfulness with the title "If This Would Be My Last Day" and sent copies to Lexie Ahrens and Gwenda Ormiston. He begins with the sentences: "I would bless you, O Lord, that you let me suffer. I would thank you, O Lord, that you let me enjoy the things of this world." He closes with the sentence: "LET EVERY DAY BE MY LAST DAY."

The disregard, underestimation and criticism from which his work often suffered even at the hands of Anthroposophic friends is entirely overcome and pardoned. Pfeiffer turns from his customary natural-scientific or biodynamic research ever more toward inner mystical experience, to occult sleep- and dream-life and towards the whole future. The former is demonstrated by his notes describing his thoughts about experiencing Christ. (p.172 ff.)[25]

Pfeiffer writes about revealing night-experiences and dreams. Once he teaches in a light-filled hall. Many chairs, coming and going, completely surrounded by flowers instead of floor or walls. "I talked and one after another left the hall. I was terribly depressed that I could not hold them and awoke. While awakening, I heard a voice: 'You fool, don't you see that they have to go because they are awakening and return to their bodies.'" He described this dream as "sweet," which shows that he was almost

25. If a slight reservation is permitted here, it is that this very intimate description of the thought element as opposed to that of experience appears somewhat underrated; anyway, according to Rudolf Steiner, there is also the very important "thought way to Christ." (See the lecture of February 11, 1919, *Inner Aspect of the Social Question*, Rudolf Steiner Press, London, 1974, ref.16. http://wn.rsarchive.org/Lectures/19190211p01.html, GA 193. Pure thought is actually spiritual substance and can also be followed as a path to Christ..

childishly pleased about the "disappointment" and explanation. And he earnestly comments further: "This is probably the best part of my self which teaches and learns on the other side, at night. But there are also hostilities so strong that I cannot take it and awaken in the middle of the night, to be back in the physical – for protection. It is strange this living in two worlds." (July 22, 1954, to Gwenda Ormiston.)

Six weeks before his death on November 30, 1961 he spoke – fittingly, one could say – about experiences of the threshold.[26]

"Now let me do something drastic. Imagine I am dead," he suddenly said to his listeners, illustrating a karmic-spiritual situation. "All of you here would now be a part of me; I would have to talk and converse with you as if you were part of my own self. I would be absolutely in tune with you… There are some people with whom I have had fights. There are some people whom I love, and others again who sometimes drive me up the wall. I am not analyzing right now who these might be, but just say this for argument's sake, so don't take it personally. There are some people who are closer to me, so that I will recognize them better after death, particularly those with whom I have established a karma, good or bad as might be. They will present their bills right away… and the same is of course true of you. When any one of you dies, whatever you have experienced is part of you. It is your inner soul environment, just as this physical three-dimensional world is your outward physical environment."

Thus Pfeiffer already anticipates the after-death panoramic experience and the following kamaloka stages and also allows his friends to take part in the most beautiful way in the impending *complete* crossing of the threshold.

---

26. "On Threshold Experience." Unedited notes of a lecture given at Threefold Farm on September 10, 1961, in *Ehrenfried Pfeiffer, Notes and Lectures, Compendium II*, Mercury Press, Spring Valley, NY, 1991, pp. 92-103. See reference 17.

And then suddenly there bursts forth a strong hope for the future, regarding the new life on Earth which he will want to lead on his return.

"Rudolf Steiner has painted the picture for us that the end of this century will be the decisive moment for all humanity. Many religions, many esoteric groups tell us the same. I don't want to be in Heaven at this decisive moment. I would like to be here on Earth to witness the turning toward the good and contribute as much ego-consciousness to it as I have been able to attain."

Will it become a life in the service of new mystery-music, to which Ehrenfried Pfeiffer's inmost being was always impelled? Certainly a further life for the spirit. And if in the Pfeiffer-life there was no lack of sharp dissonances – not to be equated with disharmonies – in the next life, this individuality will want to work with the power of a new harmony drawn from the unity which rules life after death as well as before rebirth.

May many contemporaries join this true Rudolf Steiner student in finding new ways of working on Earth, so that the growing community of free spirits can assure that the turn of the Third Millennium becomes "the Turning to the Good."

Editorial Preliminary Remarks

The Autobiography – "Fragments of a Biography": Pfeiffer wrote these notes in English over the course of a few months for Lexie Ahrens, which were part by part sent to her. He began on August 29, 1958 with the title "Fragments of a biography which will be written down as it comes to mind." After their completion they were unrevised; publication had not been considered.

Remarks by Pfeiffer in the manuscript are often between round brackets. Further marginal notes or references for Lexie Ahrens are included as footnotes. Notes and references of the publisher are between square brackets.

GA = *Rudolf Steiner Gesamtausgabe*
[Collected Edition of Rudolf Steiner].

PART I

THE MEMOIRS OF EHRENFRIED PFEIFFER

FROM MY LIFE

Fragments of a biography which will be written down as it comes to mind.

No sequence intended so far.

The young boy felt rather lonely and did not participate in the usual games of children of his age. He was frequently ill, got very easy tired and together romping with others would mean another fever and a few days in bed. So he was well protected and dreamed his own worlds, feeling embarassed, shy when the outside world entered his sphere, which, as he felt was cruel, egotistic and not artistic - esthetic at all.

August 29, 1958

Fragments of a biography which will be written down as it comes to mind

1. No Sequence Intended So Far

The young boy felt rather lonely and did not participate in the usual games of children of his age. He was frequently ill, got very easy tired and together romping with others would mean another fever and a few days in bed. So he was well protected and dreamed his own world, feeling embarrassed, shy when the outside world entered his sphere, which, as he felt was cruel, egotistic and not artistic-esthetic at all.

He loved to be alone, play his own games and, above all, wander through nature, rain or shine, hour after hour, long distances through the woods and fields, or lie on a pasture and look into the sky or on the bank of a stream and watch the fishes, snails, crustaceae in the water and the floating weeds. From these excursions fish, plants, little crayfish were brought home, put into an aquarium which got larger from year to year, and it was carefully observed how these creatures and plants grew, whether laid eggs and hatched (the water snails with a little spiral house did very successfully) or the fish produced little ones, which one day swam of mother's womb, like a gate opened. Twelve were counted on one occasion and the satisfaction was great. The plants grew and eventually produced tiny white blossoms and fruit.

The boy had piano and violin lessons and discovered that one fish (a stickleback) responded to the sound of the high E and began to swim in curves and finally jump above the water. Another lazy *Schlammpeitzger,* a long, eel-like body, would always lie at the bottom of the aquarium but get very excited when a thunderstorm approached.

There were also frogs and toads, not so successfully raised from *Kaulquappen* [tadpoles], brought home. And a thick, fat fellow with a beard, which got excited and somersaulted when the beard touched morsels of food which had sunk to the bottom. To watch all this were the great pleasures.

There were also two birds, a *Stieglitz* [goldfinch] or *Distelfink* [thistle finch], which sang beautifully and a female canary which once lost an egg while flying about in the living room (no father known.) The *Distelfink* was quite tame and very curious, studying every object. Its favored game was to sit on the thread sole [spool] of a sewing machine and to turn with it, carousel fashion, when grandmother or aunt sewed. This game enchanted the boy to sew pieces together, just to give the bird a chance to carousel.

One day the window stood open and the canary flew out, to return immediately as of being scared by the wide spaces outside.

With the nature-excusions all afternoon, after school, all spring and summer, the school-homework suffered; there was just no time for it, and the marks during the summer were not so good.

Homework was usually done in the streetcar going to school and, understandable in that shaky vehicle, on the knees the handwriting was not too good, so that he got always a half mark less for bad writing.

School was not liked, for the boy judged the teachers according to their behavior, human weaknesses, losing their temper etc. etc. The boy felt these men were actually two: a) a mortal, b), that which they taught. Since both did not always agree one with another, teachers were no authority to him, with a few exceptions, and he could not believe that that which they taught could be the truth. The teacher of religion once asked what "*ein gottgefälliges Leben ist,"* [is a life pleasing to God] answered: "to pay taxes willingly, to marry and have children." Out went interest in religion.

God, to him, was that which he felt in nature, the play of the light on the surface of the water, the murmur of the water, jumping over stones, the song of the wind, tender or storm, in the tree crowns. Here especially, he felt, was a language (of objectivity) which spoke to him and which he could understand. The chatter and gossip of men, especially when they talked about others, what they should do or did not do right, was distasteful, and so there was nothing "human" which attracted him, nor did he understand it, nor did he have interest in it. His world just did not match or meet the human world. (It took many years before he learned to appreciate the human world.) When asked what he would like to learn and to become, he would say: to look deeper into nature and to discover the finer forces in nature, in the forces and energies of nature, things about which never anything was said in school, but which he knew to exist = the causes or laws behind nature. The lessons in physics or other natural sciences were miserable – one teacher was a choleric and began to swear when physical experiments did not succeed; one teacher of biology became insane, and the course was never re-opened, and so nothing got spoiled – the boy just was not convinced that there was any truth in that which the teachers tried to teach.

Since he kept his world to himself, was never asked about and never talked about, this world was protected, and the poor teaching did no harm, for it did not touch or spoil his own world.

One experience is worth to be reported – in fact this was experienced twice, once during summer vacation at the home of a forester in Thürnhofen and the other on a pasture near the Rathsberg, Erlangen (Peculiar Karma that in 1957 the compost plant-pilot plant for Germany was built quite close to this spot.) Night, lying on a pasture, looking into the clear, starstrewn sky – suddenly the sky disappeared and the Heaven opened with the world of Being and a wondersome music sounded—the sphere harmony. The boy felt that this was not so much heard with the ear, but with the entire body, which seemed to become one with the sound, its own sound blending together with these harmonies. The boy was nine at the time. He knew that in sound something speaks to him of the inner being of man and of nature and that each thing and being could reveal its innermost and speak to him through its sound. He would therefore listen also to the sound of walking steps and know the character of man, and from the way how people talked, he could tell them how they felt, happy, depressed or else, and from here it was then only a small step just "to know" what other people thought. He astounded them often by telling them *WHAT* they thought. The isolation grew the more, for it was not always welcome to have one's thoughts revealed, and the fact that what people said and what he *knew* that they thought did not help to increase his respect.

So it came that when the school taught that the human being descends from the animal, he accepted this eagerly, looking upon man just as another animal. Indeed, less than animal, for animals in their "language" tell themselves and do not lie. To overcome this conflict and not to disrespect human beings took many years, decades in fact, but in a way predestined to become a scientist with the desire to learn the objective.

There was a friend, throughout all these years from 9 to 17, Willi Palm, who shared many of these excursions, silent. We could wander hours through the woods and know exactly everything the other thought and felt. We both loved music, and in the adolescent years went to every concert and theater when old enough to be permitted to go there. Willi died when he was eighteen, the only friend I had up to that moment.

However, the extremely sensitive ear this boy had, about whom we write, made the listening to music, if not 100% perfect, rather painful, and a special dislike of singers developed which was never overcome. Only the truly *glockenreine Stimmen* [pure bell-like voices] did not cause discomfort, and so it became after a while a torture to go to concerts and opera, a property which still prevails today. To make this understood: only such precision as f.i. [for instance] a performance conducted by Toscanini would appeal to his sensitive ear.

To go on with his sensitivity in later life would be impracticable, and so much of these refined senses got lost. The man of now almost sixty years is still sensitive and "knows" how others "feel," though he has made himself appear hardened, but he still is so sensitive to his nearer or personal environment that he suffers considerably and tries not to let people enter his sphere, to put up a wall, to appear cold or intellectual, to put up the front of the scientist, not to show compassion, f.i. [for instance], for the influences and impact of the environment would be intolerable. So the isolation is today as great as it was in childhood and boyhood – in spite of knowing now more about the finer forces of nature, the deeper meaning of the human being, etc., etc.; that is, the resulting inner conflict has never been solved.

The desire is: to experience HARMONY in everything, outside, inside, man, nature, cosmos. HARMONY we might also call Love, Peace, one in tune with the other. There is entirely too much "noise" around us, physically and in the soul (astral) realm.

To blend together with others in harmonious chords, understanding without much talking, also to be respected in one's own harmonious shell – then only true friendships begin. This does not mean that one should shun dissonance, for every dissonance demands solution, a *septime* [seventh] or *verminderter Akkord* [diminished chord] demands the octave on *Auflösung* [resolution]. In fact, a dissonance is expression of a creative tension – but it should find its solution, whereby it is necessary to say that the solution does not need to be in the same realm or on the same level – a dissonance physically, as creative tension, might loosen the wings of the soul and let it fly to a higher level where it restores the harmony.

But then, a dissonance is not disharmony or *Kakophony* [cacophony]. One should be able to *hear,* through the medium of a disharmony, the re-solution, the harmony.

This, however, requests will – as all true music derives from will – and strength to stand the tension until the solution is found. Many an instrument – alas breaks or screeches before the dissolving accord sounds. (cf. Rudolf Steiner *der menschliche Körper ist das Instrument auf dem die Götter Spielen = die Leier des Apollo.)* [The human body is the instrument on which the gods play = the lyre of Apollo.][27]

So very few people are musical, including those who believe and enjoy so-called music, for they do not have harmony.

Only with harmony one can recognize harmony.

(Goethe: *Du gleichst dem Geist, den du begreifst* [Thou'rt like the Spirit which thou comprehendest][28].

---

27. For example the lecture of Sept. 22, 1922 in GA 216. See reference 18.
28. The Earth Spirit in *Faust.* See reference 19.

2. Earlier Childhood Memories

The first memories carry back to the age of about two. We were living in a rather large, old house in the midst of a park. It was winter, and I remember seeing people ice skating on a pond, that is, I remember the motion of the people and the glistening surface of the ice and trees. About the same time, and this is probably the earliest: mice falling through a hole in the ceiling in my bed, uproar, and finally peaceful satisfaction being placed between father and mother; to be correct, I remember the situation, but nothing about the persons involved. Next event about the same time: our man-servant caught a raven and let it fly in the kitchen; the kitchen I remember because of its steamy atmosphere, the raven flying. Then there is a remembrance which is psychologically interesting because it demonstrates the automatic registration by the mind of things not understood: my parents talked about "renting out a bowling alley" at the end of the park. I do not remember the parents, but the talk and words which I could not have understood at the time. Later on I checked with my mother into the fact that this was discussed, indeed, and a bowling alley existed.

Soon we moved into another house in the midst of Zweibrücken [in der] Bayrischen Rheinpfalz, of which I remember the outside front, the kitchen door because somebody had brought a live lobster and let him crawl on the floor, and a shed: here the maid stuffed a goose with potatoes, and I remember clearly the goose held between the knees of the maid and its protests as well as the thumb pressing the potatoes down the throat; that is, the essential details.

Curiously enough, neither parents nor other people are remembered of this period. We have travelled a lot during these early years, but only one incident (age 4) is remembered: the thumb got squeezed in the door of a railroad car, and the picture of the compartment and door of this car is recognizable. Here already the trend of a kind of "geopsychic"/ or local-situation memory can be seen, which accompanied me throughout life.

Of my father I remember only one moment: he in a blue suit holding me with a warm emotion against him. I was five, and it must have been a farewell embrace shortly before his death after a long illness. It was winter and I was in the apartment of friends, looking out of the window, watching the spectacle of a military procession, music, a marching company and civilians behind a horse-drawn carriage: it was the funeral procession for my father, which, of course, I did not know. It was the specific wish of my father that the meaning of death should be withheld from me as long as possible and so, when later in school I was asked what my father did, I could not answer. Over all these years, up to the 6th year I cannot recall parents, or any other persons. I must have lived in a dream world, well protected and awakened only with the beginning of school years.

However, before this awakening only fragments of situations appear: the lancing of a glandular abscess underneath the ear: the window, the tray to receive the blood and discharge and the feeling relieved when it was opened, but not the pain prior to it; the tightening of cracks in door and windows of a bedroom and the paraphernalia by means of which was blown into the room (apparently a gas to disinfect the room) after the death of my father. Again the outside of the house, street, court, horse stable in Germersheim, where my father died, so that I could recognize it many years later.

The awakening began at just under six wears old when I went to school, a co-educational institute with plenty of girls and few boys in first grade. My memory for that which was said at the time must have been phenomenal, for the teacher would read aloud the chapter which the children in turn should read the next day. It was discovered only after quite some time that I could not read at all when I got stuck one day and the teacher asked me to follow with the finger each word and line, and I pointed to the entirely wrong place. Minor scandal.

At this time a major burst of emotion happened. I was playing in the court of the house, and somebody threw something down. At the same time mother called to come home. Since she called several times and the object hit me just then when her voice called, very angry, I thought she had thrown the object and rushed up the stairs. The glass door to the apartment was closed, and mother behind gave me to understand that I was locked out because of disobedience not coming right away. In the choleric rage which followed I pushed my right fist through the glass, suffering a deep cut on the right hand. This took quite some time to heal, needing lots of cauterization of wild growth on the scar, and was probably the first and best-remembered object lesson that it is unwise to let temper flow.

As far as I am concerned I believe I was a lively child full of activity and interest, but apparently the environment and teachers thought differently and thought I was wild and unruly.

On Sundays we were given a few pennies to put into the collection in church. Some of our gang got the idea to collect these pennies until we had enough to buy firecrackers. Instead of going to church on Sunday we let these loose in the dark street underpass under the railroad near the station. This created a major scandal. I remember the fun, and the injustice being punished for fun.

From then on I began to distrust teachers, clergymen and adults in general. The scandal, which must have been the talk of the town, Sehwäbisch Hall, Württenberg, where my mother had moved after father's death, and which influenced her to move to *Nürnberg* [Nuremberg], however, was caused by another incident. I had picked up a bad word, the meaning of which I did not even understand. That I used it was told by other children to the teacher. Big investigation, reprimanding in presence of the class by the school board, and everybody pointed to the bad child. I had now reason to distrust anybody, classmates and adults, and became a lonely, melancholic creature. Some twenty-five years later, while in London, a person from Sehwäbisch Hall told me that the teacher had expressed the opinion that an injustice was done to me and asked his friends, should they ever meet me, to tell me of his regrets for the incident. So this matter is squared; but inasmuch as it forced my mother to move to another location, it had brought about a complete change in our lives; the results of it gave my entire future a turn into another direction. Today I look back upon it, knowing how fate can interfere with one's life and change the course by some apparently devious circumstances and events.

The change to *Nürnberg* then brought this child into that school environment which he resented from the first to the last year. With the exception of two or three teachers and distasting almost all classmates over a period of ten years, one can imagine how lonely this child grew up, remembering all these years as mental and soul agony and taking refuge in nature and objects rather than in childhood and juvenile plays of children. A tremendous urge to obtain knowledge and understanding developed, but very little human relationship or friendships were established.

However, that which was taught was neither exciting nor interesting, and most knowledge had to come from books read in spare time and at night.

At night children had to sleep and put out the light. So a candle was used for reading, shaded by the bed covers so that no light could be seen coming from the cracks in the door. This went on for quite some time until once the child fell asleep and the candle set the bed on fire. Helas, this reading by candlelight did harm to the eyes, which was discovered because the boy did never greet teachers or other adults on the street for not recognizing them. First reprimandation, until one teacher had the glorious idea (after I did not even recognize my mother on the street): maybe his eyes were bad. So eyeglasses were prescribed; but my classmates enjoyed frequently to knock them off (which did not increase my happiness.)

This child and boy was frequently ill, especially with respiratory illnesses, glandular fevers, tonsil and other infections and bronchitis. About one third of the school year was spent in bed, and extended vacations were needed to build up reserves. Sport was out of question; the body was tender and the classmates just loved to torture this child, for it seemed so defenseless. Violent outbreaks of temper, in self defense, where the boy displayed strength to the damage of his torturers who got beaten bloody, earned him again the description of being an unruly child.

The vacations were enjoyed as peaceful living alone, undisturbed by classmates, in the nature of either mountains, forests or some place along the North Sea with swimming, sailing; gradually the child became stronger, and at the age of fourteen to fifteen a considerable turn took place and sports such as swimming and hiking over long distance were enjoyed.

At home a peculiar situation developed. The child loved peace and kindness above everything. The mother, who certainly must have loved her only child, alas, was very nervous, temperamental and emotional. Child and mother just could not live together, and so it was decided that the child would live in the house of the maternal grandparents and under the care of an unmarried sister of his mother. The mother lived in the same town, and the child visited her Saturday afternoon, stayed overnight and returned on Sunday noon to the grandparents. This relationship worked out very well to the benefit of all. Aunt Berta was a somewhat eccentric, but very well educated person who had seen a lot of the world, traveled a lot and had many friends, especially artists (singers), so that the child came in touch with many adults of varied streams of life, but no children of the same age.

Grandmother Babette Walter was human kindness in person and excelled in telling fairy tales of all kind, including many self-invented ones. Grandmother loved to solve puzzles, and when this did not satisfy her anymore she started to study mathematics. Since she thought with her sixty plus years she would cut a funny figure at the university courses, she had the professor of mathematics come twice a week to give her a course, from which the boy profited in his homework later on. Her influence upon the growing soul was soothing, rounding out the edges and hardships, explaining human nature. In looking backward today, I would say that she demonstrated that a human being could be fond of mathematics but need not to lose a kind, warm heart nor needed to become intellectual and abstract. It is natural that the child, being as it was, absorbed this attitude, and a great desire for kindness, humanness originated — to perceive the inner true nature of man as it was striving to enter the knowledge of deeper forces in nature. The search started early, at the age of twelve or thirteen, in both directions — nature and man. Many negative properties of man, cunning, deceiving, intellectual arguing, stubborn persisting on one point of view were sensed as part of an underworldly, even below the animal, influence in man. If the boy would have been asked by the fairy woman of fate what his choice is: sickness or honor or fame, etc., he would have answered: Knowledge turned wisdom and Kindness. About this, quite a definite concept had formed itself at an early state of boyhood. Against the background of this concept human beings were measured. One can also say the young soul went out to search for the MAN in man. The story of Diogenes[29] looking with a lantern to find a human being made a deep impression, even though the philosophy of Diogenes otherwise did not appeal.

Nürnberg had a Museum called *Germanisches* [Germanic] Museum which was often visited - this museum also had a library of alchemistic books, books of the last two or three centuries about the supernatural, appearances of ghosts and nature spirits. The librarian, an old gentleman, gave these books to the boy of fourteen and fifteen to read. Inasmuch as the boy had his own experiences of other forces and beings, he found nothing astounding or ghostly in this literature. What he read was evident; he only wondered why many of these stories were told with the attribute of fear, of doubt or of the mystical, hostile, etc., etc.

Grandfather was the element of sound reasoning, matter of fact, and again of kindness and righteousness. He was a very upright, somewhat harsh (to others) individual, in his profession known as very straightforward personality, absolutely set against any cheating or bribing. He had started life as a chemist of the 19th century, had owned pharmacies and was retired at the time when the child came to *Nürnberg*. He was about 60 then. He had a small fortune and thought this might not be enough for the child to secure a carefree future, and therefore started to work again, as a

29. Diogenes of Sinope (ca. 412-323 BC) was known as “the Cynic” Greek philosopher.

kind of Public Health – Food and Drug administrator, as we would call it today. He had a quite sovereign position, to admit or turn down new drugs, to control that physicians prescribed and pharmacies dispensed the properly admitted drugs. Since his eyes were somewhat irritable he ordered that all prescriptions and papers which he had to control must be written on green paper, for he felt the green color tolerable to his eyes. His love of nature was great, and as botanist he had extraordinary knowledge. So he could recognize and identify any grass or clover immediately from the shape of its leaves and stem even without using Linné's system of identification of blossoms.

On his frequent excursions into nature he would transmit this knowledge and love of Nature and its growth to the boy in such a way that no abstract element entered, but everything, including the medicinal uses of herbs, was demonstrated *ad oculo* [by eye].

In his laboratory he would show the child reactions which produced many color changes, and he taught the boy that colors are essential as a means to recognize substances. So in the growing mind of the child an appreciation for form, pattern and color was created which gave the later life work and study of the young scientist a specific direction.

The other interest of the grandfather was in "people," just "people." The simple, the struggling, the hardworking, not the sophisticated, super-refined and so called society type. He loved the people who were just themself and did not pretend to be something.

He disliked false, blown up authority and somehow transmitted without much talk and explanation his very same attitude and interest to his grandson. Otherwise grandfather belonged still to the 19th century and told of "his" times of the middle of the last century, Napoleon's, as though it were yesterday. The boy, having history as about the only course in school which interested him, loved these tales of eyewitnesses to history. Somehow a feeling for larger and wider horizons developed, so that he began to grasp the meaning of a perishable present and to look upon the metamorphosis of things, in time and space, as seen from a distance. In space, too, for geography and astronomy were the two other fields of knowledge which fascinated him and which were not taught at all or miserably in school. The knowledge had to come from elsewhere, books, grandfather Emil Walter, aunt Berta Walter and their friends who frequented the house. Whether mother contributed directly to this desire for knowledge is not remembered. Mother had become interested in a philosophy which much later became known to the young man, then, as anthroposophy. People who were interested in anthroposophy and the teachings of Rudolf Steiner circulated in the house of his mother. The boy did not know nor was he told what all this was. But most of these people he disliked extremely.

There were, however, a few "contacts." Michael Bauer would give a class, once a week, for many years and tell fairy tales and stories. The boy, probably 8-10 years of age, loved to go to these classes and remembers sitting on Michael Bauer's knees. There was a personality who emanated kindness and understanding, and the boy absorbed this radiance like a dry sponge. It was not so much the content of these hours, but the attitude and mood, the kind voice and the spirit of M. B. which had a formative influence on the young soul.

No word of anthroposophy was mentioned, for as he learned much later, Rudolf Steiner had instructed his mother that under no circumstances should she ever tell of anthrop. [anthroposophy] nor influence the child. The child should find his spiritual path all alone by himself. Considering the continuous friction between child and mother, this was a very wise instruction, for otherwise only antipathy and repellence would have been the result. Mother disappeared at times on very secret trips and missions (what was later recognized as attendance to cycles and lecture courses by Rudolf Steiner, *Köln* [Cologne], *München* [Munich] etc) and returned with a peculiar glow and radiance. As grandmother, the humble and simple woman, had her love for puzzles and mathematics, so had mother a great love for philosophy. She would talk about and study Hegel[30], Fichte,[31] and others, and the boy sensed that there were objective values, compensation for the emotional stress and strain pattern which otherwise ruled and was so much disliked.

On Sundays another teacher of mother's circle gave a class in plasticizing for a few children, which was very much liked. There were several artists, painters, musicians, and these were the only ones whom the boy liked of mother's friends. No doubt the love for art, and appreciation of it which permeated, had a forming and educational influence in this young life. Frequent visits to the local museum, usually together with the young friend and mate Willi Palm, enlarged the horizon.

Due to the readings and teachings of scientific popular literature and the little the school offered, the boy became thoroughly fascinated by the materialistic concept of matter, the philosophies of a Haeckel[32], the writings of a Bölsche[33] (biologist), but on the other side the warm understanding of animal life by Ernest Thompson Seton[34] was as important as the reading of abstract thought.

---

30. Georg Wilhelm Friedrich Hegel (1770-1831) was one of the German philosophers who founded the philosophical movement known as German Idealism.

31. Johann Gottlieb Fichte (1762-1814) was also one of the German philosophers who founded the philosophical movement known as German Idealism.

32. Ernst Heinrich Philipp August Haeckel (1834-1919) was a German biologist, naturalist, philosopher, physician and artist.

33. Wilhelm Bölsche (1861-1939) was a German zoologist, writer and popularizer of scientific works on nature and promoted evolution theory. Best known for his three-volume work on the poetic history of the evolution of love entitled *Das Liebesleben in der Natur: Eine Entwicklungsgeschichte der Liebe* [Love-Life in Nature: the Story of the Evolution of Love].

34. Ernest Thompson Seton (1860-1946) was a Scots-Canadian-American author, wildlife artist, founder of the Woodcraft Indians and one of the three founders of the Boy Scouts of America (BSA).

The boy felt in nature was something which he "saw," but in which science had no share, but to which he could take refuge at any time in his loneliness – Nature Spirits were his friends and mates. (Reflecting today, one may say the Divine in Nature, the harmony, the eternal laws and order stood on his side.)

In the human realm, being tortured by classmates, teachers in general, not appreciating the circle of his mother's friends, and with the exception of grandfather's house and friends observed there, he failed to discover the Divine in man, saw the animal and detestable in man, and in general had a low opinion of man – definitely formed the opinion that there was no good to be found in man, and therefore became an atheist. The general environment of the population in *Nürnberg* [Nuremberg], an emotional mass psychology of a rather low intellectual level, mob scenes, socialist mass demonstrations were a daily order; all that contributed to dislike and depreciate man. At the age of thirteen a class was given by Rittelmeyer[35] to prepare for confirmation. The boy argued that Christ was only a fable, no proof of his existence existed, the gospels were books which could not be upheld as of any value in the face of modern, materialistic scientific development. But the personality of Rittelmeyer with his kind voice and tenor of speaking and his deep penetrating blue eyes made a deep impression. It was felt that this man lived what he taught and preached. Sundays at 5 p.m. Rittelmeyer gave a service in the *Heilige Geist Kirche* [Church of the Holy Spirit] which was frequently attended, also by his grandparents. The personality of Rittelmeyer helped to create in the boy the appreciation for true humanness. At least: there was a man through whom one could find access to the Divine in man. Another preacher who was accepted was Pastor Geyer in the *Sebaldus Kirche* [Sebaldus Church]. This beautiful building of gothic

35. Dr. Friedrich Rittelmeyer (1872-1938) was a Lutheran minister and joint founder of The Christian Community (The Movement for Religious Renewal) in Switzerland in 1922, and became its first priest and leader.

art, with the works by Veit Stoß[36], the brass work, the columns, the architraves and the wood statues, f.i. the famous *Nürnberg Madonna* (in the Museum) - all these masterpieces of gothic and medieval art left a much deeper impression on the soul than all the teachings of a superficial nature at school. This experience bears out that the art-filled environment, the architectural beauty of a town is of utmost importance to the growing soul and intellect. A factor which is frequently neglected and bypassed in modern life. Architecture has definitely a formative influence upon the life and growth forces of the body. When during World War II it became known that many of these architectures were destroyed by bombing, I felt sad, as wounds had been inflicted to my own (etheric) body, and a deep sorrow overcame me. Seeing *Nürnberg* after destruction, also the house where we lived, in ruins, however, meant that no memories of these years had any physical background, no tie was left to the childhood, and in many ways it caused me to distance myself from my own youth, so that it is necessary to write about it in the third person: the child, the boy, as about an external object. Probably none of the people with whom the child and boy dealt are still alive, and so these years have become history.

We see this child and boy now living in a dual world: *the outside* – materialistic, intellectual, which was suffered as a kind of necessity, of routine, but which also in its technology, sciences, especially physics, electricity had a fascinating attraction to the intellectual mind, the *Verstand.* This *Verstand* developed into an analytical observational (cold, that is, without feeling) direction, quick grasping; the inside – the soul-life of feeling, of dreams, of ideals, living with natural forces and beings, with a dream world of human beings, with what became later known to me as spiritual and elementary worlds about which one could never speak to anybody. This dualism must have created tremendous tension which needed a temperamental outlet. It was definitely a problem to be melancholic at base and choleric at times.

---

36. Veit Stoß (ca. 1445-1450 to 1533) was a German late Gothic sculptor, engraver and painter.

Maybe the child's love for art, especially music and architecture, gothic plastic, created a balance.

Today, reflecting memories and looking backward, I am sure I possessed religion, but loathed "churches," i.e., the institutions which officially catered to a concept of God and a performance of a service which appeared hollow, superficial – with the exception of the two men, Rittelmeyer and Geyer. In the classes preparing confirmation, the child argued against the acceptance of a God and Christ, so Rittelmeyer some fifteen years later told me; he had a hard time with this heathen boy, he said, but when he looked deep down through the eyes of the boy, he saw the God and Christ force in this child, and so he did not give up and had confidence this child would find his way.

At confirmation there was a public examination in the *Heilige Geist Kirche*. Rittelmeyer asked the question: why was baptism done in earlier centuries by submerging in water and later only by touching the forehead with a moistened finger. Whereupon the prompt answer came: man had physically degenerated and softened and would probably contract a cold and brain inflammation when submerged. I still can sense the shudder which went through the assembled congregation. The other question was about the type of sins to which man is exposed, and the answer and concept behind it was and is deeply on my mind: "thought" sins = erring, illusion, deception, evil thought, doubt; sins in "feeling" = lack of piety, compassion, antipathy, ill-feeling against man and creatures; sins in actually doing and will, ill will, lying, destruction. I guess the discussion of these sins wiped out again the impression of *Aufgeklärtsein* [being enlightened] which the first answer made.

One experience of the exploring boy lasted forever: in the woods once he encountered a large, beautiful yellow toad and killed it – for no obvious reason. (fear, cruelty?) When the animal was dead, deep remorse overcame the boy, and the law "thou shall not kill" became a reality. And such was the child's path that he had to learn by committing "sins" to learn the good and to accept moral laws. Many such sins were experienced in thought and feelings and recognized as such, that even in thought one experiences a reality which may lead to deeds. Already at that time it was instinctively felt that thoughts are formative forces. To this it contributed that the child could somehow "reach" the thoughts of others and the feelings. The difference between the thoughts thus "seen" and the actual words and doings of others, of course, created a problem because these were two different things. It caused that no faith and confidence could develop in anything except nature (objective world) while the incompleteness of man was an experience, rather distressing. It was felt that only that which one creates in one's own self, by one's own efforts, would create reality, while everything else so-called human was felt as illusion.

The female influence at that time was represented by elderly persons. The difference of what we call sex did not exist; the child was not interested in it. He had no contact with girls of same age or a little younger or older. To him the woman was "neuter" and, curiously enough, "ageless." As I remember, anybody older than 20, to the boy of 12, 13, 14, 15, was "just old." There was no boyhood love to a girl as one sees so much today – the girlfriend; no dating; and the so-called facts of life were of no interest. So it happened that the young man had no idea whatsoever of sex relationships when he was drafted in the army at the age of 18 and was absolutely dumbfounded when he first heard about sex by other soldiers who, as it seemed to be customary during the war, sought relief in public houses and told about them. This caused great troubles, because the 18-year-old did not understand and got the impression that the "female" was something to be despised. It took several years before this shock was overcome. The boy had no feeling of his own body as male, and that the female body was different he gathered only from the statue of a nymph on a fountain. Other boys' talks about the female were repellent and avoided, and whatever explanations were given once in school by the teacher of religion were of no interest.

When returning from the war, *en route* home, the young soldier was invited by an officer, the only one whom he had seen displaying courage at the front, who introduced him in Marburg to a group and evening meeting of *Wandervoge*l [birds of passage – a German youth movement of the twentieth century], where also girls were present. Nietzsche[37] was read there, which did not help at all, because the sentence was quoted "*wenn Du zum Weibe gehst, vergiss die Peitsche nicht*!" [when you go to the woman, do not forget the whip!][38]

It was only later, age 20, 21, when the young man began to sense the mystery of womanhood and his first, what one may call love, flamed up at the age of 21; a very deep emotion then, indeed, to a woman 6 years his elder.

Another realm which was hidden to the growing youth was the fact that one needs to work in order to make a living. Economic values were unknown. At home money was never mentioned. It was there, and grandfather always maintained you need not to worry about the future. It is well taken care of. It was a, I cannot even say, bitter awakening when at 18 I was told: the grandfatherly fortune is lost, there is nothing, and you have to earn a living. No feeling whatsoever for the value of money had been developed. Until that time the term *"die reine Unschuld"* [pure innocence] described best the situation.

About the age 14, 15 the health of the boy suddenly improved. There were less illnesses and physical weakness, and sports such as swimming, fast and long-distance running were enjoyed. Sport events were followed with keen interest. Aviation then had started, and every opportunity was used to watch the first flights of some primitive plane. Another interesting experiment was observed. South of Nbg. [Nuremberg] were some lakes, and a schoolteacher, Wirth, made experiment to guide a boat on the lake by radio, the boat empty, the man on the shore, the boat honking a horn when curious other boats came near; this all made a deep impression. This must have been about 1911-1912, and Wirth's trials are entirely forgotten. They caused the boy to experiment with electricity and magnetism already then, far ahead from school teachings in

---

37. Friedrich Wilhelm Nietzsche (1844-1900) was a German philosopher and philologist.
38. From Nietzsche's *Also Sprach Zarathustra* [Thus Spoke Zarathustra], published between 1883-1885 in four parts. See reference 20.

physics. A primitive transmitter was built and operated in conjunction with another boy who lived across the street. Of course Morse signals was all that could be had at the time. It influenced the boy to select the study of electrotechnic when he had to make a choice of a study after completion of school.

To plan the choice of a study was quite a problem. Nothing really fitted that which lived in the deeper interests of the boy. The aunt suggested to him to become a preacher. This was out of question because of this atheism and the fact that in the preachers, with the exception of Rittelmeyer and Geyer, he felt only the untrue pathos about something in which, in a deeper sense, they did not believe themselves, therefore offering only an untrue, hollow shell or sentimentality. Also what they said did not meet the scientific age of *Aufklärung* [enlightenment].

About father he was told that he had said: under no circumstance a military career. The sea, ships, navigation as seen during vacation on the North Seas had made a deep impression and created a desire to sail on the seas, but when the time of drafting age came, he was not accepted because of his poor eyesight. So it was decided to study a practical science. Theoretical or abstract sciences did not appeal, for that which the boy knew instinctively from his inner life did not meet the texts on science. Biology might have been nearer to his desires, but somehow also did not meet the interest.

Fate, in a way, interfered.

When the boy was about 14, his mother married. Herr Theodor Binder, by the boy accepted as elderly friend, but not as substitute for the father, always spoken of as "Herr Binder," brought the news to the boy, asking what he felt about [it]. Answer: "You are old enough to know what you do." Stepfather and mother moved to Stuttgart and were visited during vacation, for it was wisely decided to let the boy finish school in *Nürnberg* and to stay in the house of the grandparents. Both stepfather and mother had become ardent followers of Rudolf Steiner and wanted to live their lives without interfering with the boy. The vacations in Stuttgart were thoroughly enjoyed, most of the day swimming and sunbathing, rain or shine – a swim during the rain or a thunderstorm was the greatest of pleasures. While it was only 4 hours' train ride, nevertheless the boy learned to travel alone and became rather independent. One good thing must be said – nowhere was he interfered with by anybody with that which he wanted to do. He became independent, because of being so alone.

Herr Binder, like grandfather, was kind and an example of righteousness. He had, alas, a very distinct opinion about others, which did not help to awaken love for human beings and influenced the boy to become rather critical of others. While this might have been a protection, in ways it made it very difficult for many years to develop human relationships. Herr Binder had a respected position as organizer in a factory, Robert Bosch[39], in Stuttgart, and so the boy became familiar with problems of industry, technology, labor management and manufacturing. He found all this much more interesting than school. He loathed school more and more. The war had started, and an opportunity offered itself to escape school even before he was drafted: to go into a factory and work as laborer (so-called *Hilfsdienst*). So he quitted school and became a factory laborer, first unskilled, then learning toolmaking. Quite naturally he learned to make a living and earned as much as to be independent and even to pay his study later on himself. He worked in a machine shop, on various machines, lathes, planers, drill presses with highly rationalized machines of American origin, so-called Cincinnati automates. He learned about the problems of labor as laborer, about the Socialists, Communists, etc., etc.

He worked a while in a foundry (explosion engines), which was not too good for his health, and repaired locomotives. Because all this in the national economy was considered *"Hilfsdienst,"* his school term continued to run, so that he got all credits without attending. This was just plain luck.

Then he was drafted, 17½ years old, and volunteered for a technical weapon pioneer or engineering corps. While he did not

---

39. Robert Bosch (1861-1942) was a German industrialist and founder of Robert Bosch GmbH in Stuttgart in 1886.

like the military at all, he was set, because of his experience with the toad (thou shalt not kill) not to do any service in the army where one would force to kill, and he is happy to report that throughout the service at the front, he had never to shoot and kill. But he witnessed a lot of killing, having to collect torn bodies and to bury them, seeing all the ravages of war – still in the "protected" shell of *"Unschuld"* [innocence] described above.

He became completely disillusioned about man, too much so, and it took many years to heal these wounds of the soul. Without the influence of anthroposophy and Rudolf Steiner these wounds might never have healed, and an abstract, cold, calculating intellectual might have developed. However, the practical years of labor and soldier enabled the young man then to stand on his own, independent, and when the revelation was made that there was no grandfatherly fortune and he would need to work, it was no shock or problem, for he had already learned to earn money.

For the character of this man it was typical that he, detesting the so-called society because of its make-believe, putting up a glossy front before an empty shell, changed to become a laborer and to learn about life and society from the point of view of the laborers. Also, he to become acquainted with the very practical problems of mechanics, shop work— even today, is considered a much more beneficial background than all school and university studies together. So he entered life well fitted.

There is no need to report about the military and war experiences. Dangers and miraculous savings of life were frequently encountered. He learned to build bridges, to blast roads and buildings, to build fortifications, and finally, to handle precious survey instruments and to work out correction tables for very badly manufactured trench mortars. More of their own people operating these things got killed by premature explosions than they did harm to the enemy.

After return from a lost war, complete demoralization of all human and society structures, he worked again in Stuttgart as laborer at Robert Bosch and in an electric installation company building switch boards, theater and other complicated installations.

It was 1919 by then, and as laborer in one of the factories he attended lectures by Rudolf Steiner about the Threefold Commonwealth[40] idea. And it was then that he discovered life, his task, he received his calling and suddenly knew what to do. He became a human being, and the youthful dream was over – he awakened.

The actual "awakening" had taken place a little earlier, but then I did not know and understand what it meant.

It was during the fall of 1918, when the German front in France collapsed. The danger of life was great, and I had the feeling that life was forfeited and I could not possibly survive this night, being under a tremendous fire, completely exposed and no shelter. Suddenly I saw the heavens opened with celestial music, and an inner voice called me by name. A supernatural voice or being said: "Your life is forfeited, but it will be spared, for you have a task to fulfill, not for yourself but for others, for humanity." It was a calling, clearly, and I knew: I am now under the protection and guidance of powers greater than I. From this experience streams forth all that which I am and became, and it was and is the task henceforth to amend the physical, the animal, yes even the man, to become worthy of it – a path never to end, most incomplete as yet (1958), a struggle full of thorns, errors, downfalls; but the voice has spoken since several times and uprighted after a fall – much love and friendship have been the reward, and I know this Love received is given not to the earthly man, but to the eternal

---

40. See Rudolf Steiner, *Neugestaltung des sozialen Organismus* [New Formation of the Social Organism], *Rudolf Steiner Gesamtausgabe, Vorträge über das Soziale Leben und die Dreigliederung des Sozialen Organismus* [Collected Edition of Rudolf Steiner's Lectures, Lectures About Social Life and the Threefold Commonwealth of the Social Organism], *Bibliographie-Nr.* [Bibliography No.] GA 330/331, *Vierzehn öffentliche Vorträge, gehalten in Stuttgart zwischen dem 22. April und dem 30. Juli 1919* [Fourteen public lectures held in Stuttgart between April 22 and July 30, 1919], *Verlag der Rudolf Steiner-Nachlassverwaltung* [Publishing House of the Estate of Rudolf Steiner], *Dornach/Schweiz* [Dornach/ Switzerland], *1. Auflage Gesamtausgabe Dornach* [1st Collected Edition Dornach] 1963. See reference 21.

value which seeks its foothold in my being. When I met Rudolf Steiner for the first time, he said, "*O, wir kennen uns ja schon lange.*" [O, we have already known one another for a long time]. I was mad then, because it was the first time I met him. NOW – I KNOW.

3. The Musical Trend and Intermezzo

If I would be asked which are the major basic trends of my desires, I might ask: for harmony. Harmony in the environment, whether human or natural, harmony of the soul, whether my own or that of others; harmony which expresses itself as kindness, for only a harmonious and inwardly free being can radiate true kindness. This desire has a background about which I will tell now. During about my 10th or 11th year it was discovered that I had some specific musical gifts: hearing the absolute pitch, remembering, so that after a few years of music lessons I could play a piece by heart, having it heard only a few times.

So it was decided that I should take music lessons, first piano, later violin. Piano lessons were given by a very temperamental lady whom I liked, and piano and music lessons (theory) were had in a conservatory, going parallel with school in the *Altes Gymnasium* [Old high school] at *Nürnberg*. The *Harmonielehre* [tharmony lessons] at the conservatory impressed me very much, because it showed the laws and principles of music, compositions, etc. A certain *Fingerfertigkeit* [dexterity] was produced, and it seems that ambitions of the teachers intended to make "something" out of this pupil, that is, to push him ahead on the path of a child-musician. It was said that I had an exceptionally good *Anschlag* [touch] and could play a piece of Bach or Beethoven with great talent. My ear was, and still is, extremely sensitive, what one would call a musical ear. So sensitive, in fact, that it causes me physical pain and nervous strain to hear any music which is not perfectly performed. Today I would say that the exactness of a Toscanini would appeal most, but the emotional, personal opinion of a performer or conductor, Stokowski[41] f.i. [for instance], would be against my grain. Int these youthful years I began to express my feelings and soul life in phantasies on the piano. This was probably a healthy outlet for the soul of the lonely child and served its purpose. The mechanical training, which of course is a necessity if one is trained to become a performer, was certainly overdone, for, after all, there was school, too, and many other interests, wander ing through nature, etc.

These varied interests conflicted. A nervous, if not to say neurasthenic child developed. Grandfather had an old master violin and viola, and the playing of these instruments was added. I remember very well that the mere physical vibration of the strings caused me agony, touching it with the fingers. The violin teacher loved these beautiful instruments, so that instead of teaching me, he took them and played himself most of the time of the lesson. This created antipathy, and gradually a state of tension developed which apparently no teacher recognized or took serious. Finally I just refused to play or to go to lessons. And that was the end of my musical career, probably at the age of 16 or 17. As substitute for the musical desire I went to all concerts and theaters (opera) at the time and probably heard all conductors of name, concert players, all pieces which were performed in these years, until a saturation point was reached at the age of 19 or 20. The sensitive ear remained. All that caused me later on to avoid to go to concerts and theaters, for if the performance was not perfect it would cause me pain and distress rather than enjoyment – because in hearing I had to play the piece myself.

In later years I had the opportunity [to] become personally acquainted with some of the famous singers of the period and had the good luck to listen to them at home. This again only helped to increase any dislike for any not first-rate performance, and especially with singing one can chase me away. Singing I could not myself,

41. Leopold Stokowski (1882-1977) was an American conductor of Polish-British extraction.

having no voice, and in school I was dispensed from all singing lessons, fortunately.

After the music training was abolished, I had spells playing the piano for hours, just to express the deeper desires or aims or dreams of a soul. These spells went on for hours, half a night. When the organ in the Goetheanum was built and the building was not finished and nobody would be there, I would use [it] for the last of these spells – and then the entire musical intermezzo was over, at least as far as own performing was concerned.

Due to this great desire for harmony, classical music of a Beethoven, Mozart, Bach would mostly appeal, but also others like Chopin, part of Mendelssohn, were liked.

The sensitive ear and musical memory was also applied to human beings, so that I can remember voices, even the sound of walking, of footsteps much better than faces. In fact, I would recognize somebody not seen for a long time rather by the voice than by his physiognomy. In the voice something of the innermost hidden being is revealed. If people would really understand and know what_they reveal of their inner problems and beings in their voices – many might prefer to remain silent.

Especially the unsolved problems come to the fore, alas. I believe that much antipathy develops because of the voices. Sympathy and Antipathy, subconsciously, is much influenced by odors or smell. But as to that, smell or chemical perception is part of the musical sphere, as we will see later. If the expression is used: I cannot stand the smell of this man, "*den Kerl kann ich nicht riechen" wie man im Volksmund sagt* [as one says in the vernacular], this only points to a dissonance perceived by the chemical senses; to the contrary: sympathy points to a harmony of chemical senses. Sound and smell, therefore, have something in common.

The greatest antipathy, that is, the stimulation of negative forces, I experience to noises, metallic, machine noises. And one can only say that present-day humanity just seems to love noises, which contain no music.

A differentiation has to be made here between disharmony or a discord which finds its solution. A *septime* [seventh] might put a strain on the hearing, but if it finds its solution in the octave, or if a *verminderter Accord* [diminished chord] is dissolved and leads to the harmonious solution, it is justified, because it is an expression of tension, of effect, of will – of that which I like to call "creative tension." It is not even necessary that the solution to harmony is actually physically performed, like at the ending of every classical music. This frequently is very cheap and easy and leaves the hearer with nothing to work with. Life does not always, in fact very infrequently, offer "solutions," and it is much better for future development and growth to finish with the discord, not to answer, but to leave a question open, hanging in the air: because this creative tension appeals to the will, to do something, to remain active and not to sit down satisfied and clap hands.

But, and this is important for the concept of harmony – the discord or disharmony *must* be creative – one *must* hear, yet unborn, the potentiality of solution. One must sense the solution.

This very principle applies to music as well as to human soul life, human relationships in general. Criticism is destructive if it only points out the negative. Criticism which heals, helps the other to do it better, encourages the other, is constructive, for it gives the potentiality for solution.

I have tried to apply this principle in lecturing: not to end a lecture with an eloquent, fulminant finale which causes only the clapping of hands, not even the desire [for a] "*da capo al fine*" [recapitulation], but to leave the last thought open, a question, unfinished, for this stimulates the earnest listener to own thought, to draw the conclusion himself. To continue in his own way where the speaker left.

When the lawn mower puts-puts all summer long, or the outboard motor sputters, or the unmuffled exhaust of a hot-rod roars: to many this is the symbol of weekend vacation and free-time activity as well as of modern civilization – musical these noises are not. Still in mechanically produced noises a certain musical element could enter. Think of the swishing sound of a scythe cutting through dew-laden grass, of the sharpening of a scythe, of the rhythm of ram hammers in the good old time when a crew of men built a cobblestone road. It is the explosion motor which has made the air musically intolerable in addition to polluting it with its exhaust poisons (the smell and noise problem again).

Maybe some engineer with esthetically feeling ears might give technological noises a twist towards something better in the future. But people's ears have hardened because of the radio, which blasts all day and is not listened to.

To have the radio on, not listen to creates a habit: not to listen to that which other people say. I have been in many gatherings when everybody talked at the same time, asked questions and never heard the answer or listened to it. This, by the way, I consider as one of the greatest insults, because it condemns the one who talks to a monologue in the presence of others and inhibits that which could develop, that which could flow from man to man, that which Goethe called the most precious thing of all: *DAS GESPRÄCH* [conversation].

The only proper answer to all that noise of our age is: Silence. Silence is more than just the absence of noise or sound. Silence can be made an active property: listening. Not only silence from without, but absolute silence also within. To be so full of *Hingabe* [commitment], devotion, unselfish perception that the own "noises of the soul" = emotions, the clattering of the gears of intellectual thinking, the roaring of the animal will and the blood instincts, too, become silent. This silence is creative. Out of it, if one really listens, the deeper inner things reveal itself. In the sounds of man and nature, the spoken word and how it is spoken, the true being reveals itself. Nature's sound, the wind rustling in the trees and shrub, the water sounds of a fine drizzling rain or a pouring cloudburst, the sweet, dreamy sounds of birds gently singing in their sleeps (yes, they too dream), the cries of pain of animals or the sounds of satisfactions, of joy of puppies when they begin to explore their world, in all that and many other sounds sentient nature reveals itself.

And then there is the human voice, the spoken word, how it is spoken and also what is spoken.

All things heard have values. It means missing a lot if one does not listen to these values. But above all: these values tell of harmony, disharmony in want of a solution or discrepancies without solution which move from sound to noise.

My ears were so sensitive that mechanical noises dim the perception so that telephoning f.i. [for instance] became often a hopeless affair, the voices through loudspeakers were never understood, and if two or more people speak at the same time, neither one could be understood. Apparently the vibration of sound overlayers itself on the "hairs," "gravel," and "fluids" in the ear.

On the other side, one has to wilfully harden oneself against the experience of something which cries deep out of the soul of a human voice and one has no opportunity to react, often not even the right to intrude into the privacy or intimacy of another being. Here again is a borderline between Nature and Man. Nature always invites and is willing to tell, to reveal. Man has the freedom and privacy of the Ego which one has to respect, not to become an intruder, and one has to have the tact to feel when one is welcome and the other opens the door of his soul and being – if and when he does: LISTEN .

Much of human *not* understanding, of problems from man to man, of conflicts is due to the fact that one overshadows with one's own soul noise the music and harmony (or disharmony) which flows forth from the other soul. This experience, however, inasmuch as the natural reaction to it is silence, to shut off, frequently had causes to become uncommunicative, to live in a protective shell, and the result will be that gradually one becomes hard of hearing in a wider sense of the word, but also "hard of speaking." To sense the deeper things, the soul of the other down deep where it is beautiful and creative, radiant or suffering, to express oneself logically and artistically, that is, musical, this gets lost: one dries up, gets old, abstract and thought shadows instead of life blood emanate.

It is only great Love, opening of the portal of one's soul caused by the warmth, understanding and listening of the other soul, which can reverse this process.

Rudolf Steiner once in preparing to give a meditation, describing the mood one should develop, said:

"Deine Worte haben mein Gemüt erweicht." [Thy words have melted my heart.]

Gemüt [heart, mind or soul] actually is that property of soul which swings and lives in the musical mood as described in my childhood being. *Gemüt* is that which modern life tends to destroy, to harden. The English language has no adequate word for the concept, "*Gemüt*"; it has not many words for sounds, to describe sounds or noises. Even in the negative such words as " "*schnalzen, schmatzen*" cannot [be] properly translated. Sometimes one reads only, "he made small noises with his mouth."

Gemüt is that which lives in radiance and warmth of soul, in true, not sentimental feeling – but even the German language has degraded *"Gemüt"* to the bourgeois, "*Gemütlichkeit"* [congeniality or agreeableness] which is a passive property, an offence to the true "*Gemüt.*"

Should be continued [noted Pfeiffer].

4. Rudolf Steiner Enters My Life

By far the most important of anything which entered my life and brought about a complete turn, as well as it determined the future course to be taken, was the meeting with Rudolf Steiner.

My first contact was one of which I knew nothing. At about the age of 8, I developed some kind of spasms (*Stimmritzenkrampf*[42]) which began in the middle of the night and almost chocked me to death, so that after a short awakening I fainted. My mother, already then an ardent follower of Rudolf Steiner, asked his advice, and within other things, he gave the prayer for children, a little modified from the published version. This was meant to take away the element of fear. I remember clearly that the spasm was always anteceded by a state of extreme fear (caused by the wrestling for air), and I remember how that state of fear recessed, so that by an effort of will I could overcome the next attack and from then on had no more.

---

42. *Stimmritzenkrampf* translates as laryngospasm and is the uncontrolled/involuntary muscular contraction (spasm) of the laryngeal cords.

Mother, and later the stepfather, were devoted followers of Rudolf Steiner. He, however, had advised my mother never to speak about anthroposophy to me and to let me find my way entirely alone.

In 1916 somehow I was brought to a lecture by Rudolf Steiner in Stuttgart, probably to a group meeting with guests, for I remember that the audience was small. In this lecture Rudolf Steiner spoke about hearing: that one actually hears with the entire body, with the fluid system as well as with bones (the skeleton vibrates even physically, and the fluid system responds with denser and less denser compression.) Due to the musical inclination I was quite familiar with these phenomena of inner hearing, and so the lecture was listened to with interest, but told "nothing exciting," that is, made no specific impression.

In 1919, after return from the war and after the socialistic revolution in Stuttgart had settled, at the time when I had decided and started to study electrotechnic and physics at the *Technische Hochschule* [Technical College] in Stuttgart and had already practical experience as laborer, as described previously, I saw an advertisement of a lecture by a certain Dr. Carl Unger. "*Vom mutigen Denken*." [About Courageous Thinking]. That "*Denken*" [thinking] is necessary was impressed upon by the classes in physics and mathematics when the professors taught of the "clear, cold, reason as the foundation for a scientific approach to nature and man." That courage is an ideal to be striven for became an experience during the war years at the Western front, because I had seen plenty of cowardice, fear, but very little of courage. In fact, I remember only one officer and a few otherwise very humble and modest enlisted men who had displayed real courage, and returned from the war with the impression that men in general do not have courage, an experience which had added to the disillusion in general after the protected child and youth's life. To develop courage in thinking: this was a concept which immediately attracted me. Carl Unger spoke with enthusiastic words about thinking. He quoted from a certain Rudolf Steiner's "Philosophy of Spiritual

Activity"[43] – *Philosophie der Freiheit* [Philosophy of Freedom]: "*Im Denken halten wir einen Zipfel des Weltge-schehens.*" [In thinking we hold a corner of world events]. *In diesem Augenblicke* [At this moment] I forgot Unger, but faced my own self and its destiny, and my future spiritual path and desire stood clearly before me. I must seek the man to whom thinking opens the portal of life, who demands courage in thinking and leads to the recognition of Freedom (of will, of doing.)

So I came home and told mother of this quotation and the book from which it was quoted. Silently she walked to her bookcase, opened it (which before had never any interest to me, and I did not know what was in it) and gave to me the *Phil. der Freiheit*. "Maybe this is what you heard about." I sat down and began to read. Forgot night, forgot day and read, read until I had finished. Barely appeared to the meals. Returned and asked, is there more of this man – whereupon gave me: *Knowledge of the Higher Worlds*.[44]

Again, forgot day, night and read and read until I had finished. Undreamed-of horizons of a path – of thinking, will, into the world of the unknown, the spirit by awakening of one's own inner senses – observation of the spirit nature in man and nature, not speculation, but the path to actual seeing it, as a scientist would proceed:

A new world had opened. I knew by instinct, by the resonance of my entire soul, that here was the path to be taken to find the answer to all my problems and questions. That this other world can be experienced, by one's own free will and effort, can be observed, studied, this determined my entire future. Before, I had read poems of Christian Morgenstern,[45] *"Wir fanden einen Pfad"* [We found a path], and I knew I had become a *"Wegbruder"* [brother on the way] of his. I had found the path upon which — in freedom I could

43. *The Philosophy of Spiritual Activity [Freedom*]: *Fundamentals of a Modern World Conception*, GA 4. See reference 22.

44. *Knowledge of the Higher Worlds*, GA 10. See reference 23.

45. Christian Morgenstern (1871-1914) was a German Anthroposophic poet and humorist.

find myself and recognize the world. Within a week's time I had devoured, in addition, *Occult Science*,[46] *Spiritual Guidance of Mankind*,[47] and decided to attend any lecture on the subject of anthroposophy. There was the difficulty that personally, emotionally I did not like the people of my mother's environment. They were not scientists and did not speak the language of the academic world. The artists of the group I could digest better, for they did something, painted, and one could look at the paintings as upon phenomena. But when they started talking or philosophizing, it gave me the creeps, for I felt: this was just another way of speculation, of *Ausklügeln* [puzzling out]. I had developed, and still have, a very fine sense of differentiation between that which a man "thinks, speculates, *klügelt aus*" [puzzles out] and true inner observation and experience. Already then, and more so today, only that counts to me which is spoken out of experience, of doing the path actually rather than to construct theories about it.

Then could have developed a very critical moment, measuring actual experience against that which was said and lectured about anthroposophy, more or less as commentary or quotations, learned, acquired or read, not digested and made manifest. But before this critical moment became conscious, Rudolf Steiner. appeared in Stuttgart and lectured to the laborers of the Robert Bosch *Werke* [Works] (of which I was one), to the *Daimlerwerke* [Daimler Works] and to many others, in public and private, on the Threefold Social Order. And this was great revelation. With the knowledge of the spirit, you can actually *do* something. You can make it practical, you can build a world on firm grounds.

There was this young man, thin, hungry (the war years had left the scars of starvation and malnutrition,) searching, disillusioned, with no faith in God nor humanity, taught to use only cold logical reason, and now he experienced there is a MAN who has experienced what he says, who lives what he says, and who lives it not for his own personal ambitions, but who lives a life under sacrifice

46. *Occult Science*, G.A. 13. See reference 24.
47. *Spiritual Guidance of Mankind*, G.A. 15. See reference 25.

of his own self for the benefit of the world, of a future which to build he has given the tools and instruments of recognition: No other decision was possible but to follow, to surrender completely and to become one of them who helped him.

During this year 1919 I followed every step and lecture of Rudolf Steiner, not being a member as yet of that group whose behavior I disliked so much. But then it appeared I had to overcome this dislike and to move right into the center of the movement for which Rudolf Steiner stood. I swore to myself to devote my entire life to make Rudolf Steiner's world of ideas manifest and my own.

There were many clever, well-talking people about Rudolf Steiner, and there was this shy, silent young man in the background, like a shadow, ready to follow.

Two events stand clearly before my mental vision: A lecture by Rudolf Steiner in the summer of 1919 to the labor unions in the *Gewerkschafthaus* [Trade Union Headquarters]. The Communists had assembled their agitators and speakers with the Marxistic dogma against the message of Rudolf Steiner's new social order.

It was a hot day, and Rudolf Steiner had a hard struggle of the minds to overcome. He was on the platform, perspiring profusely. The laborers sat at tables, each with a glass of beer in front of him. The Anthroposophists, a few, were on the balcony as silent observers, because it was a laborers' group meeting. I felt sorry for the man on the platform and asked the waitress to put a bottle of *Überkinger*[48] and a glass in front of him. He interrupted his speech and gulped it down at once. I knew at that moment: the unknown little student and laborer, it is his task to help this man wherever it is possible, to get things done. This was my decision of which a whole lifetime resulted in the service of anthroposophy: to help, to make it work, practical, not to speculate, nor to watch from a balcony, but to step right into middle of it, not to care what others did or not did and – if nothing else – just to offer a glass of water when it was needed.

---

48. Mineral water.

The other: when the Marxistic dogmatist had so much opposed R. St's. ideas that he had to withdraw from any other lecturing to the labor unions and search for other channels, I stood near the platform when he descended and heard him say[49]: "At the present moment it will not be possible to penetrate onto the way to a new social order that I have begun; we must first establish the spiritual life anew, and from now on I shall dedicate myself entirely to the tasks of the spiritual life." (The exact date of this utterance I can, alas, no longer establish; in any case, it happened around the time of the breaking-off of discussions with the trade unions.)

Another event happened during the summer of 1919: visit to the so-called branch lectures, at first as guest at no. 70 *Landhauss-trasse* in Stuttgart. On this occasion the young student was personally introduced to Rudolf Steiner, which was followed by his words. "We have already known one another for a long time." As this was the first personal introduction, I could not understand how we could already know one another for a long time and was quite angry about it. Only years later the meaning of these words dawned upon me – namely, that they did not concern physical acquaintance, but knowledge of the eternal worth and destiny of the personality that stood there before the great teacher.

In Autumn 1919 (or even earlier) Herr Binder was appointed by Rudolf Steiner to take over the financial reorganization and supervision of the building project at the Goetheanum in Dornach, whereby mother and stepfather were prompted to move to Switzerland.

My first journey to Switzerland at Christmas 1919 remains an unforgettable day. First the half broken down, overcrowded trains with hour-long delays; in Karlsruhe I had to climb through the window into a carriage just to be able to come along, which provoked violent protests from the man in the red cap. Because of the collapse of Germany all respect for authority was lost, and I was determined not to give up my seat. Fortunately the train departed at that moment. The arrival in Switzerland. The parents first took the

49. Pfeiffer continues his biography in German text.

hungry youth into the station restaurant, and for the first time in many years he had real bean coffee and genuine milk – a great experience! The peace in the town of Basel, the serenity of the people, no rushing about, no cursing; all this awakened the feeling of homecoming. Arrival in Dornach late in the evening, so that one could only see the Goetheanum in the night light from a distance, rising from over the hill. The next morning, the first walk up the hill to the Goetheanum:

I knew: here is your home, what lived throughout your youth as a dream-spirit-world, what your ideals are and your strivings to manifest them in the physical, harsh so-called reality or earthly world – all this has found a home here. You have arrived on Earth and awakened. It was two months before my 21st birthday.[50]

The first Goetheanum building as seen on a rainy December morning melting with its green Norwegian slate roof into the grey fog is an impressive sight. Its architecture has been much disputed, liked or disliked. To whom the spirit world is an experience, not an abstract thought, it appeared as a visible message from this other world – a manifestation extending from the realm of ideas (a reality according to Plato, to Goethe) into the material physical world. Rudolf Steiner had frequently pointed out the "materials" should be used in such a way that they don't act as a wall, limiting, but as windows leading in eternity. I knew at once that here was a home, the home of that for which I stood at the time, when the youthful seeker of the truth had ascended to the hill of the Goetheanum. Rudolf Steiner had selected the green Norwegian slate which he saw once traveling in Norway and liked it because of its living quality, changing with sunshine or rain or fog its color, always blending together with the air, sky and clouds. The building therefore appeared wide open, upwards.

The woodcarving of its entire out- and inside spoke of human hands. Rudolf Steiner was proud about the fact that during the war, on the island of peace in the political turmoil which Switzerland was after all, that citizens of all fighting nations and peoples peace-

50. The text in German ends here and the text in English continues.

fully bridged the world dissonances and worked with their hand to complete the building which had started in 1913 and was near completion of the shell in December 1919.

The glass windows, colorful and artistically carved out of glass with a dentist's grinding wheel-like tool, were in place. Entering the building in its half-*dunkel* [darkness], with colors transparent from the windows cast over the woodwork – an unforgettable impression. Nothing the like, as interplay between color and form, woodwork existed anywhere else in the world, now, or earlier.

Rudolf Steiner was on a lecture trip, expected to return for Christmas. The Christmas plays were in preparation, where I should play Joseph and the *Stern* [star] singer (with great agony and stagefright, as it appeared later on), prompted by Rudolf Steiner whenever I got stuck. This first performance before people by the shy youth was quite an ordeal. Stagefright made me forget my lines, so I wrote them on the *Sternscheere* [star scissors]. But – it was necessary to expand the *Scheere* [scissors] to its greatest extension, and the little ladders upon which the lines were written disappeared far out of reach of the eyes. Rudolf Steiner, sitting in the front row, supplied, prompting, the words.

Being a student of technology, I was interested in the technical, constructive problems of the Goetheanum, and an immediate friendship and co-operation established itself with the then-architect of the Goetheanum, Aisenpreis[51]. Many nights into the wee hours were spent together to discuss the problems. There was especially the problem of the stage construction, of the stage lighting and upon my proposition of ventilation. I always felt adequate ventilation should be supplied to any room where people assembled, for I felt (today I know why) oxygen is an absolute must also for the brain, for attention, for listening; it breeds harmony and understanding, while lack of oxygen breeds disharmony and an-

51. Ernst Aisenpreis (1884-1949) was the German-born architect who became Chief Architect for both Goetheanum buildings in Dornach, Switzerland.

tipathy. Inasmuch as I had practical experience with stage problems and the installation of stage lighting from my labor-working days, I was presented a second time to Rudolf Steiner as the one who could do these technical jobs at the Goetheanum. That I was not quite 21, and probably still very young and green, did not enter the discussions. I did not know at the time that Rudolf Steiner had already prior to this vacation trip discussed my coming to Dornach with my mother and stepfather and had asked my stepfather almost every day, "When is he coming?"

In this interview Dr. Rudolf Steiner invited me to come to Dornach for good and to begin the assigned job the sooner the better. He went, and this was typical for him, as I found out many times later in regard to other problems, into all details of the physical arrangement: to return to Stuttgart at once, to get an immigration visa and permit to work in Switzerland; he produced a timetable and selected the train, estimated the waiting time for the visa and: "You will, of course, need something to make a living; you should therefore receive 300. – Sfr./month for your work, but should be entirely free how you want to organize the job." Once the job decided upon, full authority was delegated to me, and I could freely dispose of all means and employees needed to carry out the assignment. There was never any interference by anybody, and when some nosy guys tried to interfere, Rudolf Steiner shunned them off. The salary was one of the best-paid at the time to anybody at the Goetheanum. Much later I was told that in a finance meeting the question was brought up that this young lad is being paid way above his rating and youth, but Rudolf Steiner turned the critics down: "Well, he will be working for us at all times in the future, so what." Rudolf Steiner wanted his coworkers to be well-paid and free from want and financial worries, a principle which the administration in later critical years could not always adhere to.

It appeared that it took six weeks instead of the originally planned two weeks to return, and again Rudolf Steiner asked almost every day, "When does Pfeiffer come?"

Arrived the second time, for good. Rudolf Steiner outlined at once the task and his concept for stage lighting, which was quite different from the customary technique at the time.

5. Rudolf Steiner as the Creator of a New Art of Stage Lighting[52]

It has been about twenty years since Dr Rudolf Steiner gave some indications which led to the development of that interplay of color known to everyone who attends a Eurythmy performance. While previously, Eurythmy programs displayed uniform lighting interrupted by just a few nuances – red-white, red-white-blue, white-yellow – for whole program parts, as a result of those indications a technical solution was sought for stage lighting that permitted very fast changes and transitions.

Dr. Steiner expressed to the writer of these lines that he envisioned for the stage lighting in the Goetheanum an arran-gement that would produce as diffuse a light as possible, similar to soft daylight with its light and color changes. He pointed to a skylight in the old *Schreinerei* [joiner's workshop] and challenged him to notice how the stage would change if the sun shone through or a cloud passed over the sun or it were a dull day. "You should study the color display that arises when the sun is suddenly obscured by a cloud, or emerges again from behind a veil of clouds." Stage lighting was to be patterned after this to have as "scattered" a light as possible. Light artificially concentrated through lenses, such as produced by a spotlight, has the character of something unnatural. For the stage of the first Goetheanum

---

52. At the wish of Pfeiffer, his article entitled "Rudolf Steiner als Schöpfer einer neuen Bühnen-beleuchtungskunst" is included here. It first appeared in *Das Goetheanum: Wochenschrift für Anthroposophie* [The Goetheanum: Weekly Journal for Anthroposophy], Dornach, *19. Jahrgang* [19th Year], Nr. 10, *3.* March 3,] 1940, *S.*[pp.] 75-76; *Bühnenbeleuchtung zur Eurythmie* [Stage Lighting for Eurythmy], published by Georg Wurmehl, Dornach 1969. Reprinted (in German only) in Rudolf Steiner's *Farbenerkenntnis* [Perception of Color], GA 291a, as *Eurythmie-Beleuchtung* [Eurythmy Lighting], *S.* [pp.] 385-394. See reference 26.

building, which was also the small cupola room with its architraves, pillars and cupola painting, one should aim to flood it with multi-colored illumination coming, if possible, from all directions. The figures should be surrounded in a cloud of light and color. For this purpose one should work with special lighting intensities and six colors (white, red, yellow, blue, green, violet.) In order to achieve such a saturation of brightness, lights should be placed six meters high laterally behind the pillars in addition to footlights along the full width of the ramp.

On the basis of these few indications, the installation of the stage lighting of the Goetheanum was begun. Diffusion imitating daylight was achieved by departing from usual routines of stage technology. At that time one mainly worked with flies, spotlights and similar devices, i.e. directed light broken up or regulated by means of reflectors and lenses. We built special light fixtures with convex instead of concave reflectors, covered with matt but pure white chalk. This enabled us to achieve a specially soft and intimate mixing of color tones. The light fixtures were set up behind the pillars of the small cupola so that nothing could be seen from the auditorium. Since a light source stood behind each pillar, the whole space was fully and equally flooded with light from the side as well as obliquely from behind. An intensive colorful and yet soft mood could be achieved. The only six-meter-high arrangement made possible a richness not achievable with the high rigging lofts of normal stages. The closest to this effect on the usual stage would be with a cyclorama.

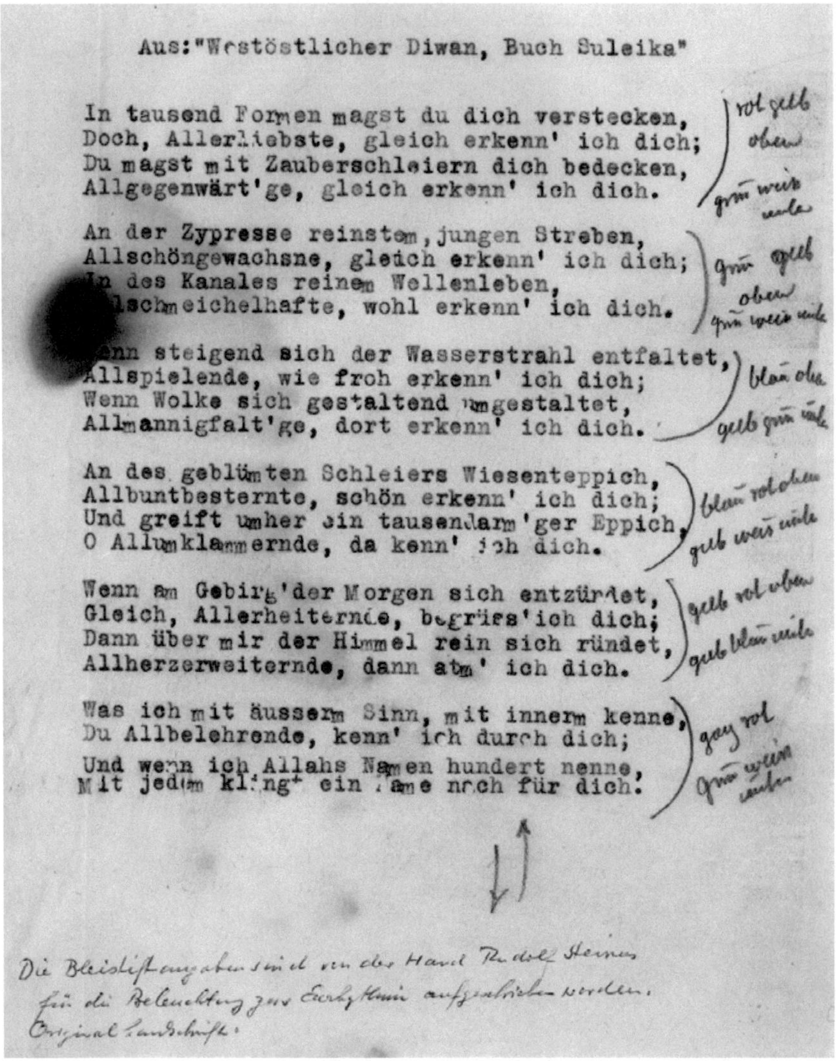

Aus: "Westöstlicher Diwan, Buch Suleika"

In tausend Formen magst du dich verstecken,
Doch, Allerliebste, gleich erkenn' ich dich;
Du magst mit Zauberschleiern dich bedecken,
Allgegenwärt'ge, gleich erkenn' ich dich.

An der Zypresse reinstem, jungen Streben,
Allschöngewachsne, gleich erkenn' ich dich;
In des Kanales reinem Wellenleben,
Allschmeichelhafte, wohl erkenn' ich dich.

Wenn steigend sich der Wasserstrahl entfaltet,
Allspielende, wie froh erkenn' ich dich;
Wenn Wolke sich gestaltend umgestaltet,
Allmannigfalt'ge, dort erkenn' ich dich.

An des geblümten Schleiers Wiesenteppich,
Allbuntbesternte, schön erkenn' ich dich;
Und greift umher ein tausendarm'ger Eppich,
O Allumklammernde, da kenn' ich dich.

Wenn am Gebirg' der Morgen sich entzündet,
Gleich, Allerheiternde, begrüß' ich dich;
Dann über mir der Himmel rein sich ründet,
Allherzerweiternde, dann atm' ich dich.

Was ich mit äusserm Sinn, mit innerm kenne,
Du Allbelehrende, kenn' ich durch dich;
Und wenn ich Allahs Namen hundert nenne,
Mit jedem klingt ein Name nach für dich.

From Goethe's *West-Eastern Divan VIII. Book of Suleika.*

The pencilled notes above, in Rudolf Steiner's original handwriting, indicate his directions for the lighting of an Eurythmy performance.

Thyself in thousand forms thou mayst conceal,
Yet all-belovèd, straight thou art known to me;
Thou mayst fling over thee some magic veil,
Thou, the All-present, straight art known to me.

In the young cypress's most pure aspiring,
All-burgeoning-beauty, straight thou art known to me;
In the canals' pure life of waves untiring,
Thou, All-caressing, straight art known to me.

If beamlike flung in air the fount escape,
How gladly, All-sportive, thou art known to me;
If the cloud shape itself but to reshape,
All man-fold, in it thou art known to me.

In the pied carpet of the meadow shining,
All-diverse-starred, how fair thou art known to me;
Does ivy fling her thousand arms entwining,
O All-embracing, there thou art known to me.

When on the mount morn kindles, thou straightway,
The All-rejoicing, greeted art by me;
When o'er me deepens the pure dome of day,
All-heart-dilating, thou art breathed by me.

What lore through outward sense or inward came,
Through thee, All-teaching, has been known to me;
And Allah's hundred names if I should name,
A name for thee with each would sound to me.*

Goethe, March 14, 1815

**The Ghazel is a litany of love parallel to the invocation of Allah by his ninety-nine other names.*
[Translation by Edward Dowden, President of the English Goethe Society. Published in 1914 by J.M. Dent & Sons Ltd., London and Toronto, pp. (97) 142-143.] See also reference 27.

The use of six colors gives rise to effects beyond those of merely the blending of blue and red for violet or blue and yellow for green. An intense green, for instance, can never be achieved through blending. This is particularly apparent when one not only carries out the lighting of a space, but takes note of those small changes created on a colored costume or veil by varying, mixed-color lighting as, for instance, in Eurythmy. A "green" from a mixture of blue and yellow would bring out, for example, the yellow on a yellow ground and bright-red veil quite differently from a pure green illumination, which has a more dimming-down effect. While a light-blue veil in the same situation forms more of the resultants of green with "green," though the blue+yellow will intensify the blue, the yellow will dim it almost to grey. Thus innumerable variations are possible if one notes the interplay of the lighting with the colors of the costumes and veils. Lighting can accentuate, dim and extinguish. Depending on its change, the same garment can appear almost solid in space, or as a surface image, or even be lost, dissolved in an intensive fullness of color.

After the technical installation was so far advanced that all the light fixtures had found their most advantageous positions, with a switchboard that allowed for mixings at any intensity, Dr. Steiner quiety arranged a special stage-lighting rehearsal in order to study the color effects. A chair was placed in the middle of the stage under the small cupola with colored veils and costumes laid on it and illuminated by single colors at full strength. This yielded important insights regarding intensity. Intense red lighting from all sides can make a light-red garment appear almost white, but a red of identical shade disappear. The same with blue on blue, green on green. A sudden change to a most intensive red after green can make a red garment look black for a few moments, as long as the after-effect in the eye lasts. Indeed, through sudden determined changes the active capacities of the eye can produce all manner of "subjective" effects. All this was researched at this rehearsal in late summer, 1920, and final instructions given for color strengths. Anyone who saw the stage lighting in the old Goetheanum will remember in what fullness of light and color the whole space could shine. An unforgettable experience for those who could let the essence of the continuously changing colors work upon them. For example the *Prologue in Heaven* (Faust) took about 40,000 W.

One of the most important innovations in the realm of stage lighting was without doubt the suggestions of Rudolf Steiner for a color intensity which until then had not been striven for. One can certainly say, with regard to the earlier conventional stage lighting of the naturalistic theater, it required courage to undertake this journey into the realm of pure colors.[53] As opposed to merely mood-setting sunset, afternoon or midnight stage lighting, Rudolf Steiner began with illumination of the Eurythmy stage suitable to the soul and spirit of the character of the performance. What still alienated some in his early audiences was the frequent sudden change—without gradual transitions. But contasts don't seem to be present and justified only in the spirit or soul. They also arise in and around nature. One need only think of the above- mentioned suggestion to observe the play of color as a cloud passes over the sun. It's not so much a matter of seeing the sun and cloud, but rather of studying how objects on the ground or in a sun-illuminated space change. In such a case there are often quite sudden transitions, rich in contrasts. The blue colors are suddenly lost in uncertainty, darkness. Only the bright yellow and white lights still flash forth; at the moment when the sun reappears, at one stroke blue and violet return to their original strength, while the lights, on the contrary, lose something.

Thus also the fact of sudden color changes reveals the pure essence of light. Altogether, Rudolf Steiner's way of applying stage lighting is the consequent artistic expression of what insight can be developed, perhaps from Goethe's Color Theory or his lectures on color, into the essence of light and color.

Now it would be wrong to think and speculate that the color changes for Eurythmy were puzzled out or that all these observations of the effects of coordinating costume, veil and lighting were

53. Since this time the use of a color-symphony has become more and more known on other stages.

premeditated. That could not be the case, because Rudolf Steiner's lighting was often written spontaneously into the textbook; it was never tried out on the stage whether this or that suited better. The lighting with its color nuances was determined the moment Rudolf Steiner was given the respective text or music selection. It was an *a priori* element of the composition or poetry. This came to expression in the way the lighting instructions were given, e.g., for pieces of music. Often only with a movement of the hand: "When the music goes like this (a broad raising, slowly climbing hand movement) you must use *this* color; when it goes like this (a horizontally undulating gesture), then *that* color." The stage-lighter had the task of emmpathetically interpreting in color the mood and movement of the melody according to the gestures and instructions. "With those notes (a prominent staccato movement) red must be added as well," etc. The first time the Eurythmy figures were introduced in a lecture and their movement, character and feeling discussed in connection with costume and veil, Rudolf Steiner was asked whether the colors given to the Eurythmy figures also determined the stage lighting. Rudolf Steiner denied this, but added that every verse of a poem had a basic mood; one is tuned completely to A [Ah], another to I [Eee], still another to a consonant. This basic mood comes to expression in the lighting. With the lighting of the upbeat and final measure (whether silent or with music) these basic moods are repeated one after another, forwards or backwards. Often Rudolf Steiner wrote out a sequence of sounds in color. I can likewise make the observation that the color sequence had a most intensive connection less with the veil or costume, than often with the sound sequence of the Eurythmy form that was followed in space.

The stage lighter must then become a Eurythmist himself in order to follow the forms and carry out the change at the right moment. Rudolf Steiner also left it to the stage lighter to find the right mixture of the blending nuances. He appealed to the artistic impulse. This kept the stage lighting from becoming something rigid or schematic. On the ordinary theater stage, the stage lighter is found amidst his machinery; the equipment and its respective resistance and current figures are indicated in a textbook. The man often sees the stage incompletely or not at all. For the new art of stage lighting, this is unacceptable. Here, it is a matter of following the movements on the stage with alert attention and accompanying them through color Eurythmy Thus the stage lighter becomes an active co-player perceived by the audience through his effects. He represents an essential part of the harmonious effect of the whole.

If one wants to have a remote idea of the lighting effects of the old Goetheanum stage, two photos may be seen of the space under the small cupola. One is taken with stage lighting, i.e., scattered light from all sides; the other, with the central 8,000W ceiling light.[54] In the first case, even in the black-and-white photo one can observe the soft mood, avoiding hard shadows through light saturation of the space, the gentle and yet plastic transition of the architrave and pillars. Especially noticeable is the "true-color," natural appearance of the cupola painting this made possible. By use of the six-colored lighting, every color of the cupola painting (just as of the moving figures on the stage in performances) came into its own. In contrast, the centered, concentrated lighting is selective, partisan and produces hard shadows. The reconciling element of a color-saturated space is lacking, and one is faced with angularity.

The essence of Rudolf Steiner's indications for stage lighting has been preserved for us. In a scene from the Mystery Dramas portrayed Eurythmically, Rudolf Steiner instructed the stage lighter to give each person a particular basic lighting. Each person should be enveloped in his or her individual garment of color, and on stepping forward lend this color character temporarily to the whole scene. Perhaps much more could have been created, especially for the Mystery Dramas, since that period from 1920-1924 was devoted mainly to the development of lighting for Eurythmy. A wide field for artistic undertaking still lay open here. The burning of the old Goetheanum destroyed much here, also. The harmonious accord of architecture, light reflected by wood, the painting of the

---

54. See the illustrations on pp. 116/117 in: *Das Goetheanum als Gesamtkunstwerk* [The Goetheanum as a Total Work of Art], Dornach 1986.

cupola and the most intensive flood of color with whatever was happening on the stage could not be restored again. Whoever experienced this at the time saw, for a few short years, possibilities in the realm of color which now, like the king's daughter in the fairy tale, await reawakening. For purely technical reasons, much could not be carried out on the new Goetheanum stage as it was before. Here the givens of a purely functional stage must be reckoned with. Above all, that harmony within the small cupola room could naturally not be attained again. What, however, survives is the living memory from which the new art of stage lighting can develop further.

*

One fundamental idea was that light should be used diffuse, like sunlight coming thru a window and as light appears in nature but not concentrated by lenses as in floodlights. "In light which passes through a lens and is concentrated, there is an element of untruth," he said. I had great fights later on with the performers, who wanted to have floodlights upon their persons, but I never gave in, defending Rudolf Steiner's original instructions. This is the way I learned to become stubborn and persistent and to carry out an idea. I believe I was not much liked by others if I did not yield to their whims.

It was at the same instructive meeting that Rudolf Steiner said to me, "*Halten Sie sich immer an Frau Doktor*" [Always follow *Frau Doktor*, i.e. Marie Steiner], a task which some ten, fifteen, twenty years later caused many problems. At the time Frau Marie Steiner[55] paid but little attention to the young man; he was just a stage hand.

It was clear to me that the technological part of the stage lighting, as far as electric installation was concerned, could follow routine construction principles, but that the instruments for the light-

55. Frau Marie Steiner-von Sivers (1867-1948) was a Russian-born Swiss actress and speech artist, leader of the Section for the Arts of Eurythmy, Speech, Drama and Music at the Goetheanum, who became Rudolf Steiner's second wife in December,1914.

ing had to be built by ourselves, for there was, at the time, just nothing developed which would fulfill the demands of Rudolf Steiner – including the switchboard. So, a workshop was set up in the *Kesselhaus* [Boiler House], where the electrician Bollinger and an apprentice, Stracke, began to build the various apparatus according to my specification, and often I had to put on hand myself.

As office, with huge drawing boards, we used the East wing of the Glasshouse, where originally the huge Glass windows were carved. The West wing, some twenty-five years later to become the home of the laboratory, was still used for glass carving. It was mainly Frau Turgenieff who worked there, a Russian of great artistic talent, and a Polish Lady (S.) whose name I forgot [=Emma Stolle].

This office had huge dimensions: one round room, about 27 feet high and 30 feet diameter. Herr Aisenpreis had his drawing desk there, and I occupied the other half of the room, getting used to large dimensions. Once, much later, when I had to use other offices, and especially right now with only a cubbyhole of office, I always missed these dimensions.

Having thought and experienced so much while wandering thru field and woods, I learned to think and ponder while walking, never liked sitting before a desk, and this large office suited my peripatetic trends just right.

Rudolf Steiner had created a new art – Eurythmy – the art of motion of the body in tune with the inner motion of the spoken word. Dance is not the right term, for it is not of the nature of the ritual temple dance of old and, of course, Eurythmy has nothing to do with modern dances at all. The formation of a sound, vowel or consonant, releases finer motions within the human body, fluids, skeleton, muscles – the expression of the sound via the larynx, vocal chord, mouth and lips, carried outward by the breath, is only a small fraction of the entire process which leads to speech. In Eurythmy, the attempt is made to express, through motion of the body members, the original force or law which lives in the production of sound. (It would be simple to describe this in terms of etheric and astral body, but I am trying at this stage of affairs to avoid the Anthroposophical terminology; this will be introduced later on).

When I came to Dornach there was only a small stage, temporarily, in the *Schreinerei* [joiner's workshop], the workshop where the woodwork, lumber etc. was prepared for the building. In this *Schreinerei* was a lecture room for Dr. Steiner's lectures parted from the stage by a blue curtain. This hall would hold about 300 people. The stage had one foot-ramp and two *Soffitten* [flies] and most primitive switches to switch on or off white, blue, red or yellow bulbs. Usually a whole section of the Eurythmy performance was clad in white-yellow, another in blue-red, etc. That is a rather monotonous setting.

Rudolf Steiner explained that he would like to follow the mood of a verse or poem, a line even or any specific motion, with color changes of the lights. This necessitated the building of rheostats easy to handle that would "play" colors in lighting like one would play tunes on a piano. What technology had to offer was much too clumsy and heavy to allow fast, flowing, dynamic changes. I decided to build a system of fluid rheostats to be operated by a short keyboard (a kind of color-piano) which enabled to mix the different colors of the stage lights instantaneously and in every direction desired. This color keyboard was finished and put to operation in May-June, 1920. While it had still many faults, it was an instrument to play color and to be used for that which Rudolf Steiner wanted to develop as color–light–scheme to accompany Eurythmy. At the main rehearsal he would then indicate the color changes to the poems, verses, bars of music, motions – changes which followed one another in swift succession. He would write the colors in the books of poetry to be performed, which I handed to him, or the notes of music, sometimes even only indicating with a gesture which sequence he wanted. I had built a little cubbyhole with the color piano near the left corner of the stage, sitting on a footstool and having the full view of the stage. Some of the Eurythmists would come into that corner to view the stage, and I must say we had a jolly good time in this corner. During the rehearsal Frau Marie Steiner had an armchair on a platform in the audience section, to watch and give instructions and to recite, herself. She was not particularly interested in my work at the time, taking it for granted that Rudolf Steiner would tell what to do with regard to the lights and I would carry out accordingly. I had a free hand to carry out the instructions by Rudolf Steiner and don't remember that I have ever been corrected or reprimanded. In fact, nobody showed much interest in this specific work, taking it for granted. The role assigned to me was like to a *Heinzelmännchen* [elf], whose help one takes, but never sees it.

Rudolf Steiner would come to the main rehearsal which was, if possible, run like the performance with little interruption and sit beside Frau Marie Steiner, observing the procedure or performance, give advice as to veils, colors, movements. It was a perfect example of cooperation, where everyone concerned did his share without much coaching, arguing, etc. These main rehearsals were quite different from the anteceding study and trials where, to the contrary, much discussion and arguing went on – in the absence of the master. Since I always, and still, dislike arguing, I did not attend the pre-rehearsals, but only the main rehearsal, taking in a way a chance that things worked all right at the performance the next day. It was at one of these rehearsals that Rudolf Steiner called me for the first time by my Christian name (Ehrenfried). Climbing out of my cubbyhole and walking up to the throne, as we called the setup where he and Frau Marie Steiner would sit, I heard the following discussion: Frau Marie : "*Was rufen Sie da?* [What did you call him then?]". Rudolf Steiner "*Was haben Sie dagegen, Ehrenfried ist doch ein schöner Name.*" [What do you have against it, after all Ehrenfried is a beautiful name.] Frau Marie, which was very typical for her attitude in general, did not like such informality as done by Rudolf Steiner, to call somebody by first name. In fact, I remember only three cases when he did, and it made me very happy to feel included. Anyhow, a personal relationship had developed which cannot be otherwise labeled as that he took a fatherly interest in my little affairs and being. A few days later I met Rudolf Steiner in a small passage to the left of the stage. He took both of my hands, drew me somewhat near and looked deeply with his dark eyes into mine and said, "*Sie nehmen es mir doch nicht übel, dass ich Sie Ehrenfried nenne.*" [You do not mind that I call you Ehrenfried]. This again was so typical for Rudolf Steiner, who respected so much the freedom of the other, that he excused himself for calling the other by his first name. It was at this moment, when we met eye to eye, that I perceived something of the true being Rudolf Steiner, his eternal being, and I felt that something of it flowed over to me and filled my whole being and heart, something from or for which I lived henceforth. While many saw in Rudolf Steiner the great lecturer, the teacher, the esoteric teacher, the Initiate, the man far above on a pedestal, I saw henceforth the human being, the man who struggled, who fought, who suffered, who loved, whose kindness was above any other kindness I ever experienced in life. I experienced also the shyness, that mysterious force which plays from human being to human being when one soul opens its gate to another, as one does in true love. I "recognized" Rudolf Steiner in the sense as is described in the Gospels when the to-become-Apostle men saw Jesus and "recognized" the Christ, which became the cause of their Apostolic mission. So I recognized the spirit beings and powers in that moment which acted through the man Rudolf Steiner. A very tender relationship emanated from this, tender especially because I did not belong to the *Haute volée*, adepts, big-shots of the Society. Years later, 1938/39, and almost another ten years later, by way of an exchange with the then ailing Marie Steiner shortly before her death, I had an exchange of thought about this "recognizing" of Rudolf Steiner, and she confirmed that she had a similar experience, which prompted her to follow him and prepare his path. I know from a few remarks that another personality, close to him, Frau Doktor Ita Wegman[56] had the same experience.

---

56. Ita Maria Wegman, M.D., (1876-1943) was an Indonesian-born Swiss physician, leader of the Medical Section at the Goetheanum and founder of a clinic in Arlesheim, Switzerland, in 1921.

*

The stage lighting was perfected and worked out in more details until the final illness and death of Rudolf Steiner. The task to establish the same principles in the Goetheanum was difficult for many technical reasons, but was finally solved. One night Rudolf Steiner came alone to the building for an inspection and trial to see what the new installation would do. This was a peculiar experience – he alone in the audience space – *Frl.* [Miss} Käthe Mitscher[57], the untiring stage manager of the Eurythmy performances, was sent away, and so we tried and tried many different combinations, and when all lights were on, some 25,000 candle powers, Rudolf Steiner said: "more light." It appeared then that we had reached the maximum capacity which the electrical facilities, transformers and supply of current would give, and there was no way to increase because there was just no more current. Such problems were discussed as to make a person (indicated by colored veils and costumes over chairs on the stage) completely disappear (red light with utmost intensity on red veil and costume) and to create all kind of contrasts. The person should appear and disappear from a "cloud of color" wrapped into color which changes continuously with the mood of that which is said.

It was as Rudolf Steiner was sitting there and drinking in all the light and color, becoming color through and through. And so I felt, as in the teen-ages everything became music, harmony or dissonance, I felt now that color can transmit a similar experience: the harmony, or dissonance which demands solution, that which is so dryly called the weaving light and color. I felt that one cannot only bathe the figures on the stage in color, but one can completely penetrate it, dissolve it or make it tight, physically hard or transparent, so that the actor actually emanates that which he performs as color and light as he speaks the word and makes the motion (as in Eurythmy.) I knew, and Rudolf Steiner guided, how one could create an impression so that one could release – visibly – that

---

57. Käthe Mitscher (1892-1940). For a short biography, see webpage: http://www.lichteurythmie.de/leblauf/mitscher.html.

which emanates as color from the etheric and astral body, to become perceptible to the spectator.

This was the art of stage lighting which Rudolf Steiner wanted to create in the Goetheanum, adequate to the entire purpose of this building. And we had *one* performance, late at night, on this memorable day, at least, with no spectator of this new art of the light and its colors.

Alas, circumstances later on prevented that this art ever could be developed.

To me it meant, as I had – as a youth – once seen open the heavens and heard the heavenly music and harmony, I had once seen the light and the weaving colors, and I knew from experience what it meant when Rudolf Steiner taught about the light "*Des Lichtes webend Wesen, es erstrahlet...*" [The Light's weaving essence, it radiates...][58], *The Portal of Initiation, Sc. 3.*

Preparatory to this moment probably was that I had read, during the last year in Stuttgart, on weekends where my parents had a weekend house in Sillenbuch, with my parents Goethe's *Farbenlehre* [Theory of Color] and made Goethe's experiments, just looking at the phenomena, with no speculation about it.

In the Anthroposophical movement there were many study groups on Goethe's *Farbenlehre,* which more or less repelled me because of the abstract, intellectual, pseudo- scientific approach to the problem. One talked *about* the light and color, but actually did not experience the Light – Experience was what counted to me, not speculation, theory *about* a thing.

In all these years there were probably only two or three occasions that people ever asked me: and what did Rudolf Steiner *really* intend when he created the Art of Eurythmy–stage lighting? Marie Steiner, fourteen years later, was one. A few years ago, artists at the Goetheanum and the then man in charge of the stage

58. Footnote by Pfeiffer: It would be necessary to speak now of the rainbow experience, but this cannot be clad in words as yet.

lighting asked me to give a lecture on the subject[59] to a small group. It was then that the word dropped: well, this what Pfeiffer. says casts such a new point of view that it seems we had been moving in the wrong direction. I had noticed this to come for many years, but saw no possibility to interfere with the procedures – anyhow, life had brought other tasks – but the circumstances which led to my resignation to continue stage lighting at the Goetheanum some seven years after the above-described scene with Rudolf Steiner were such that I could not possibly resume any contact or activity in this direction, and so that Art of Stage Lighting which Rudolf Steiner wanted to create belongs to the lost arts.[60]

With his art of lighting on the stage for Eurythmy and Mystery Plays, Rudolf Steiner had a specific purpose in mind: to surround the performer with a color-filled space which was in continuous fluctuation according to the mood (*Stimmung)* of the spoken word. In order to understand this, one could imagine a landscape or room which is penetrated, filled by sunlight. Then clouds move, intermittently covering the sun, and light and shadows are changed – only that in this case the clouds are colorful, and we would have not only the interchange of light and shadow, but the play of colors.

It was obvious that – in order to produce the desired effects, also the technical arrangement of light and color spending [emitting] equipment had to [be] constructed and designed in such a way that swift changes were made possible and enough intensities, as candle power, were made available. On a small stage this is no problem. On a large stage, as the one to build into the second

---

59. On February 22, 1955, in the Goetheanum. The essay first appeared in 1940 in the weekly journal *Das Goetheanum* [The Goetheanum], then in *Bühnenbeleuchtung zur Eurythmie* [Stage Lighting for Eurythmy], published by Georg Wurmehl, Dornach, 1969. Reprinted (in German only) in Rudolf Steiner's '*Farbenerkenntnis* [Knowledge of Color], GA 291a, as *Eurythmie-Beleuchtung* [Eurythmy Lighting], S. [pp.] 385-394. See reference 26.

60. Footnote by Pfeiffer: It is possible that this continuation does not quite match the previous pages because there is an almost 2½-month interruption in writing, from September to November, 1958.

Goetheanum, there were technical limitations a) by the size of the stage opening, b) by the height of the light-emitting fixture above the stage floor, i.e., the ceiling height, c) by the available electrical current (kilowatt). Since light diminishes at the rate of the square of the distance, it was obvious that the ceiling height was a set condition. In planning the stage of the second Goetheanum, the portal opening height of the stage was set as of six meter. Accordingly the light fixtures would be dimensioned. This meant at maximum intensity the full use of the available electric power. This would have enabled the operator of the lighting to meet the purpose of Rudolf Steiner's lighting art.

Alas, the artists demanded different. For the sake of historical truth I must state here, as much as I regret to do so, that very little understanding for Rudolf Steiner's original idea was shown. One artist demanded as only item "plenty of red;" another one, very ambitious, could not have the stage opening and width large enough for her little or inflated ego, demanded and finally forced a portal opening of 9m and accordingly a larger width and ceiling than the one which was technically provided for. This reduced the light intensity to exactly one half of the planned one and made it impossible ever to achieve the effects which Rudolf Steiner had in mind. There was not enough power available to adjust the equipment to this demand. This writer, since he found only deaf ears, could not carry out the original impulse and decided to resign. The regret that he could not carry out the task assigned by Rudolf Steiner influenced him so much (one may say hurt him so much) that he wanted never to deal with any of these problems, even though some twenty-five years later he was asked to give advice. This event was a typical illustration to the very interesting problem that the artist has not only to be an artist, performer as it may be or a creative artist with imagination, inspiration and ideas, but he has also to master the problem of the material with which he works. Not even the best violinist can give a perfect performance if he would have an instrument built from knotty, unseasoned wood, or a painter having colors which are not light-fast and are dull (cf. Leonardo's unsuccessful attempts to create new, brilliant but not lasting color.) To coordinate artistic creation with the technology of the available material is an absolute must, and the artist becomes only a master if he can harmoniously blend his art with the material and can find that material which gives his art performance the adequate foothold and environment.

This principle applies to all and every art, even the art of living, or the "art" of being a human being. While technology should not rule art, Art should cast its beauty upon technology and create such means as will favor this art to the best.

The artist has to be a technologist lest his creation becomes [a] perishable piece [of] work. The genius has to become a talent too, has to make painstaking efforts to create adequate means of expression. No Eurythmist serves the spiritual impulse of this art, as a visible expression of the spoken word, who believes that the flaying arms and moving body are all that is needed. A Eurythmic performance remains incomplete, even with the most beautiful movements, colorful garments and veils, as long as these are surrounded by dull, weak light and color and not bathed into an almost unearthly intensity of light and color. The true artist would have to yield to and accept the given technological conditions, without which this aim remains incomplete. To demand the impossible is *not* Art. To use the available, possible means in such a way that it becomes integrated part of the performance *is* art. Then the artist has mastered matter, as Michelangelo did when he carved a David out of a misshaped block of marble.

This deed of Michelangelo was one of the greatest masterpieces of artistic creation, if for nothing else, then at least for the reason that he had overcome gravity and created a free- standing figure that is standing on its feet as a living man and not using such supports or crutches as one sees frequently in monuments, a lean-to to a pole, tree, or, which is worst, a stick or iron rod along the back or through the belly of a horse to hold the structure.

Art which masters the material does not need crutches.

*

Well, this period which started with my assignment to come to Dornach and was intensively connected with the preparing of the technological arrangement at the first and second Goetheanum had come to an end after about seven years, two years after the death of the great master.

In the meantime, other situations and conditions had arisen, so that for the writer no problem or hardship was created otherwise; but the regret that the original impulses could not be carried out does not relieve him before his own conscience of the feeling of a failure. However, as Rudolf Steiner once said, One who is striving esoterically can admit only two reasons for giving up a thing once begun: a) the recognition of an error, b) the fact *"daß einem der Stuhl vor die Türe gesetzt wird"* [that one's door is barred with a chair]. Since in this case the reaction of others concerned was such that he could not carry out what he wanted, the second reason applies.

This in a way influenced the writer such that in the future he tried to adjust his beginnings and to conduct his behavior and aims in such a way that the danger of the chair put outside was reduced to a calculated minimum. This meant that he had to adjust his goals to a reachable distance in accordance with his means, talents, abilities and to strive for something which he could achieve, so to say, on his own steam – alone or with the help of understanding and cooperating friends. Within other things, he learned that he had not only to convince himself, or as one would say in U.S.A., to sell the idea to himself, but that he had to create enthusiasm for the execution of his ideas.

That I have not been able to create interest in the stage lighting idea Rudolf Steiner's and understanding for the involved technicalities was due to several factors, one being my own shyness in the contact with human beings. I liked to listen, but if there were more than three people, the throat just felt strangulated. The other reason is one of fundamental difference between the method of approach of the so-called artist (Eurythmist in this case) and of the one who underwent at the same time a scientific and Anthroposophical training. Doing the technical job as outlined was looked upon as something inferior, since electricity was involved; this belonged anyhow for many to the "underworld"; so one did not understand or accept the one who handled this "material" as anything worth of consideration.

At many occasions, the annual meetings of the Society, f.i. [for instance], the arts and artists were always highly appraised by some speakers, but little recognition was given to other work. In this lack of recognition for the work of the scientific mind, the researcher, I see a major reason that the Anthroposophical Society and the Goetheanum has today an "art" (we don't need to evaluate how good or perfect it is,) but has very few scientists which can devote a full time to their assignments as the artist could. They always had to earn something as a side issue in order to maintain their contribution to the Goetheanum. Who doubts this statement may study the annual financial reports and compare the sums which were allotted to the arts and stage work with the sums which were allotted to the laboratories.

One satisfaction could be had, though, which outweighed all other disappointments of a Cinderella existence otherwise in these early years. At one general meeting, I believe it was in 1921, after once more the artists had been appraised by many, Rudolf Steiner mentioned one should not forget the work Ehrenfried Pfeiffer has contributed with the stage lighting to the arts at the Goetheanum. But hereto is to say that Rudolf Steiner had always an open interest in the activities and growth of this young man.

*

6. Study – Study – Study

The first few months of the year 1920 were completely absorbed with construction and erection of the stage lighting equipment at the Goetheanum. When these duties eased up with regard to the time element and were concentrated more or less to the weekends, the desire appeared to pick up again and to continue academic studies. Before coming to Dornach, my primary interest was physics with emphasis on electricity and electrical engineering. Two semesters were spent at the *Technische Hochschule Stuttgart*

[Stuttgart Technical College] besides the practical shop work. My primary interest was still with physics when I asked Rudolf Steiner whether and how I should continue my academic studies. To my great surprise and even some protest, Rudolf Steiner suggested chemistry as major object. While I see today that chemistry = the knowledge of the world of substance, the material out of which nature builds its life and bodies, and the knowledge of the functional relationship of these substances has been, and still is, in the truest sense my inner calling and disposition, I did not accept this at once when Rudolf Steiner made the suggestion. Even though I had been even genetically or inherited prepared, for my grandfather was a chemist and pharmacist, and my father, who died when I was five, wanted to become a chemist but was not permitted so by his guardian, who forced him into another profession.

Rudolf Steiner took matters in strong but kind hands, and at the beginning of each semester I had to come to him and show him the *Vorlesungsverzeichnis* [course catalog] as well as give a Resumé of the previously achieved. He emphasized time and again the need for practical, laboratory, experimental work. He would select few theoretical courses, but much laboratory practice and courses in experimental chemistry and physics. But the range of his suggestions went much further, including full courses in mineralogy, physical chemistry, botany, geography of plants, ecology and, again to my surprise, national economy, history of trade, *Handelswissenschaft* [commerce], yes, even psychology, and as a special course: psychology of the masses. When I called his attention to the fact that he had selected two full-day practica in one period, he just smiled and said: "*Oh, Sie werden das schon bewältigen.*" [Oh, you will manage it all right.]

So, we look back upon a very busy student during these years 1920-1925, attending the courses and practica at the University of Basle and at the same time doing stage lighting at the Goetheanum and attending all lectures and courses given by Rudolf Steiner in Dornach, Stuttgart, Austria and elsewhere on the continent, but not in England or Norway or Sweden (the latter for lack of spending money.) This was a very active period of learning, absorbing, of discussion of that acquired with contemporary friends, of activities to create an Anthroposophical youth movement and of aims and preparations to establish a center for Anthroposophical scientific research at the Goetheanum.

The hunger for knowledge of this young man was enormous. It is quite clear, looking backward, the academic studies as far as theoretical knowledge is concerned remained incomplete, and only in much later years it became a must to catch up on this things. The laboratory work was done at all times with great enthusiasm. Hereto contributed that in inorganic and analytical chemistry Prof. Fichter presented his matters with great enthusiasms. His courses belonged to the real joyful part of the academic years. Courses in theoretical physics and physical chemistry offered more of a headache. Were it not for the great devotion and admiration for Rudolf Steiner, this young man would have landed in the midst of the quantum theory, of studies on Beryllium (which was Fichter's speciality and pet), of silicon chemistry, which has become such an important branch today, or of applied organic preparatory chemistry of synthetic plastics, for he was present when his neighbor at the laboratory table produced one of the formaldehyde–phenol polymerizations for the first time in history. Without the diverting influence of anthroposophy, I would have landed, as said, in the midst of the coming atomic energy research.

Rudolf Steiner advised to put down everything I learned on one page of my diary and to put down that which anthroposophy has to say on the subject on the opposite page; to keep, so to say, double bookkeeping with the aim towards integration whenever the proper time has come. Not to speculate or to build theories or hypotheses, but to let the facts speak as phenomena. To collect as many data and facts as possible and to have not narrow, but widespread interests.

"This way you will gradually collect material for a thesis; you will then, in due time, be able to evaluate it." I followed this advice up to the present day. This method prevents the dangers of abstraction.

It was, at the time, and – alas – still is today in high vogue with many of our so – called Anthroposophical scientists to point out, following Rudolf Steiner's concept, the Goethean method of phenomenalism, that is, to collect phenomena and to let the phenomena speak rather than to work with hypothesis. The way these discussions were handled in Anthroposophical meetings and study groups, ever since 1918, to me was simply repellent. I felt they make a hypothesis even out of phenomenalism. They make this an *Erkenntnistheorie* [Theory of Knowledge] about pheno-mena instead of simply collecting data, informations, to let facts speak, question and answer. It is of course a human trend that he wants to explain; if he has no explanation, he makes one, temporarily. Thus gradually an Anthroposophical hypothesis or speculation develops which in no way is better than any other materialistic hypothesis.

My mind operates different: I can be quite happy by seeing, observing, and maybe at first even not understanding. I can feel at ease having a question not answered. But I would feel the impulse to enlarge my field of vision, of phenomena, evt. [eventually] creating such experimental arrangement that more phenomena can be had and observed. Once more in my life I felt alone, because many of my environment speculated, which I detested, but few were willing to go the path of the experimental approach to observe and to create phenomena.

I like to illustrate my method a bit more.

When Rudolf Steiner in a lecture spoke about any subject, of nature, of man, of the earth, discussed a personality, I would immediately go to a library or search for books to find out what does the world know about this stone or plant or the biography of this man, or the history of this or that period. The Anthro-posophical or spiritual point of view I had through Rudolf Steiner. The material background I collected from the world. This way a *umfangreiche* [comprehensive] knowledge built itself up during the years, a treasure from which to draw whenever the occasion occurred.

My mind was always active, eager to learn, to collect information, always open to accept more. No theory or hypothesis was allowed to block the view or to shut up a possible channel of investigation.

The mind does not get tired, nor does it need rest – this in distinction from the body. In the active, *observing* (N.B., not speculative) mind we have a source of eternal youth.

To observe, and to put the mosaic of visible, i.e., observable phenomena together and wait until gradually out of the pieces of this picture-puzzle a pattern develops, creates a productive tension. This kind of waiting is by no means a passive property of the soul, but is stimulating. This tension is the motor to continue search; in fact, one will discover that there is no end to it. It leads from the space-and-time-limited to the endless, to eternity. Most human beings are afraid of eternity and therefore seek crutches, seek a foothold for the mind instead of free moving, limit their scope of investigation and build mental cages instead of watching the endless horizon. Logic and reason have their proper place in the planning of the investigation, in the evaluation of information received, in the discovery of the pattern, but they should not be misused in the setting of boundaries or the limitation of the scope of searching. Theories and hypotheses limit the scope, are crutches for the mind, no matter whether these theories are based on a materialistic concept or use a spiritual background. Observation and experience free ourselves and lead to realities. Explanations are always bound to time, space, our present status or level of knowledge. It needs courage to live and dwell in a world which can be experienced, but not explained. As soon as the fragments of our knowledge fall into pattern, we KNOW. Higher beings, it is said, live in the adoration, *Anschauung* [contemplation] of God. They do not think or speculate *about* God, but they know God as they see Him. So we can live in the *Anschauung* [contemplation] of Nature, but do not need to speculate about nature.

*

7. The Last Years with Rudolf Steiner

The first Goetheanum Building had something of an unearthly beauty. Its forms, architecture, architraves, capitals, colors of the cupola painting and the unique glass windows "spoke" to the human mind, appealed to it, challenged it. It had educational value, for the viewing and perception of the forms awakened constructive "building" forces in the soul. One was not left alone there, even if one happened to be the only person standing in the big hall. Gothic architecture reflects the mood of the prayers rising to God, with its swift arches bridging through the air space, as in the clouds. Gothic architecture creates a similar mood as one can experience on a rainy or misty day in the giant woods of fir and spruce in the *Schwazwald* [Black Forest] or Voges Mountains. Romanesque architecture has more firmness, is less lofty, but draws the soul within to contemplation and meditation. So the Goetheanum architecture appealed to the spirit within and united it with the cosmic spirit from without. The walls acted not as separating walls, and because of the colored window carvings one felt drawn into light and color, rather looking *through* all that into another world, passing the threshold between the physical and the Spiritual: the door was wide open.

The metamorphosis of form, from the simple to the complicated and returning to the simple, of the architraves, sockets and capitals of the columns spoke the language of evolution: the same laws were described by Goethe in *The Metamorphosis of Plants*. The same laws of metamorphosis comprise the evolution, rise and downfall of civilizations, of all growth. Rudolf Steiner had truly manifested a building in physical appearance adequate to his philosophy and teaching. His entire life-work and its results were condensed in architectural forms. One could experience that this building was part, essential part, of Rudolf Steiner's being.

When the fire broke out at New Year's Eve 1922/23 and destroyed this Goetheanum with all its beauty and treasures, part of Rudolf Steiner's being and body was destroyed. Ten years of his life with all hopes, aims, creation were wiped out in the course of a few hours. The shine of the colossal fire (the building was entirely of wood) rose skyward and attracted the curious from near and far; it could be seen 30 miles away and farther, to the Voges and Black Forest as well as Swiss Jura Mountains. The fire started in or near a ventilation shaft accessible from the outside (i.e., another part of the building) in between the outside and inside shell of the South Wing. Whether arson was the reason has not been "legally" established. But Rudolf Steiner had many a time pointed to the need of the protection of the building, for prior to the fire there were many heated attacks against him, the Goetheanum, by a local Catholic priest, who went so far as to publicly announce from the pulpit: "So many intellectual sparks have gone hither and thither against anthroposophy and its creators that it is now high time that a physical spark would eliminate this scourge on the Hills of Dornach."[61]

It could be quite imaginable that a weak, imbecile mind, under the suggestion of this expression of hatred, would feel compelled to take matters in his hand and to act, to make history.

A dark cloud of smoke poured forth from the White Hall above the original source of the fire, which was discovered only when the fire had already spread to hopelessness to save the building. The first men therefore entered the White Hall, being deceived by the smoke pouring forth from the ventilation openings. One man was felled by the smoke and carried out of the building. At this moment Rudolf Steiner arrived, who had returned home already after the New Year's Eve lecture. The fire was first discovered some twenty minutes after the last of the audience had left the building.

There was this man, felled by the smoke, lying in the South Entrance to the Goetheanum.[62] Rudolf Steiner had arrived and attended to resuscitate this man. Later on, when the insurance questions were discussed and settled, witnesses heard, one not very

---

61. See GA259, p. 64 at reference 28 for the fire. See also *Der Europäer* [The European,*] Jg.1* {first year,] *Heft Nr. 5* [Issue No.5], *März* [March] 1997, *S.* [p.] 6ff. at reference 29.

62. Max Schleutermann; also GA 259, *S.* [p.] 63 at reference 28.

tactful adjustor asked Rudolf Steiner: “It is known that you are clairvoyant. Why did you not use your clairvoyance to discover the original site of the fire and to guide the crew directly to it instead of losing precious moments?” Whereupon Rudolf Steiner answered: “If one serves spiritual principles as I do, one is obliged to lend all possible knowledge to rescue a human life in danger, even though one’s own work and life would be destroyed in the meantime.” Such is the codex of ethic as it applied to Rudolf Steiner. He mentioned, however, afterwards that this event was part of the machinations of dark forces who knew that he had to adhere to this codex and brought about that this man felled by smoke was thrown in his path. This writer has been witness to this event.

The hopelessness to stem the fire became apparent after a short time, and some more-or-less precious material which could be carried by hand was rescued. Within other things, the huge curtain was pulled out, and the models which served for the architecture and wood carvings of the Goetheanum were saved. Adjoining the Goetheanum were the *Schreinerei,* the workshop, the temporary small stage and lecture hall used during all this year from 1914 to 1922 and still at use today. This huge wooden shop building harbored also the studio of Rudolf Steiner where he worked and where the Christ statue proper was placed for completion, as well as in an adjoining studio the entire group representing man. These statues were carved in wood, much on it done by the hand of Rudolf Steiner himself and his faithful helper Miss Edith Maryon.

Sparks of the great fire fell on the roof of the *Schreinerei*, and the main efforts during the night were concentrated to save the *Schreinerei* and Studio. A pear tree in front of the *Schreinerei* got thoroughly singed. Some overeager members thought to “rescue” the Christ Statue and broke open the one side of the wall of Rudolf Steiner’s studio to carry the statue in the open, which then lay on the grass and some vegetable-garden beds. This was done without asking Rudolf Steiner’s consent, and he was terribly upset about it, in addition to the sorrow about the destruction of ten years of work. Rudolf Steiner wandered about the burning building, giving advice here and there, accompanied by Edith Maryon. Frau Marie

Steiner had to stay at home because at the time she was confined to a wheelchair and could only watch the fire from a distance, from the garden of the Villa Hansi, where they lived.

It speaks for the greatness of the master that in spite of becoming witness to the destruction of his work, he could see and point out the beauty of the rage of the elements. The huge carved-glass windows of the great cupula were stained with colloidal metals contained in the glass in order to produce its color: the red and purple with gold, the blue and green with copper. This process of producing the stained glass was the secret of a company in Paris, France, based on some medieval traditions. (The shopmaster who supervised the glass flux and the addition of the metals to produce these intensive colors had died during World War I, and it appeared later on that nobody knew how to produce these intensive colors.) Due to the intense heat, these metals in the glass became volatized and added their typical flame colors to the fire, so that wherever the broken glasses melted, the flames were intensively stained in various shades of green, blue, purple and orange. Rudolf Steiner pointed out the beauty of these color phenomena. After the fire, the curious collected many chunks of the glass, now covered with films of the metal oxides, as memory, but it speaks for the *Weltfremdheit* [unworldliness] and lack of *Geistesgegenwart* [presence of mind] of these collectors that nobody came forward with a chunk which could be analyzed to discover the formula of the glass when it became apparent that the manufacturer was not able to replace the original glasses for use in the second Goetheanum.

The thousands of people who milled about the fire and ruins made the impression of a stirred-up ant heap. Rudolf Steiner was left alone; only Miss Maryon would stay close to him. To the multitude, Rudolf Steiner was the great teacher of spiritual wisdom, the creator of new arts, the esoteric teacher or Initiate, the clairvoyant who could bring down secrets of the spiritual world. That there was also a HUMAN BEING who could suffer, had a feeling, a heart, who might need consolation in the moment of greatest distress, whose heart was broken in this night, did not seem to occur to anybody. I saw and experienced in this night the Human

Being Rudolf Steiner and attached myself to this little group: Rudolf Steiner, Miss Maryon. The few words the master uttered spoke of this great suffering and grief, and consoling words were spoken by the young man.

The spiritual loneliness of the Great was witnessed, and a vow rose in the heart of the pupil never to desert the master, nor his work, nor the MAN, especially the man. This created a bond still in force today and for all eternity to come. It was the second time that I "recognized" Rudolf Steiner. When it became apparent that there was nothing left but the smoldering ruins, Rudolf Steiner withdrew, completely exhausted and broken, to a room nearby and appeared at dawn again. It was then that this young man talked again with the MAN Rudolf Steiner, directed by an inner voice and compassion to find the words and appeal to strengthen the broken heart and to point out what the necessities of the hour were. Because the man Rudolf Steiner was broken, his heart had received a deadly blow and his physical strength had faded. Miss Maryon, who also was witness, never recovered from the shock and began to ail and died after a few months. The words which were exchanged must be left to silence, because they belong to the most intimate of experience when a great soul opens. But the result was that in a superhuman effort, Rudolf Steiner carried on and showed no weakness when he faced the members and his usual entourage and continued the work, lectured the next evening.[63] It was spiritually and physically important that the continuity was not interrupted.

In writing this I do not want to say that other friends and members did not share the grief – in fact, all were thunderstruck – all did want to continue. But there was a moment, darkest moment of despair, which could be overcome only by forces of Love radiating from one soul to another. Mission accomplished, the young

---

63. Lecture VI in the cycle *The Origins of Natural Science,* GA 326. See reference 30. Described here in Part III, p. 223 by Dr. Paul Scharff, "...about the Night of the Fire."

man withdrew again into the background or shadow to let others take over in the limelight of events.

*

When clearing away the debris, it appeared that the concrete foundations and first floor were so damaged by the heat that they had to be scrapped completely and an entire new approach to the rebuilding was needed. Rudolf Steiner decided for obvious reasons on concrete; but also artistic reasons were involved, for concrete could be poured into any shape, so that what was the "spirit" of the building could be expressed in forms of concrete.

"Of course every material has its own laws, conditions, expressions and therefore needs to be shaped differently; the new Goetheanum will be entirely different."

The will to build a new Goetheanum was strong throughout the membership of the Anthroposophical Society, and Rudolf Steiner was urged to give advice, prepare a model. Architect Aisenpreis, supported by others, architect Ranzenberger prepared the physical arrangements; the members collected funds in addition to the insurance sum of some 3.2 million Swiss francs in order to get started.

This sum did not cover anywhere the time and effort, not to speak of the artistic value, of the first Goetheanum. It covered only the value of the material. Would one want to estimate the actual even economic value of the first building, an estimate of 10 million Swiss francs would be more adequate. The riches of donations which could flow before World War I were no more available during these years of economic postwar disasters, of inflation, of reshuffling of nations. The raising of funds therefore was not easy, led to many heated discussions; the entire next ten, maybe seventeen and more following years suffered under economic restrictions; then World War II came. It is my opinion that the Anthroposophical movement has never recovered from the blow, and the responsible treasurer had a hard time to carry out all future intentions and to make both ends meet.

The plastic model of the new Goetheanum could never be completed by Rudolf Steiner because of his occupation with the reconstruction of the Anthropos. Society, and then, finally, his illness prevented him to spend the necessary time. So a model resulted which was only complete in a few details, West-portal, South and North side, but the East wing was a torso and many details, of windows f.i. [for instance] needed to be guessed, as well as the internal structures and architecture of the great hall.

The new model therefore remained a torso, and so is the second Goetheanum. It would be much better to acknowledge this fact before one's own conscience.

The first Goetheanum had two cupolas, a larger holding the audience, a smaller the stage; the side wings were designed to hold two more lecture halls, of which one was completed, and many small dressing-rooms and offices. Originally the stage was meant for the performance of the Mystery Plays, and in fact the entire "stage" was a scene in itself, of the mystery–sun temple. The idea was to have the Christ Statue and [Lucifer and Ahriman] groups on the East base of the small cupola, in an about two-third circle of columns swinging around with "seats" for the hierophants representing the leading spirits of culture epochs; the round cupola above with its most beautiful paintings rested as a dome celestial on these columns; capitals, architraves, the seats carved by hand in wood: indeed a magnificent setting.

The difficulty from the technical point of view was how to build into this setting such technicalities of a stage as stage lighting, trapdoors for props, smaller scenes which did not request the magnificent setting of the "temple" scene, other apparatus which is necessary on a stage; a ceiling f.i. [for instance] with soffits. There was no possibility to suspend something from above, the painted cupola; and a transportable flying ceiling would be needed. The basement space underneath the stage floor was entirely inadequate, with insufficient height for any object to be let through the trapdoors. When I arrived in 1919 with as little or as much practical, technical knowledge I had acquired prior about stage construction, I saw the problem at once and also was greeted by the then-acting architect Aisenpreis with the words: "we have a problem there, how can it be solved." The architects, artists, helpers of Rudolf Steiner had beautifully carried out the artistic model and idea of

Rudolf Steiner, but of the technicalities of a stage otherwise, even for the scenes of the Mystery Plays, there was no proper concept.

I even doubt that these earlier builders ever had properly discussed the problem with Rudolf Steiner. This was not the fault of the master, but he was insufficiently orientated; one cannot expect that he should tell every detail. In the execution of the basic idea he was certainly expecting competent advice. When the stage problem was brought before him with the ideas which had developed in discussions between Aisenpreis, myself and probably others whom I don't remember, Rudolf Steiner lent a willing ear to the project.

For the construction of the second Goetheanum it was at once decided to avoid the difficulties which the first Goetheanum offered and to construct a stage wing proper according to the standards at the time, with all technical paraphernalia connected with it. This decision gave the new Goetheanum its pattern: a huge audience space, to hold about 1000 people (seating capacity), for as Rudolf Steiner pointed out, this was the upper limit of space where an intimate contact between a speaker and the audience could still be maintained. (I may say right here that the unfortunate acoustic conditions of the large hall make such intimate contact with the audience almost impossible, as I, as speaker, later on could experience, myself; others might be of different opinion, but having lectured all over the world in many different halls, I know what the difference can be.) Then there was the stage wing proper. The idea to have a permanent setting for the temple scene was given up; the Christ Statue and group therefore had not the place in its dominating center position as it had in the first Goetheanum. It was a great pity that this question was not discussed with Rudolf Steiner, because the solution which was later on approached, after the death of the master, did not do justice to the original idea.

Since the beginning of the first Goetheanum the new art of Eurythmy and speech had developed. This, too, requested a "stage." And so it was decided to have the technically well- perfected stage.

Dressing-rooms, rehearsal and exercise rooms were needed, and this all was incorporated in the new project. Most of it had to be decided upon during the last illness and thereafter. During the long illness there was a moment of hope. Rudolf Steiner had, in

February, 1925, already ordered a wheelchair, in order to be able to leave the study, where he had been in many months of confinement to bed, in order to inspect the work at the new building site which had begun. It never came to pass. The architect, Aisenpreis, had to make all decisions himself and tried his best, supported by very incompetent advice of some artists, by much criticism from others. Having had my office and drawing table side by side with his, I participated intensively at these discussions, pointed out the acoustic impossibilities already on the drawing board, to no avail. Nobody would listen to the young man. The older generation of the leading members of the Society were so surrounded by the air of self-importance and self-esteem that they just "owned" the Know How. How different were the few discussions I had with Rudolf Steiner: always open, listening to propositions and entering every detail of the problems under consideration. After many fruitless discussions, a mood of resignation developed, deep sorrow. In order to save the honor of the architect Aisenpreis, who was later on often blamed for the inadequacy, f.i., [for instance] of proportions of the windows of the second Goetheanum, I may state that also his share of resignation became apparent. What we finally have as the new building was a compromise.

In many matters of the Society, that similar self-importance of members became evident, overrunning frequently the suggestions made by Rudolf Steiner, theoretically saying yes, yes, but in fact carrying out one's own intention and quoting Rudolf Steiner only when and if, and only to the extent as, a remark of his seemed to support one's own intentions or opinion. This had became so bad that Rudolf Steiner frequently pointed out that he had been treated as "*quantité négligeable*" [negligible quantity] in the Society, that he desired cooperation with others who really carried out *his* intentions.

At the occasion of the obituary for Miss Maryon, he pointed out that there was a modest helper of his who always carried out his intentions and tried to feel herself into that which lived in him. No wonder that Miss Maryon had lived in closest contact, being always present in the studio where Rudolf Steiner worked and only leaving silently when others entered to have a talk with him.

At one time she even had saved his life when he slipped on a high scaffold and dreaded to fall down quite some depth (some 30 feet.) This same Miss Maryon had called me one day in the studio after the fire, and when it became apparent that she would succumb to the illness which had started because of the shock of that New Year's Eve night of 1922/23, and explained that she considered it her task to be around Rudolf Steiner to protect his welfare. She would not live much longer and asked therefore that I and another person would take over in said protection of Rudolf Steiner. Again I had to admit to resignation, for soon thereafter another person close to Rudolf Steiner, took over (the name shall not be revealed)[64] and told me in unmistakable words that I should stay away, for this person would completely take care of everything. My role was then only, with others, to become a kind of physical body guard, inasmuch as an attack already prior to the Goetheanum Fire had been made during a public lecture tour in Munich. The people who physically tried to attack Rudolf Steiner after a lecture in Munich belonged to the Society of Thule, a group out of which many years later the Nazi Philosophy under one Rosenberg [*The Myth of the 20th Century,* 1930] originated. Already in 1921 it had become a custom that always a young man followed Rudolf Steiner, especially on a trip. Günther Wachsmuth, Andreas v. Grunelius, myself functioned in this capacity, and in Dornach a regular bodyguard was established. This gave several occasions, in the automobile, to travel with Rudolf Steiner between Dornach and Stuttgart and to come in closest personal contact. It was on these occasions that Rudolf Steiner, even without being asked, for I tried to be as silent and unobtrusive as possible, that Rudolf Steiner opened and spoke about the deepest things, esoteric problems, which belong to the most precious treasures of my life, influencing my entire future and attitude towards anthroposophy.

*

In the development of anthroposophy several distinct phases are visible depending on the development of Rudolf Steiner himself,

---

64. Refers to Ita Wegman, as Pfeiffer indicated to Lexie Ahrens elsewhere.

the tasks he assigned himself apparently in consultation with a carrying-out impulse of spiritual inspiration. This impulse was received, acknowledged by people who felt drawn near to Rudolf Steiner's philosophy, communications of matters and events spiritual, esoteric teachings. At first when Rudolf Steiner began his Anthroposophical career, he worked with small groups and individuals. The preparatory period is described in his autobiography, in his "early" writings, in some of his letters, especially to Hübbe-Schleiden.[65] Rudolf Steiner worked with an independent German branch which sprang originally from the Theosophical Society. He definitely did not just accept and continue the lore and teachings of the Indian-tinged Theosophy, but created his own teachings based on immediate contact with the spiritual world and beings, established the Spiritual Science of Anthroposophical orientation (this his own term: "*Anthroposophisch orientierte Geisteswissenschaft.*") [Anthroposophically-oriented Spiritual Science.]

It is not my task to describe this development as a historian, but for the understanding of later developments and my own participation in it, it is necessary to outline a few points.

Let's say the teachings of the Spiritual Science proper began about the turn of the century (1900). In the introduction to one of his basic books Rudolf Steiner used the sentence: "*Seelische Beobachtungsresultate" auf wissenschaftlicher Grundlage* ["Results of soul observation" on a scientific basis]. He gave results of these observations of the soul and Being of man, and the spirit as well, as he taught the way how to obtain knowledge of a Higher World. The point of departure was the philosophical idealism of the 19th century, foremost Goethe's world perception; but others, Schelling, Oken, Fichte, Hegel and many today forgotten philosophers; poets (Hamerling, Fercher von Steinwand, etc); scientists (Haeckel) formed a background. The method he used was one of observation – observation of the spirit and its manifestation and description of the observed, exactly the method of the scientific method as it should be used, without speculation, hypothesis or abstraction. The

---

65. See *The Story of My Life*, GA 28; Briefe [Letters], Bd. [Vol.] I u. [and] II, GA 38 u. [and] 39. See references 32 and 33.

method can be called the phenomenological because it rests with the description of the phenomena, does not try to add the speculation element of a human thinking, which falls short of reality. Speculation and hypothesis (theory) always fall short of reality because they continue in the human mind when the phenomena are incomplete, and the mind tries to bridge the gaps in order to explain. It was Goethe's perception to let the phenomena speak, and therefore Rudolf Steiner could link up and use Goethe as a starting point. Goethe, in a fairy tale [*The Green Snake and the Beautiful Lily*] and in his poem "*Metamorphosis of Plants*" had touched fundamental principles of the spirit-nature of man, development (growth) in nature, and continued in his theory of color.

It is obvious that the method of observation of the spiritual world cannot be the same as the methods of the material world. The material world we can observe with our senses, the sphere of sense perception of the three-dimensional world in space, of that which can be seen, heard, felt, smelled, tasted, weighed, measured, analyzed, enlarged with instruments – all of which lead to the development of modern science (natural science,) and the results can be applied in technology, engineering, physics, chemistry, biology and all the descriptive as well as basic sciences.

It is likewise obvious that a spiritual world, the soul being of man, the development of personality (the Ego), the spirit being in man and in the world (including the cosmos), the fate, or karma, destination of man – all of that which does not belong to the physical, three- dimensional world, weighable and measurable, accessible to material instruments and analysis – all this demands its own proper senses of perception which are not the physical senses, but spiritual sense organs. To develop these in a way which makes them "exact, scientific," was Rudolf Steiner's endeavor: to enter the suprasensible world in terms of exact observation, free from speculation and illusions.

The Western world and mind had developed natural science and its applications. It was therefore specifically geared to "scientific methods." This is what Rudolf Steiner wanted to create: an approach to the spirit to meet the spirit exactly on the scientific grounds which is proper to the spirit.

In this aim anthroposophy is entirely different from any Eastern teachings, even though Rudolf Steiner had, especially in the beginning, to use such terms as karma, etheric, astral, theosophy etc.

He also had to point out the existence of an hierarchical order, of independent spiritual beings, of an elemental world of beings. In the center of this concept stood the Being of Christ, not as something which was inherited by traditions, religions, churches being handed down from century to century, whereby the picture of the original faded out more and more, but as a reality which could be very concretely experienced.

It is my modest, but very sincere opinion that in all these endeavors Rudolf Steiner exceeded by far everything by way of Knowledge, of wisdom which heretofore had been given to – let's say – the general public. For all this was preserved and kept in esteem in the so-called Mysteries – a Knowledge to which only a few well-prepared Initiates (of older and newer times) had access. It was Rudolf Steiner's opinion and commission that the development of the world and man, the turn our time took towards an extreme materialism and materialistic explorations of the spirit, of man, of the cosmos requested the counter-move by the spiritual exploration based on Spiritual Science.

Now let's return to the phases of the Anthroposophical movement. At first Rudolf Steiner taught what he could "bring down" from spiritual observation. He found willing ears to listen, to accept, to try it out themselves, to develop organs of spiritual observation. During this earlier period, the separation from the Theosophical Society and its teachings of Eastern color (without the Christ as center being) took place. It was the German element which, because of its history, upbringing as a people of thinkers, philosophers, artists was especially receptive. German in a wider sense, including all Middle European Countries and extending somewhat East (Russia before the revolution) and West (France, England, U.S.A.)

Up to World War I, gradually anthroposophy had developed as a complete edifice and had also laid the foundation, the Goetheanum in Dornach, Switzerland in 1913 as the physical center and building for this concept, the renewal of the Mysteries and the renewal of an art based on a spiritual concept. The members of the earlier phase, naturally, were such that they felt attracted by the esoteric, the occult, the mysterious, the *inner* world. They were men from all layers of human society, but very few so-called "exact" scientists, natural scientists, least physicists, more chemists, physicians, engineers were present.

The World War I brought a complete upheaval of all human affairs and situations. Many began to realize that maybe materialism as philosophy and science might not have the answer to the human, the social, the cultural problems of the world.

The pre-war, pre-1914 bourgeois satisfaction and complacency had been pierced, broken down. Innumerable values had been destroyed. The best, enthusiastic, hopeful youth had died. This brought an awakening of many to search for eternal values. There was a great surge towards anthroposophy all over Middle Europe and a tremendous influx of new elements with new and other desires. There was also the social problem: how to organize human society. The dark shadow of Bolshevism rose, and the Western World was not adequate to solve neither the social, nor the spiritual desires of the war-torn countries. The political solutions which were attempted, as f.i. [for instance] with the peace treaty of Versailles only led – as history has demonstrated to - new conflicts and another war.

The active followers of Rudolf Steiner, which did not want to sit back in order to develop their own spiritual organs or absorb the wisdom of anthroposophy for their own satisfaction, wanted to apply anthroposophy in all realms of human endeavor, social life, education, art, science, religion, civilization as a whole. So the place of anthroposophical applications in science, medicine, schools, social life, economy had started. Not all of these beginnings were lucky, successful or survived. Especially the social and economic endeavors were under a bad star. Members active in these fields brought their problems before Rudolf Steiner, asking for advice. His time and strength was taxed to limit of the humanly endurable.

Students at universities formed study groups in anthroposophy. During the years 1920-1921, a *Hochschulbund* [University Federation] was formed, which did not succeed. There was great enthusiasm, but not enough knowledge. The youthful barnstorming, flight of ideals was too much in a state of fermentation to be able to settle into a permanent pattern. A youth movement followed which found itself opposite to the aims of the older generation. The youth felt itself understood by Rudolf Steiner, but not by this older generation. Since the continuity was interrupted and the youth at that time revolted against history, it wanted its own channels of activity. In the Anthroposophical Society in Germany, or middle Europe, rather, this led to the formation of a separate society within the Anthroposophical Society. I participated actively in the formation of the *Hochschulbund,* [University Federation] less so in the trend of separation. For at that time there were two distinctly different trends.

One, in Germany, towards an all-embracing youth movement governed by a Goetheanistic and, as I must say today, rather an intellectual approach towards anthroposophy.[66] For – what remained of this impulse and survived is a system of lecturing about anthroposophy which I must term more or less a commentary based on thinking, explanatory or thought experience. Many clever words were said, and gradually a speculative, combinatory element crept in. This method of approach was termed by Rudolf Steiner himself the "Stuttgart System,"[67] for in Stuttgart lived the largest group of members representing it and forming centers of activity. It is true that this system bore its fruits, and out of it the active-will schools (Waldorf School to begin with), clinics, sanatoria originated, all to the good.

The other approach, in Dornach, voiced only by a few to which I may count myself, we may term the esoteric impulse,

---

66. [Ernst Lehrs.]

67. *The Fateful Year of 1923 in the History of the Anthroposophical Society: From the Goetheanum Fire to the Christmas Conference: Addresses – Meetings – Documents, January to December 1923,* G.A. 259, Rudolf Steiner Verlag, 1991, p. 271. for mention of the *Stuttgarter System* ["Stuttgart System."] See reference 28.

which later on led to the new formation of a Society of which, one year after the fire of the first Goetheanum, Rudolf Steiner became the first president. Before that time Rudolf Steiner had been the teacher, but had not assumed office in the Society. Then he formed a board (*Vorstand*) in which he took active leadership in order to gain decisive influence upon the affairs of the Anthroposophical Society. This esoteric impulse was voiced by a few, above all Frau Dr. Ita Wegman, Albert Steffen, Dr. Günther Wachsmuth; Frau Marie Steiner, as the companion of Rudolf Steiner, participated in everything. But there were also others less known, Mieta Waller-Pyle, Scott Pyle, Count Lerchenfeld, Wachsmuth's brother Wolfgang and his wife Hilde, Frau Harriet v. Vacano from Stuttgart, Dr. Maria Roeschl (Vienna originally) who later moved to Dornach, Dr. von Baravalle; Kurt Piper, the poet; Emil Leinhas; who joined this impulse. My parents, mother and stepfather Elsa and Theodor Binder, myself.

Our aim was to create a renewal of the Mysteries at the Goetheanum, to emphasize the inner, esoteric activity, to tune ourselves to the demand and needs of the spiritual guidance. I can speak only for myself in this connection: the question was not so much "what can I do in the outer world, to stir up activities," but "what should I do to carry out an original spiritual impulse, being guided, becoming an instrument for the spiritual impulse, make myself worthy, not to let my own self speak, but rather carry out that which the spirit objectively commands." This esoteric impulse was very well received by Rudolf Steiner A group of twenty-four people was selected to whom Rudolf Steiner, in three meetings, gave fundamental instructions. It is my opinion that the later "*Vorstand*" and the specific new foundation of the General Anthroposophical Society in Dornach, Christmas 1923, originated out of this impulse. Four participants of this group became members of the *Vorstand* – the group as such ceased to exist, and all others went on to carry out their tasks independently one from the other. This formation of the Society at the Goetheanum was Rudolf Steiner's answer to counterbalance the intellectualising Stuttgart system. Many members of the Society might find this report strange, but then, they do not know, and could not know what went on, so to say, behind the screen. It is my sincere opinion that up to the present day that which Rudolf Steiner meant with the new esoteric impulse was never understood.

Before World War I, Rudolf Steiner had given special instructions of an esoteric nature aside from that which is contained in the books and so called cycles, lecture series and public and members' lectures. These esoteric instructions were given to a few selected. It would not be correct to say these were the more "advanced" Anthroposophists, even though some believed it to be so; but it was that desire to receive messages, communications of the spiritual world proper which dealt with a higher, not materialistic aspect of earthly and cosmic things.

The word "esoteric" means to receive special instructions and knowledge which by profane ears and thinking would be meaningless. The word was first used to describe a selected group of Aristotle to whom Aristotle taught what he could not do in the general and public dissemination of his philosophy (cf. definition in Webster Dictionary.)

This member had two desires: a) inner development, deeper insight into the undercurrent of man's development, as individual and in history; b) to come together with a special bond, even in ritualistic and cultic form. Dr. Steiner hinted this development in his autobiography. He connected that what came to pass to traditional remnants of esoteric striving in the past, especially of a spiritual stream called Rosicrucian. The mystical personality of Christian Rosenkreutz who stood for a spiritual, not materialistic understanding of man and the world, for inner experience, had set the pattern. Nevertheless, Rudolf Steiner created his own method, independent from so-called occult or Rosicrucian societies. It is a malevolent distortion if opponents of anthroposophy call it a cult, a sect, or mysticism. To do this is a gross misstatement. No such thing as a secret society was meant or existed.

However, members who participated in these special instructions sometimes felt inflated, thought to be something specific, raised individuals for having a knowledge which was not publicized. When World War I broke out, Rudolf Steiner stopped these special classes, for as he said: "In a time when political and other emotions of hatred and destruction were overtaking the world, no proper environment existed anymore for such peaceful endeavor." After the war, because of the attitude of some members who had participated, Rudolf Steiner could not continue. He stated to me once, "*Nach meinen gemachten Erfahrungen werde ich mich hüten, diese Dinge wieder aufzunehmen.*" [After my past experiences, I would not dare to take up these things again.] He spoke frequently of the members "*die auf ihren kurulischen Stühlen sitzen.*" [that sit on their ivory thrones] I believe that much of the revolt of the younger members against the older generation was instinctively, subconsciously based on the antipathy against the attitude of those on the throne. [*kurulische Stühle*] For there was a deep esoteric, spiritual desire in many of the younger. There were, of course, also the others, who did not want to go deeper, but to entertain intellectual acknowledgement of Anthroposophical truth. All this created many conflicts, and Rudolf Steiner tried to hold this struggling, counter-acting body together.

The Dornach impulse, let me call it this way, wanted to give Rudolf Steiner a platform where the truly esoteric, inner impulse could find an abode again. Frau Marie Steiner, who had participated in the previous attempt, was disillusioned and would not take an active part in the newer proposals.

A small group of young people brought before Rudolf Steiner a certain impulse so that he felt he could react upon it – this happened independent of the Dornach impulse. The Dornach impulse was brought before Rudolf Steiner especially by Ita Wegman, Wachsmuth, myself on one side, Albert Steffen apparently somewhat different; Dr. Vreede in her way also brought something, so that Rudolf Steiner felt compelled, to the surprise of many, to include her in the *Vorstand*. While Rudolf Steiner revealed to me much about his inner feelings, I was much too young to do anything else but to stay silently in the background. But in talks with Rudolf Steiner I had frequently brought up the matter of the need for a new spiritual and esoteric impulse.

My share was not so much with regard to the Society, but a) to renew the Mysteries, b) to make the Goetheanum the center of this renewal, c) a special problem which I wish to outline now.

Already in my teen-age I had a special desire to know something about the deeper forces in nature, especially those which work in life and growth and are transcendental beyond the reach of purely physical energies as in electricity, magnetism etc.

I had formed a mental image that our modern civilization and social structure was based upon the progress of natural science, of technology. I could only see that the application of this physical science as in physics and chemistry, in the theory of warmth (thermodynamics), of electricity, of magnetism leads to a civilization which bears in itself the prefix of destruction, climaxes in ever farther-reaching use of implements of destruction, war machinery, an economy of selfish profits, of individual advancement in disregard of the interest and feeling of the other human being. I could see only that in spite of increased technical means of traveling, of communication, human beings drifted farther apart; that they lacked the impulse to develop a unified social body that is "humanity" rather than races, tribes, power groups, interest groups, nations. Everyone shared in nature's gift only to the extent as it suited his own personal interest.

The method of science, in a materialistic sense, is based on *analysis*, splitting apart (today atom-splitting and fusion, etc), disintegration, separation, dissecting, and all the procedures which have to destroy and take apart, to work on the corpse rather than to grow, to develop, to synthesize. That the human mind was captured by these methods of breaking apart: in that I saw the source of our present situation. My question, therefore, was: Is it possible to find another force or energy in nature which does not have in itself the ductus of atomizing and analysis, but builds up, synthesizes? Would we discover that constructive forces which make things alive and grow, develop adequate building-up methods of investigation, evt. [eventually] use this force for another type of technic applied to drive machines, then because of the inner nature of this force or energy we might be able to create another technology, social structure, constructive thinking of man rather than destructive thinking. This force must have the impulse of life, of organization within itself as the so-called physical energies have the splitting, separating trend within themselves. My question to Rudolf Steiner during October 1920 and spring 1921 therefore, was: Does such a force or source of energy exist? Can it be demonstrated? Could an altruistic technic be built upon it?[68]

When these questions formed themselves in my mind, I met in Günther Wachsmuth a life-long friend who pondered about exactly the same problems.

Some discussions with Rudolf Steiner were carried out individually; others we both together had with Rudolf Steiner.

My questions were answered as follows :

Yes, such a force exists, but is not yet discovered. It is what is generally known as the ether, not the physical ether, but the force which makes things grow, lives, for instance, in the seed as *Samenkraft*. [seed power] Before you can work with this force, you must demonstrate its presence. As we have reagents in chemistry, so you must find a reagent upon the etheric force. It is also called formative etheric force, because it is the force which creates the form, shape, pattern of a living thing, growth. You might try crystallization processes to which organic substances are added. (This has been done, and the results described elsewhere, known today as the method of sensitive crystallization). It is possible, then, to develop machines which react upon and are driven by this force. Rudolf Steiner then outlined the principles of the application of this force as source of a new energy. In the presence of Günther Wachsmuth at some other time, he outlined the principle of the four etheric formative forces, light ether, chemical ether, life ether and warmth ether (somewhat different than in the so-called Warmth and Light course before Waldorf teachers)[69] and pointed to a book by [Pandit] Râma Prasâd, *Nature's Finer Forces*,[70] which described some of it.

Wachsmuth, in turn, wrote his book on the Etheric Formative Forces.[71] To me the task fell to start experiments. In this, the coop-

68. Cf. GA 107; also *Der Europäer*, v.I, no.6, pp. 8ff.

69. GA 320 and 321.

70. London, 1913.

71. G. Wachsmuth, *Die aetherischen Bildekräfte in Kosmos, Erde und Mensch* [Etheric Formative Forces in the Cosmos, Earth and Man] v.2, Dornach, 1926.

eration between us, the seed for the *Forschungsinstitut am Goetheanum* [Research Institute at the Goetheanum] was laid. I had to perform certain experiments which [I] do not feel at liberty to describe. The result of these experiments were reported, whereupon Rudolf Steiner said with utmost earnestness: the outcome of the experiment points to another force, not the etheric one, but an astral one (i.e. forces which live in sentient matter, nerve, brain.) That the experiment did turn out this way is the answer of the spiritual world to him, and it means that the time is not yet ready to make use of the etheric forces. I asked when will the time be ready; Answer: when the social conditions are such that no misuse of this force can be done for selfish purposes; that would only be the case if the Threefold Commonwealth order would be practiced at least over a few territories on earth. Until this time, experiments in the direction of using the etheric forces would not be successful, or should not be done.

Since we live today in a world which is farther away than ever from the solution of the social problems, where selfishness and personal advantage, profit and national conflicts because of them have the upper hand, since especially the Anthroposophical Society has never put the solution of the social problem in front of all its aim[s] and not contributed that which was demanded by Rudolf Steiner to be done, I see no other way but to bury the instructions with regard to the use of the etheric force deep down in my chest, probably to take it with me to [the] grave, with the hope that other times will come, other circumstances, other ages and lives, where the time then will be ready. My conscience is deeply moved, but I have to obey higher reason, for this means that for the time being the world must go on with the use of energies which have the power]of] death and destruction in their essence, and it is only to be hoped that the world learns the hard way, by endless suffering; that one day it will awaken to accept the mission of life, of living together in peace, of mutual acceptance and coordination.

Everything else we developed in Anthroposophical natural science, experimenting, had to remain with the first step, the demonstration of the presence and existence of formative forces. Only in the use of the biodynamic method of soil improvement could we go a step farther. How this developed is described elsewhere (in *Wir erlebten R. Steiner*[We Experienced Rudolf Steiner]).[72]

But I must consider all this as piece work as compared with THE ONE great task: the discovery and application of the etheric energy. So my life work, as interesting and productive it may have been, must remain a torso, incomplete. It remained to work for anthroposophy, a philosophy of the living versus a philosophy of the dying, of disintegration, to make a dent into the onslaught of materialism, to help to "change the mind" of the people of the world.[73]

*

8. The First Years after Rudolf Steiner's Death

On March 30, 1925 I walked up in the morning to the Goetheanum. I had had a disquieting dream about the beloved teacher the night before. It was a typical early spring morning, brisk, sunshine and clouds chasing, and it was as a tender light would spread out and flow over the landscape.

At the door of R. Steiner's studio, where he had spent almost six months under the diligent care of his coworker and physician, Dr. Ita Wegman, was some commotion. The door stood open: Rudolf Steiner had just died. A whole world of activities, hopes for future instruction, farther building up of the Goetheanum, of the School of Spiritual Science, of the Anthroposophical Movement, collapsed. There were, as yet, very few people around: these who had done the last services and attended to Rudolf Steiner: Frau

---

72. See *New Directions in Agriculture* by Ehrenfried E. Pfeiffer, pp118-129 in *Rudolf Steiner: Recollections by Some of his Pupils*, Edited by Arnold Freeman and Charles Waterman, *The Golden Blade*, London, 1958, iv + 188 pages. This volume is a translation of *Wir Erlebten Rudolf Steiner,* [We Experienced Rudolf Steiner] edited by M. J. Krück von Poturzyn and published by the *Verlag Freies Geistesleben*, Stuttgart, who retain the copyright. See reference 34.

73. [At the end of this section Pfeiffer noted in pencil:] "A sleepless night helped to get this down, writing from 1 to 5 a.m. I feel happy that it has been said. Should I suddenly die or not be able to complete this biography, I feel it could stand now, incomplete, though; but it can stand."

Wegman and two of her assistant physicans. Dr. Wachsmuth, Albert Steffen had left. The death came sudden; Marie Steiner was in Stuttgart and was recalled by phone. A few of the guards. I entered hesitantly to see Rudolf Steiner on his deathbed, facing the Christ Statue. A few galley-proof pages of the medical book, in which he had set so much hope, lay on the bed covers. I helped with whatever was necessary to be done, dumbfounded and lost otherwise. Soon the deathwatch was organized, Rudolf Steiner bedded for the viewing which went on and on, thousands of members coming from all over the world to pay their respects. His countenance had changed; one recognized the effects of suffering, but a divine beauty and freshness lasted for several days: this was the physiognomy which had been carved by deepest spiritual insight, determination, love and kindness and much suffering, physical and spiritual. Even a complete stranger could see the great personality which had used this body.

The last ritual before his cremation was performed by Rittelmeyer, accompanied by music and speech chorus in the presence of well over a thousand mourners: an unforgettable impression, too deep to be described, even today (1958) after so many years. Dr. Wachsmuth, Groot, Pracht and this writer were the pallbearers, performing their duties with broken hearts.

Soon thereafter everyone had to return to his job and routine, and it became apparent immediately that there were deep personality conflicts between the main leaders of the Society. In fact, the whole history of the Society thereafter was a continuous array of personality conflicts. These were strong personalities, set in their minds, who had to continue the work of Rudolf Steiner – as a whole, in the Society, the Goetheanum, the sections, in the large horizon as well as in many details. The building construction work of the second Goetheanum had begun. There was only a rather incomplete model left, many details not yet worked out and in need of imagination more to guess rather than execute the intentions of the master. So it was with the whole edifice of the Anthroposophical Society, with the education towards spiritual experience and insight of Rudolf Steiner's most closest pupils or disciples. For these existed, some as good as unknown and unaccepted by the gross of the society. What Rudolf Steiner has left as teachings was complete, a whole world and concept in itself, based on sound and acceptable principles which could be followed. What was left – human beings – all were full of intentions and good will, but they were HUMAN, and therefore not complete. The work Rudolf Steiner had intended with regard to the new foundation of the Society and the Goetheanum had started but a little more than a year ago and was by no means complete. It was given into the discretion, authority and initiative of those who were in charge of the Society and its branches to continue using their individual judgment. Rudolf Steiner had left no directives whatsoever, what and how it should be done. A movement based on the principles of a philosophy of free will could not be left in another condition but this, to exercise free will. It is useless to ask: why did Rudolf Steiner leave matters as they were, did he not expect his death, etc., etc. I am convinced that in due respect of the decisions made by free will, he could not act differently. Whichever would or should become of this work of Rudolf Steiner, it could become only because of and through the followers who tried to carry out the original intentions according to their abilities, knowledge, initiatives.

That which Rudolf Steiner wrote about the human Ego in an incomplete manuscript, preface to Fichte's *Wissenschaftslehre* [Science of Knowledge] – he wanted to write a *Wissenschaftslehre* himself, too – can be superbly applied to the entire situation. What the members, the Society, the Goetheanum make of it– this will count before history, form a future, or fade away. I quote therefore these lines from the unpublished handwritten pages:[74]

"Neither the views of the individual person nor those of whole circles of people are unrelated when they appear one after the other: they develop one out of the others and determine each other. It may (…) well be that the kernel is unchangeable, but that it

---

74. At this place of his manuscript, Pfeiffer left a gap marked "missing." Thus it is uncertain which sentences from Steiner's commentary on Fichte he meant to cite. The ones offered here are the editor's suggestions. Quoted from *Beiträge zur Rudolf Steiner Gesamtausgabe* [Contributions to the Collected Edition of Rudolf Steiner], *Heft* [Issue] no. 30, Dornach, *Sommer* [summer] 1970, pp. 28ff. See reference 35.

merely assumes different forms depending on the narrower or wider horizon of the individual, (…) so that what is altered may be valid for an earlier outlook, but no longer for a later one.(…) The Knower: in him we must seek the fundamentals of knowledge insofar as they can be considered as certain. The source of certainty (…) is the knowing person.

"(…)When Fichte stated that the pure essence of the ego came through determining oneself, this is said in a very arbitrary manner, for the ego does not merely determine itself, but also other things (…) But in every case it is always active. Its whole being consists in its activity, and this can be expressed in the phrase: the ego is active (…) Unless it makes itself into something, the ego is nothing at all, it is as good as non-existent (…) If the ego is to become imbued with will, it must make itself into a willing ego, and so with all its activity. Its 'what' is its own product."

The personality conflicts began immediately. The Society split into different sorts of activity, regrouped itself at times and split again. Much momentum was lost this way; many valuable personalities, too tender or too proud to fight, disappeared. Others survived and fought. It is not my task to judge, to accuse or to excuse.

At the time of Rudolf Steiner's death I was a young man, university studies not yet completed, full of desire to do something, to be active and helpful, too young as yet to be invited to any responsible position or to have something to say; "human" enough so that many of the top leaders confided in him their problems. He tried to build bridges, to see only that the current would sway away such trials. So I participated in everything, but without taking a stand. There was one field, however, where I could create, independent: to build up a center for Anthroposophical scientific research, experimentation, laboratory work and application of the learned and acquired in biology, biochemistry and agriculture. My whole upbringing, education and directions given by Rudolf Steiner had led me and enabled me to take this phase upon my shoulders – to try at least to make something out of it myself. Thus the start was made to a research laboratory, as it was called then later on: *Forschungslabor am Goetheanum, Chem. Biol. Abteilung*. [Research Laboratory at the Goetheanum, Chemical-biological department.]

First Years

In quick succession various states of growth were passed: a box underneath the bed, a closet, a space in the *Glashaus,* [Glass house] a room over a shed of the Weleda A.G.[75] in Arlesheim. Already during Rudolf Steiner's illness experiments had started to demonstrate formative forces. These experiments concerned more the formative principle as transmitted by animal substances. During the year 1925, a course was given to a youth group at a place called "Holle" in Arlesheim. I participated with a simple demonstration of chemical experiments and of basic phenomena as the first attempt and approach to a *Substanzlehre* [theory of substance] in following a Goetheanistic concept, that is, to let phenomena speak and explain one another without burdening the demonstration with any theory or hypothesis. During this course, which was well received even though it was my first trial in such matters to teach, I noticed a young woman who seemed to follow each experiment with keen interest, more intense than anybody else. I had the feeling that there was a personality who had a special gift for experimenting and would devote her entire being and life to it. This was Erika Sabarth, who became my life-long coworker in the laboratory, in Dornach, in Holland, in Berlin and finally in U.S.A. Mrs. Sabarth had the extraordinary gift that she would just "touch" the right thing; an instinctive fingertip feeling which was the more valuable and important because the field of research we entered was new land, exploring unknown properties of matter.

The first experiments with the sensitive crystallization method had started ; my reasoning and Erika Sabarth's fingertip feeling let us do just the right thing. Selection of chloride of copper, a glass plate of 9 cm diameter for the crystallization, plant extracts and blood addition, and all the other things which are reported in the literature on the method.[76] We had the incredible luck (or guid-

75. A.G. = *Aktiengesellschaft* [joint-stock company] the equivalent being public limited company (plc) in the UK.

76. See in addition the bibliographic references in Alla Selawry, *Ehrenfried Pfeiffer: Pioneer of Spiritual Research and Practice.* Translated by Joe Reuter and edited by Gerald Karnow, M.D., Mercury Press, Spring

ance) that the first crystallizations already contained all fundamental principles of the method. Out of piety to this fact, we have published in books later on exactly these first crystallizations of the Agava americana, the camomile, the waterlily. The Agava am. and waterlily were selected because they belonged to my favored plants.

Later on it took many years of painstaking, even boring detail work to prove that our first assumption was correct in every detail, and no other arrangement would lead better to the desired demonstration of formative forces. (The details of the method are known and have been widely publicized; therefore they need not be reported here).

Had we not hit the right arrangement at first, the entire method might never have been discovered and we might have lost ourselves in trials, errors and unessential details. It was one important factor in our cooperation which has been overlooked, misunderstood, misjudged frequently by many, even quite close other coworkers, that it was just this blending together of thought, reason, vision or imagination (if the term may be permitted here) with absolute trueness and devotion in following up the idea by experimental trial which had led to results. A mutual devotion to the work, undisturbed by the criticism, doubts of others – just the faith in the correctness of our idea and the perseverance to demonstrate it empirically with reasonable results: out of this cooperation grew the laboratory which became my one great love of this life, never deserted, never given up.

Simultaneously another coworker found her way to the laboratory: Erika Riese. She was a botanist and gardener at heart. With great enthusiasm she could welcome each new growth in the experimental garden, or teach botany or collect herbs which we needed for our experiments. While Erika Sabarth was the more

---

Valley, New York, 1992. Originally published as *Ehrenfried Pfeiffer - Pionier Spiritueller Forschung und Praxis, Begegnungen und Briefwechsel – Ein Beitrag zu seiner Biographie*, [Ehrenfried Pfeiffer – Pioneer of Spiritual Research and Practice, Encounters and Correspondence – A Contribution To His Biography] Philosophisch-Anthroposophischer Verlag Am Goetheanum, Dornach/Switzerland, 1987. See reference 2.

introvert type, devoted to things and ideas and with difficulty making contact with others, Erika Riese had the gift to make friends and to be very sociable.

Both had and still have one property in common, to carry out an idea, i.e., to make it work no matter how new, off the trodden path or unusual this idea would be – as long as it lent itself to some experiment, it was performed. Both had one property which I don't possess at all: they were excellent draftsmen and could draw, illustrate and letter in the most artistic way.

Erika Riese had to stay in Dornach when I moved to the U.S.A., but is still in charge there of the plant experiments and the seed–breeding which we started in 1926.

Dr. Günther Wachsmuth, the head of the Science Section at the Goetheanum, had little time for laboratory work because he was at the same time secretary-treasurer and fully occupied with administrative burdens. Through his books, especially the one on Etheric Formative Forces, he had contributed and set a certain pattern, and as organizer he brought together the various, often rather divergent opinions of all the groups arising out of anthrop. scientific research and agriculture.

Occasionally he would come to the laboratory and we would discuss problems, and he would benevolently try to protect the lab. against criticism, of which there was a lot, and help financially.

At the same time, when storms and fevers raged over the body of the Anthrop. Soc., we could work quietly and undisturbed, i.e., objectively, in the laboratories, for we made it a point that Society problems, frictions, oppositions or party–groupings should never enter into our work, should not be discussed even, while we worked together. This enabled us to a very efficient cooperation, because our chief and only interest was to forge research ahead which would give information on formative forces.

While as member of the Anthroposophical Society, we were, of course, involved in Anthroposophical Society problems and decisions, we had to attend meetings: the lab. was a place of peace and productive work and still is today, after almost thirty-five years. No "Society" problem ever interfered with any laboratory or other enterprise for which I was responsible. All my coworkers at all times felt this responsibility that the WORK stands above personal opinion and interest. I am proud about the fact that quite a few coworkers have faithfully stood to our enterprise, over many years, here as well as abroad.

This is mainly to be credited to the fact that we all followed a main idea for which we worked, and that we all felt that monetary profit and/or personal opinions and personality conflicts have to be subordinated to the execution and perfection of this idea. The idea was that we wanted to demonstrate the value, the practicability, the stimulus for research which comes forth from Rudolf Steiner's spiritual and not materialistic concept and his specific guidelines given for our task.

The gratitude for Rudolf Steiner's impulse, to make it work, to make it practical—that was the motor which time and again made all of us recover from downfalls, errors, hangups and go on and on.[77]

77. "Not at all complete much more comes to this chapter." [Note by Pfeiffer at the close of this text, on the last page of the MS.]

A Soliloquy[78]

Ehrenfried Pfeiffer

When future tasks are discussed, I always have to think of Dr. Steiner and a small scene which took place in the spring of 1924 in the garden of the restaurant "Pfau" in Freiburg i. Br. We had interrupted the drive from Stuttgart to Dornach and sat there having afternoon coffee. Dr. Wegman was there, next to Dr. Steiner, Mr. and Mrs. Leinhas and Pfeiffer. In the course of the conversation Dr. Steiner turned to me and said: "A main cause for my impulses not becoming effective is that the members are unable to listen to what I said but want to express themselves and especially that they do not want to accept the people through whom I have to work according to karma…If only two would stick to me, then, I believe, I could accomplish my task."

From other remarks one could derive that it was most difficult to find those two. Not that the pupils and admirers of Dr. Steiner did not want to follow the words and wishes of Dr. Steiner, again and again one could experience:

1. When a revelation of the spiritual world was given, that this or that could not be done or accomplished, that it was said: yes, wonderful, grand, but that essentially the original impulse was bypassed and altered. The members who were given a task said "yes" with the head but in their actions they behaved so that it appeared as though they knew better.

2. That persons to whom Dr. Steiner told something or gave a task, were immediately attacked by others, maligned, corrected, as though they were unsuited and unable to accomplish what Dr. Steiner had charged them with. From his insight and from his karma Dr. Steiner had trusted a person – the others knew it better and had a thousand causes and objections why it could not be done – instead of helping those involved.

---

78. First published in *Ehrenfried Pfeiffer, Notes and Lectures, Compendium I*, Mercury Press, Spring Valley, NY, 1991, pp. 1-4. See reference 36.

To such situations Dr. Steiner's remarks mentioned above referred; they were expressed with much suffering and I believe that much loss of strength was caused by this, which led to his illness.

How much, for example was fought against the founding of the youth-section and its leaders, with the result, that of the many hopeful souls only few still have the strength to risk something; that there is hardly a following of Anthroposophical speakers and teachers; that many of the most gifted ones have drifted into the Christian Community.

Dr. Steiner gave suggestions for the development of a discipline of knowledge of substances (materia medica) and medicaments.

As we started with this many years ago in a working group, it resulted that every physician knew it differently; that one could not come to a uniform teaching and conception, or that not even – in spite of many beautiful and interesting single cases – clinical patient-histories and medicine-descriptions were being collected. Therefore the Weleda to this day does not possess the basic tests and reports for their medicines, the physicians do not have the "vade mecum" demanded by Dr. Steiner; the younger generation lacks a teachable system of Anthroposophical medicine.

At that time a certain physician was given the task to travel round to collect patient-histories for the remedies. After some time he returned and had a thousand reasons why this could not be done.

In my own work I have experienced the same. Where I could pursue a task given me by Dr. Steiner quietly with the help of immediate coworkers, something could be achieved; for example, with the new types of grain; there usable plant-forms exist today, only the loss through the war is regrettable.

In another realm, in that of crystallization research, a very peculiar experience was had. Crystallization research was started in order to study the "*Anschauende Urteilskraft*" [power of perceptive judgment] with regard to life-processes: that is, to become more familiar with the etheric and formative forces. Under the pressure by some coworkers and the audiences, consisting at first of Anthropososophists, it was demanded to develop the crystallization more and more as "proof" for the formative forces. It had not been my original intent to publish the work. But it was talked about so much, that I preferred to make the work public in my own words. Through this "providing of proof" was necessitated, that is from a method started to develop the perceptive judgment, an analytical, scientific method resulted. It was estranged from its original spirit and when the medical application came, the majority of the Anthroposophical physicians demanded that the path of "proof" be followed instead of training the imagination. I have complied with this demand out of a feeling of duty, more or less successfully.

One day, in 1939 in winter, (I cannot present this in any other form), a delegation of spiritual beings came to me and said approximately the following: "We are the beings which are needed in order to work within the physical and chemical forces in nature in such a way that the formative forces become visible. We have aided you in your striving because we hoped that thereby the force of imaginative perception (*bildhafte Urteilskraft*) in those persons who came in contact with it would be developed. We feel that we should cooperate only in the task of cognition of the etheric. You have engaged in paths where you demonstrate etheric formative forces, but other people want to make from this proofs along materialistic lines. This is not in the original intention of the spiritual world, which wants to replace materialism by imaginative cognition."

The consequences which I had to draw from this conversation, were that I can personally perform and ask to be performed only such crystallizations, where that which the spiritual world revealed as abuse does not enter.

This entails that there is hardly any possibility for publication because my friends demand the "characteristic of proof" of publication. I mention this only as an example how one can contribute something towards the solution of a problem, but cannot continue because the proper acceptance of the matter recognized (*Erkenntnisse*) is not present.

This is what Dr. Steiner has emphasized repeatedly: that one can go only that far as there is understanding for it. He also mentioned this, for example, for the necessity for a Michael Festival:

"As much as it is necessary that such a festival is arranged, as much will I care that it is arranged only when people are available who are ripe for it."

Asked what the requirements were and how many at this time – 1924 – would be ripe for it, he mentioned a one-digit number. The requirement: fully awake consciousness.

Written in May 1945

(The following was written in Fall/Winter of 1945/46)

What wants to be said with these words is the following: although a man can develop himself within himself, on his own accord, it will be possible insofar as his karma and external circumstances permit. He may get quite far on this way of development if he is active enough, that means that his astral body can refine itself, he can obtain significant cognitions, and he can develop deep insight and understanding of happenings. But this still remains his own path of cognition. In the true nature of man it lies, however, that such development becomes effective also outwardly, that is, is transformed into deeds. The person in question assumes tasks with this. From himself he can only present the total of his personality. From the accomplishment of tasks in the physical world he needs:

a.) Acceptance by others

b.) Co-operation by others.

c.) He can be listened to, that others listen to his ideas, and these can give a certain satisfaction.

d.) If the ideas he expresses are good, satisfaction can only then result, when these good ideas are accepted by others and lead to corresponding deeds. It belongs to the suffering of a spiritually cognizant man when his insight is listened to but not taken to heart, i.e. the listeners then return to their order of the day.

e.) In the listener such forces and desires are awakened, that he wants to partake in the effects of the spiritual cognitions, that he wants to cooperate and convert into deeds of his own, that is that he not only wants to do, but actually does. From the actually doing a true social contact develops. He thereby becomes a helper, a co-worker and, because purely spiritual tasks are in question, he can do this only out of his own decision, he cannot be forced to do it, he must himself resolve to do it and the grade and intensity of his cooperation depends entirely on his own personality.

It is a deeper pain which one who tries to act out of spiritual insight experiences: that the suggestions are listened to and are accepted, may even be praised, but that they, naturally, are modified, but often modified in such a way that nothing is left of the original.

The originator then gets into a situation where he can no longer participate, because something is being done which has very little to do with the impulse entrusted to him.

He will then experience that the fulfillment of his task is totally handed over to others and that he is either too weak or that it is not within his destiny to be able to succeed.

From this he will learn to strengthen himself or to search for other ways. In social cooperation, success depends upon the degree of cooperation of all. It is as though in a group of men working in a field the speed of the work, of hoeing or weeding is not determined by the fastest or most skillful worker, but by the slowest. Thereby a condition of tension arises. This tension can lead to experience, can also lead to loss of force, can contain both. All this must still be thought of on a basis of the good will of all coworkers to cooperate. That is, that this social organism is not yet hampered by anti-social, destructive impulses.

In the cooperation of men and groups of men true "humanity" arises. So far I have tried to describe an objective line of thought, which, I believe, can be accepted as a basis by each single human being. In the personal life of the writer several examples can be cited which can illuminate all phases of a spiritual and material, social and anti-social co-operation.

As an example, the work of the biodynamic endeavor will be referred to. In this I have acquired (may I say in all humility) far-reaching knowledge and experience. These are available and people have expressed the desire to start something on the basis of this experience. I have consented to cooperate with and aid such enterprises to the degree that I have placed myself into some things assuming personal responsibilities in them. In certain cases such a working connection proved to be valuable and something good resulted. In other cases, those who wanted to do something confined themselves to creating a certain situation and left the doing to me. In some countries biodynamic organizations were created which worked according to my plans but were absolutely independent, where I did not have to push. It is there where people developed creative forces from their own impulses and from their own will creative forces.

Here in America a situation evolved from which one can say only, (and I use the word very cautiously), one had much desire, had also shown the start of some action, but had left the real doing and execution up to me to such an extent that my forces were thereby exhausted. In the American B.D. Association very little was done in the last years, only that which I could do myself, or what the others could do under my direction. From most of the interested parties one hears only that they do not have time for it or that circumstances do not permit them to do something, except in the case of our literature. There, where I myself stand actively in the economic life, conditions are not much better, because my employees or friends, which are in a relationship of quasi-employment also de facto, accomplish very little. In other words, there are today in America, in spite of all efforts, so few qualified B.D. enterprises that you can count them on the fingers of one hand. The peculiar situation is this, that the intellectual scope of the work is far-reaching, the social scope is nil. From the 25 or so young men with whom I had occasion to work in Kimberton in the course of the years, none remained in agriculture and still less became active and developed coworkers. One could best characterize this as an intellectual success and a social failure.

Now I am asking the reader of these lines for a serious and honest advice: what consequences should I draw from this, how shall I behave under these circumstances from now on?

A similar, although not as significant condition has resulted in the Anthroposophical realm. In that realm also one receives constant communications and confirmations how important it is what one is doing, how valuable it is for the movement, or, in order to bring this into an often-used formula: "we need you." In spite of this, very little is done in order to make this "we need you" possible in the physical-social realm.

The Heart as a Spiritual Organ of Perception and the Etherization of the Blood

[The following lecture by Pfeiffer was given in Spring Valley on December 17, 1950. It is the first of three lectures, which after his death were published under the title *Heart Lectures* (Mercury Press, Spring Valley, 1982 and 2009). Pfeiffer prepared himself for nine months before delivering this lecture. The great responsibility for this theme may be noticed from the utmost care in which the train of thought appears. Pfeiffer wanted to look through the notes of the lecture, but did not get back to it and left it to his friends to undertake the eventual publication. (See Lecture I in the booklet *Heart Lectures*, Mercury Press, Spring Valley, New York)]

Last time I reported about our compost activities in California. Today I want to go back to a more Anthroposophical subject, but since interruptions are coming, it will not be a course as in previous winters. However, it will be a related series of lectures.

Several years ago I lectured here at the farm concerning the nervous system of man. The endeavor was made to build a bridge between the physical organs and spiritual forces. I had intended to go on and talk about the rhythmic and metabolic systems, but difficulties intervened. If one studies metabolism – the exchange of substances – this is a complicated matter needing knowledge in the field of physiological chemistry. It is too likely that misunderstandings will creep in if the listeners do not have such a background of knowledge. Such a study of the rhythmic system also requires a deep insight into physical functioning.

The human heart and blood constitute one of the most far-reaching of subjects. Dr. Steiner spoke of the etherization of blood[79] that takes place there, i.e. the transformation of matter into etheric forces. One can quote Dr. Steiner, but one would like to understand why and how he was able to speak about such things. Today the science of physiology has only very little evidence re-

79. E.g., on October 1, 1911 in Basel, see G.A. 130 at reference 37.

garding the function of the heart. But occult groups other than the Anthroposophical know these secrets of the heart, and some groups do not want them made known to others. So we feel it a kind of challenge. Also, Rudolf Steiner, in the *Spiritual Guidance Of Mankind*[80], speaks of the need for a science which will be able to observe the working of Christ in Nature. This is something far in the future. So as an Anthroposophical scientist one feels that one wants to study the human heart as an organ where a bridge is being built between man's physical body and spiritual entity.

Sixteen years ago I met a leading occultist[81] (he is not publicly known). He works in a realm which is not Anthroposo-phical, nor is it a realm of black magic but rather grey, in between and nearer to the dark than the light forces. This man, a medical man by profession, told me a story: He said that Dr. Steiner's illness – according to research of himself and his associates – was due to the fact that Dr. Steiner wanted to tell more regarding the spiritual function of the human heart, and other occultists did not want this known at present. So they brought to bear on Rudolf Steiner forces against which he was unable to defend himself, and he became ill.

This knowledge which Rudolf Steiner had concerns "the fifth chamber of the heart"[82]. The idea is that in our time there are certain changes taking place in the heart, by which gradually a fifth chamber will develop. In this fifth chamber man will have a new organ which will allow him to control life forces in a different way than is possible at the moment.

It is known that there is a kind of endocrine action in the blood. There have been found traces of a sort of "suprarenalin," like adrenalin, indicating that the heart has a kind of gland function. Rudolf Steiner was willing to tell more regarding etherization,

---

80. cf. footnote 105 on p.172 in this book.
81. Presumably in the U.S.A., when for the first time in 1934 Pfeiffer undertook a lecture tour.
82. An indication from Pfeiffer. Of the four "chambers of the heart" see *inter alia* R. Steiner's lecture of March 21, 1911, in G.A. 128. At reference 38.

and the heart as a dual purpose organ, both physical and spiritual. The heart is not a pressure pump, but an organ in which etheric space is created so that the blood is sucked to the heart rather than pumped. He also said that it was important to change the scientific concept from the idea of the heart as a pump to something else.[83] It is difficult to bring evidence on this point which can be presented. The matter needs more study; it is no help to quote Rudolf Steiner.

The key to the problem can be found. I want to try to make a gradual approach to it in several lectures. Among the things that Dr. Steiner gave on the subject is what he said to the workmen on the Goetheanum in a lecture on June 6th, 1923[84]. In discussing the blood circulation and the motion of the heart, he said that with some people the heart is not quite in its proper place. He said that in the case of dancers, the heart is moved from its proper position on the left to the right side. When this happens it makes man more perceptive in an inner way to the influence of his surroundings. He also said that in modern man there was such a disorganization of the blood circulation that he was able to go to the movies and not faint. An old Greek would faint immediately in the movies, because of their disturbing influence on the circulation.

Together with the wrong concept of the heart as a pump is connected the fact that we have a wrong social life today. A healthy social life can develop only if the old pump-concept is removed and is replaced by the proper one. So this is a subject that should interest the student of social problems. Rudolf Steiner said that a true cognition in this regard would also make it possible to build machines that are in accord and in harmony with the human being and not destructive to him. He said that only when people know that it is the invisible in man which moves the heart, will it

---

83. See the lecture of March 24, 1920, G.A. 312, *Spiritual Science and Medicine* at reference 39.

84. See G.A. 350, *Workmen's Lectures* at reference 40.

be possible to construct proper machines and to solve the social problem.[85]

In Nature there are three principles. One is the principle of form, the second is the principle of substance, the substance that builds form – and this includes color. We can describe any object by looking at its form and color. This is true as long as we are merely looking at an external object. However, there is the possibility also of abstract geometrical thought-forms. But these are not found in Nature, in Nature there is always the marriage of substance and thought-form. In Nature we see the two principles of the Creative Entity. In the form pattern we see the thought of God, and since forms are in a constant process of change and development it is a picture of Creative Thought. In substance we begin to find our way into another realm of Creation, because substance is a realm which has been emanated (with the help of the Thrones) out of the Spiritual Substance of the Creator. Thus every substance was the Spiritual Substance of the Creator. The Creator is not matter, but is the power which acts in matter, i.e., will. In every substance we find the emanation of the Will of the Creator.

These are deep problems, which we neglect. Approaching them requires an attitude of worship, of beginning to sense the holiness of the problems which we approach. If we have such an attitude we are able to discover the Will of the Creator in matter, and the Thought of the Creator in the forming of matter. Only if we are able to approach the holy of holies in Nature can we overcome and begin to transform matter. Then we realize that in taking substance, in breathing and eating, we are moving into the holiest realm the human being can perceive.

Form and substance in Nature are brought together by a process of growth. Form is filled out by matter through nourishment, metabolism. Thus there is a third entity which brings about the moving and changing of substance into form. This is the principle of motion in its widest meaning. It lives in the background wher-

85. Here Pfeiffer points to an essential component for the development of the "Strader-technology" of the future.

ever there is growth and development, it is Cosmic Motion. This Cosmic Motion exists in every body and organism, animal and human. This Motion is the Third Power of God into which we look if we look through metabolism and circulation into what is behind them. If we look into the Spirit we see this motion as something embedded in the Feelings of the Creator, say rather the Heart of the Creator. There is nothing but harmony in the Heart of the Creator; out of it comes every motion that exists.

In the human form, which is "the image of God," we find the Thought of the Creator, the harmonious Heart of the Creator, and the emanated Substance of the Creator. Goethe said that if our eye were not of the sun nature we could not recognize the sun, and if we were not of God's Nature we could not recognize God. There is in our thought the possibility of perceiving the Thought of God in our organs. In the exchange of substance, metabolism, we participate in the Will of the Creator. And in circulation we perceive something of the harmony embedded in us by the Creator. But all these are given to man to be used by him. Nobody is influenced by the Creator. This implies a responsibility: we will use them properly or misuse them. The fact is that we all do both.

Now to the heart problem: Physiologically it is an outstanding organ of the body, anatomically it is a system of muscles. We have muscles in our arms, legs, etc.; these are fibrous tissue which bear up our structure, for it is due to our muscles that our skeleton is held together. The heart also is definitely a system of muscles and as such connects with the astral body. But the heart is a different muscle because its fibers are laid down differently[86], and also it is a hollow muscle. I think it is the only hollow muscle in the body. The fact that it is a hollow sphere brings about an inner motion, because there is empty space inside.

86. The heart musculature is horizontal, whereas normally only the voluntary muscles are so, while the involuntary are longitudinal. This means that in the future, the functioning of this organ will be under human control.

I have spoken in the past of Rudolf Steiner's exercise for learning imagination: You form the image of a sphere, metamorphose it to a central point, and from this center again out to a sphere. You can think of concentric circles getting smaller until they become a point and then enlarging again. One day you will try to apply this to the outermost cosmos. Then you will feel it concentrate, with everything into the earth, and then the earth itself will contract finally into the central point of the sphere. Then you will experience the central point of your own heart as the central point of the sphere. This has to be experienced; just thinking about it is of no value. If you have this as experience, you then expand again, and what expands is not the vast cosmos but it is you. Then if you are objective and are strong enough, you find that you face yourself on the Threshold of the Spiritual World. And if the Guardian allows you to pass, you then see how small you are. This new sphere which expands is an incomplete and spotty cosmos, some parts of it more outlined, some less so. This is not depressing but is an objective experience. You see everything that is spiritual radiating out, you feel its radiating power; and you also experience other, dark spaces.

What you have done is to concentrate your entire God-made Cosmos to a center, and from this center radiate outward what will some day be a new cosmos. This is what makes the heart move, the motion which radiates out from the heart. This is what Rudolf Steiner was ready to give and what the occultists opposed giving out. In fact, Rudolf Steiner has given it in a meditation.[87]

The same occultists to whom I referred earlier said when we were wrestling about these things: "We have discovered since the death of Dr. Steiner that unless this knowledge of the center of the heart is made known, there will be no salvation for the human race,

---

87. For example on July 6, 1924, see G.A. 317; *Curative Education Course*, at reference 41. Compare also the letter of R. Steiner's to G. Wagner of December 1903, in G.A. 264. *From the History and Contents of the First Section of the Esoteric School 1904 to 1914: Letters, Documents and Lectures.* See reference 42.

but only destruction." One can call this sensational, or one can say, "How deep a secret, that even the dark forces have to recognize it."

The etheric center of the heart draws the blood towards it and then pulses it out again. Here is where substance is transformed to ether, and Dr. Steiner says forms rise up to the etheric brain and thence to the physical brain so that it can function and so that there may be harmony in the organs of the body. The organs and their functioning are regulated by what takes place between the etheric heart and etheric brain. Through this heart muscle, with a hollow sphere and an etheric center inside it, pulses the blood. The blood enters the heart with its four chambers. Between the second and the third chamber it goes to the lung to be regenerated, and from the fourth it goes out to the body again. There is no pulse in the main vein which brings blood to the heart – there is no pressure – it is taken from every vein by suction.

In the lung, with its oxygen, the blood is touched by the outer world. The old, poisoned, used-up blood goes back from the lung as regenerated blood. There is really a constant dying and regeneration. New blood is really born. This is a marvelous process of which we know practically nothing. The heart is the only muscle that only gets tired once (except if diseased), and that is in the moment of death. This shows the eternal youth force in the etheric heart; the heart lives entirely in cosmic rhythms. It lives in relation to the time of the cosmic migration of the sun in the zodiac.[88] In addition, the heart also takes up nourishment from the blood. What we eat goes in part to the lymph system, and in part to the liver, but finally, all that we eat goes into the blood. So this human blood (blood proper and the lymph) bears nourishment and takes away the breakdown products of the body, and also it is the regenerated substance that pulses from the heart into the body.

---

88. In healthy adults there are generally four heartbeats to one breath; the number of breaths per day corresponds to the total number of years that the vernal equinox needs to pass through the zodiac: 25,920. The number of heartbeats per minute corresponds to the total number of years that the vernal point takes to advance one degree of the zodiac: 72.

What we eat has a tremendous influence on the heart. For example, if we drink alcohol[89] this passes unchanged into our blood and can be measured exactly. This alcohol circulates through our entire body as a foreign substance. This substance imposes something on the heart. Red wine, for instance, has the effect of opening the capillaries to the head. Thus more blood comes to the head so that it, in a minor way, is illuminated. People have more life in their head, so they get a lot of ideas and have warm feelings. If they pat you on the shoulder at such a time, you do not take it seriously, because you know that it is simply that these capillaries have been opened. On others, it has other effects; for instance, Goethe liked a little red wine and wrote some very good poetry when he had had it.

We see that alcohol brings a change, that it disturbs the entire heart function. Also, with alcohol we impose something on the liver which hardens it. Changes in the heart take place with everything we eat. The secret of digestion is that we do not take foreign matter into our system, but all foods are broken down and their forms are changed. Indigestion takes place when this process has not been carried out. This imposes action on the heart. The heart has the task of regulating everything, and the blood mirrors everything that happens in our body. The kidney in a healthy person is able to filter out sugar from the blood. Then at another point, in the glomeruli, the blood reabsorbs the sugar. It is necessary that the sugar be out while the blood is being purified in the kidneys; then it is returned. Through the lung the blood is regenerated, through the kidney the blood is purified, and the heart cooperates in both these processes.

Dr. Steiner said that in older times the spiritual experiences took place mainly through the lung. In the lung, man took the other world into himself, so that God could be a concrete concept for him. This relationship ceased in the 19th Century. Since the 19th Century man no longer experiences the forces of God through

89. cp. lecture of R. Steiner's of March 20, 1913, G.A. 145 at reference 43.

breathing in. So he finds in matter a God-forsaken world. Dr. Steiner added that since the 19th Century man experiences something of the spiritual world through the kidney.[90] The kidney does not experience the outer world directly, but by way of the inner world. Dr. Steiner once called the kidney the brain of the metabolic system[91]. If the kidney is disturbed, the retina of the eye is disturbed, and also we get high blood pressure. High blood pressure occurs when the astral is drawn too much into the blood system. This process can be influenced by medicines, but medicines cannot help the underlying spiritual and regenerative forces that are needed. So it is a good idea to learn how to behave so that we do not tax our kidneys too much.

Rudolf Steiner said that through our kidneys we perceive only our own self-created spiritual world. Therefore kidney-ideas, if not spiritualized, are ideas full of fear, ideas of incompatibility, ideas of clairvoyance. If we trust the kidney without learning about the etheric heart, the regulator, we learn only about atomic destruction of man and the world.

If the kidney does not purify the blood, it means an accumulated burden on the heart. Hence a proper diet, with not too much sugar, etc., is important. But you meet people who keep to a proper diet and follow the book in everything and still look worn out, passive and the like. This condition is caused, not by diet, but by lack of spiritual activity. This is the disease which eventually breaks down the heart. The blood is affected not only by external impressions but by every emotion, fear, joy, etc. Adrenalin production is changed by fear and rage. It is now recognized that short-tempered persons have their adrenalin function affected by this condition. Joy in turn has other effects, and our blood is influenced if, for instance, we are not able to feel joy when someone speaks objec-

---

90. In lecture 14 of July 28, 1923 , "Lung Knowledge or Kidney Knowledge," pp. 243, 255-261, G.A. 350: *Lectures to the Workmen* at reference 40.

91. On June 8, 1912, G.A. 137, *Man in the Light of Occultism, Theosophy and Philosophy*. See reference 44.

tively well of us or others. Moral effects work on the contraction and expansion of the capillary vessels, and the emotional, moral, soul life influences the composition of the blood.

Then there is the question of spiritual experience: At the moment when a person becomes spiritually active (this means not only to think logically, but to be spiritually active), at that moment the composition of the blood changes again. Rudolf Steiner once suggested in this connection that one might measure the nitrogen content in the blood and kidneys of a dozing person and a person who is trying to solve a mathematical problem. Furthermore, in proper meditation there is a spiritual process which breaks down used-up products in the blood. A basis for life and health lies in there being enough spiritual activity to be able to transform used-up substance into etheric substance. Moral joy and pure thought can do a lot of good in this connection.

With every pulse of the heart a certain amount of substance is absorbed, is taken away as physial pressure and added to the etheric substance. This then begins to radiate outwards. Dr. Steiner said that a clairvoyant could see the amount of radiation that goes up from the heart to the brain, and if a person knew this, they would be ashamed to fall asleep at a lecture in the presence of a clairvoyant. The radiation from this etheric organ of the heart is actually developing into a spiritual sense organ. A new sense organ is developing in this etheric heart, and this is the only organ by which man is able to sense and to recognize the Etheric Christ.

I can think, "Not I, but the Christ in me." Such a thought may stimulate us to healthy feelings, but in itself this is not enough. There has to be something which goes through our will, and since our will is combined with metabolism to produce etheric substance, so "Not I, but Christ in me" has to work through the etheric heart, transforming substance into pure ether, pure radiance.

For us there is an experience of the heart similar to the way in which, in the old Mysteries, the sun was experienced. We experience in every heart a sun. The sun shines on all people; it shines on the fields of the earth; it shines on other planets. And all the time it is consuming its own energy. The sun dissolves matter and transforms it into radiant energy. Its light can be seen everywhere in our earthly cosmos. The same power that dwells in the sun wills to live in every human being.

If you become aware of the heart as a spiritual organ, you begin to develop the power to see the Etheric Christ. You do this by realizing that that force in the heart is the same as the force in the sun, physically as well as spiritually. If you take this as a reality, there will still be conflicts, but there will also be the realization that your entire picture of the world changes. The force from the heart is a force which will be good.

Now, daydreaming a little, let us imagine what would happen if all those responsible for the political future of the earth, war or no war, etc., if all these were not to use kidney thinking, but the radiant power of the heart. How different the future would be. But of course, this has not been developed yet, and we have to suffer the consequences of kidney thinking.

All that we can do is to be aware of the forces of the etheric heart. Because these will shine, they will be perceived from other planets and will increase the brightness of earth. In fact, the earth will only become a star through that process.

Systole and *Diastole*

Two colored sketches by Ehrenfried Pfeiffer
from his Heart Lecture of December 17, 1950

The first publication of these sketches of Pfeiffer's take place with the kind permission of Paul W. Scharff, M.D.

Systole

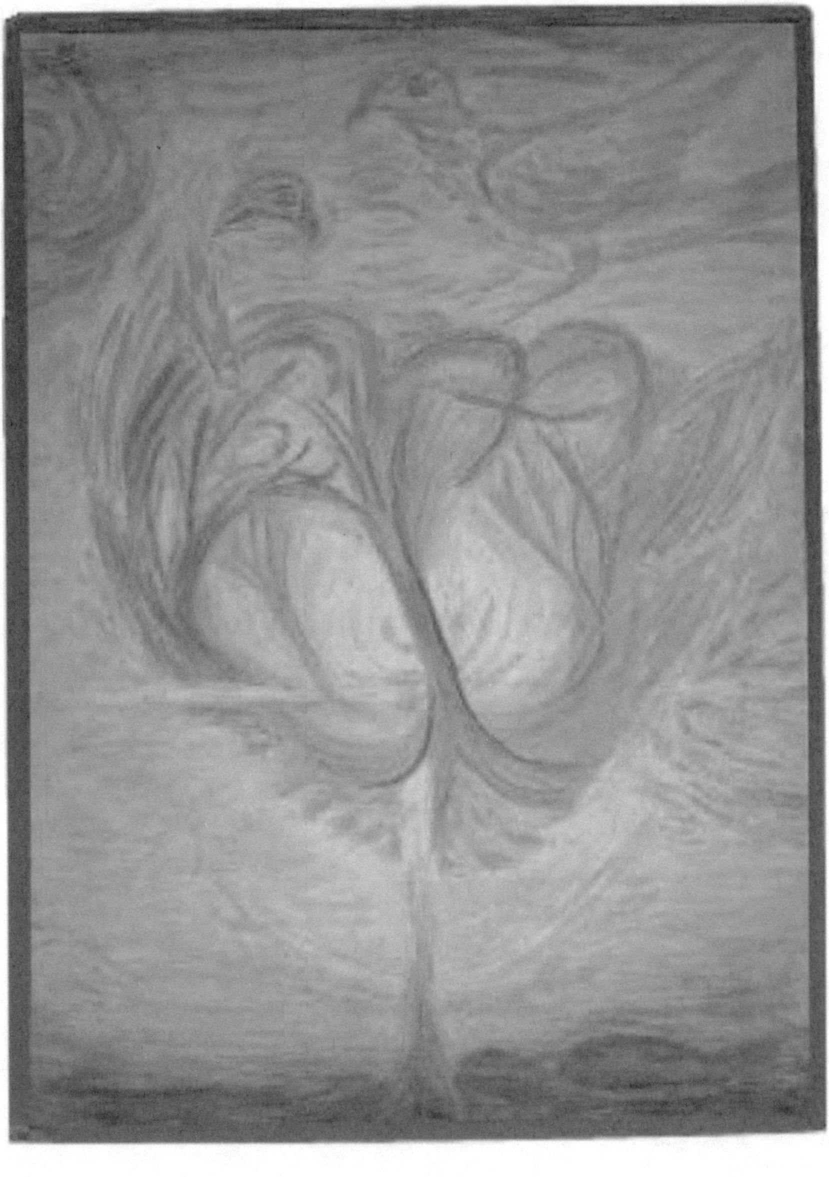

Diastole

In regard to making anthroposophy live in our own selves, not just as something abstract, I would say that if we only just glimpse at this etheric organ of the heart, we will have begun to make anthroposophy live.

It is a peculiarity of the heart that it is the only bodily organ which is self-maintaining. This is because the blood going through the heart also nourishes the heart. The coronary vessels around the heart are like hands holding it. These coronary vessels nourish the heart and take away the used-up substance. They must be the most overtaxed vessels of the body. In modern man, scleroses and thromboses, diseases of the coronary vessels, are most widespread. This is because the etheric is not able to take up the impact of physical things on the heart. So it becomes stiff or clogged. We suffer a sudden end. Modern scientists also know that fear or despair bring about an increase of these diseases. These diseases come because the heart does not get proper spiritual nourishment.

[At this point, the speaker showed paintings of the etheric heart. He ended by saying:]

I have been working on this lecture for about nine months, and it is still incomplete. I received the possibility of speaking at all from working on this sketch. If you forget everything else I told you today and only experience the fact that you have in you a creative sun which actually radiates light and warmth, you have already achieved a lot.

*

“This is a problem of nutrition”

[After R. Steiner’s return from Koberwitz, where in June, 1924, on the estate of Count Carl von Keyserlingk, he had held the Agricultural Course (GA 327), Pfeiffer, who had been unable to attend, had the following conversation with Rudolf Steiner which renewed the memory of an earlier conversation with his teacher. Pfeiffer’s description (in the third person) is to be found in the article *New Directions in Agriculture,* reprinted in “Rudolf Steiner – Recollections by Some of his Pupils,” *The Golden Blade, 1958, p. 118ff.*]

When Dr. Steiner returned to Dornach, however, the general situation was discussed with him. When I asked him whether one should immediately begin experiments regarding the new method, he replied: “The most important thing is to make the blessings of our agricultural preparations available to the largest possible areas over the entire earth, for the healing of the earth and in order to improve the nutritive quality of its produce to the utmost respect. That should be our first objective. The experiments can come later.” He obviously thought that the proposed methods should be applied at once.

This can be better understood against the background of a conversation I had with Dr. Steiner en route from Stuttgart to Dornach before the agriculture course was given. In this conversation, he first pointed out the need for a deepening of esoteric life, and in this connection mentioned certain faults typically found in spiritual movements. Pfeiffer then asked, “How can it happen that the spiritual impulse, and especially the inner schooling, for which you are constantly providing stimulus and guidance, bear so little fruit? Why do the people concerned give so little evidence of spiritual experience, in spite of all their efforts? Above all, why, in spite of theoretical insight, is the will for action, for the carrying out of these spiritual impulses, so weak?” Above all, Pfeiffer wanted to get an answer to the question as to how one could build a bridge to active participation and the carrying out of spiritual intentions without being distracted from the right path by personal ambition, illusions and petty jealousies. These three negative qualities had been named by Rudolf Steiner as the main inner hindrances on the path. Then came the thought-provoking and surprising answer: "This is a problem of nutrition. Nutrition as it is today does not supply the strength necessary for manifesting the spirit in physical life. A bridge can no longer be built from thinking to will and action. Food plants no longer contain the forces they need to give people." A nutritional problem whose solution would enable the spirit to become manifest and realize itself in human beings! With this statement as a background, one can understand why Dr. Steiner said that "the blessings of the biodynamic compost preparations should be made available as quickly as possible to the largest possible areas of the entire earth, for the earth's healing."

With this perspective one must regard the whole Koberwitz agricultural course:[92] that here was given an introduction to understanding and practicing those powers which will re-introduce the spiritual forces, often called cosmic forces, into the plant world.

---

92. G.A. 327. See reference 45.

The True Basis of Nutrition

[The last lecture given by Pfeiffer in Switzerland at Dornach was held on October 10, 1958. The complete title is: *Unternatur und Übernatur in der Physiologie der Pflanze und des Menschen – die wahre Grundlage der Ernährung*. [Sub-nature and Super-nature in the Physiology of Plant and Man – The True Basis of Nutrition].[93] Although not all the desirable evidence could be produced, nevertheless this little-known lecture with its fundamental points of view and legacy-like character is included here.]

Honored friends,

Points of contact between anthroposophy and the so-called sciences[94] are especially evident in a problem which deeply concerned Rudolf Steiner, one which we frequently do not recognize as a problem, or at least do not understand why it should be the subject of an Anthroposophical lecture: namely, the problem of nutrition. Nutrition is connected with our physical existence. It is also connected with the manner in which our body can be the carrier of the soul-spiritual, and we will see in the course of the lecture that this relationship is of a fundamental nature for both our material and spiritual nature.

I will first have to begin with a few very primitive concepts in order gradually to introduce the problem. If you look into a textbook on nutrition or at a newspaper, or even at one of the lectures in which Rudolf Steiner spoke about nutrition to the workers at the first Goetheanum, you will first find that man needs various substances: protein, carbohydrates, fats, mineral substances, and of course water.[95] These substances are contained in everything we

---

93. Spring Valley: Mercury Press, 1981. (Transated by G. F. Karnow, M.D.)

94. See Steiner on November 4, 1910 (GA 115): "Science must necessarily err when it is not led by occult science, which everywhere supplies guidelines for what we can gain by physical research."

95. See the Discussion of February 23, 1924, in *From Elephants to Einstein…Answers to Questions*, G.A. 352, Rudolf Steiner Press, London, 1998, pp. 143-163 (Reference 46).; also the lecture from January 23, 1924 in GA 352.

ingest; in bread, in meat, in vegetables, and in fruits. It is generally considered, especially by the older scientific teachings of nutrition, that these substances then give our body its material nourishment. Today there is a branch of science called biochemistry, which studies the chemical processes in the course of life. It was for decades the stepchild of physiological chemistry, but just in the last thirteen years it has advanced so significantly that after reading Rudolf Steiner's lectures about nutrition and at the same time studies the new findings in biochemistry, one has the impression that here the points of view come into contact, whereas in the older characterizations of nutrition there are great conceptual differences with Steiner's views.

Actually, we cannot talk about nutrition without talking first about digestion. I must say that my special interest in the problems of nutrition simply came about because whenever I had the opportunity to wait somewhere with Rudolf Steiner when I accompanied him (once in the train station in Basel, waiting almost an hour for the train connection, and also in other situations,) he always began to talk about nutrition and the use of nutrition. I was at that time a young man totally involved in the study of anthroposophy, and at first considered it a little boring that Rudolf Steiner talked again and again of eating – because I still lacked the great spiritual horizons. That was the starting-point for this lecture. From that point a work has since emerged, a work about which one can say that in general, it takes thirty-three to thirty-five years before one starts to grow in wisdom and understanding.

Now to the problems of nutrition and digestion. I will first represent the viewpoints of modern research in the area, in which I must report on some studies, some exact biochemical studies. As I said, one speaks essentially of proteins, carbohydrates, starches, sugars and fats. In nature, these substances are prepared in the plant, mineral and animal kingdoms. They are taken up by man more or less through chewing and the digestion. In the mouth, while chewing, a new reaction begins through the so-called sense of taste, thereby initiating via the nervous system a whole sequence of processes which then influence almost all of the bodily organs, increasing digestive activity. Rudolf Steiner pointed out, for example, that one should not gulp down one's food, because then, especially, these processes are disturbed; this can be biochemically verified.

These foods are then digested: in the stomach, a part is predigested, and then processed further in the duodenum and other parts of the small intestine. Now comes the moment which is exceedingly important for us. The foods are broken down. With the exception of salt, no single food remains as it entered the mouth; each one is taken apart: proteins are broken down, carbohydrates are transformed by the body fluids into sugars, which in turn are transformed, and the fats are similarly broken down. In this field there has come about a change in the views of exact biochemistry which also enables us as scientists to understand better what Rudolf Steiner said and recognize its depth. The proteins are broken down into amino-acids and peptides and the fats into fatty acids and glycerol. The resulting substances are then taken up from the intestine and pass over into the lymph or blood systems, and some of them are then transported to the liver.

Now comes the point with which I have even today, in my scientific and academic lectures, the greatest difficulties with my students. These students, who are already prejudiced by their education, have the greatest difficulty in understanding what is actually going on. The average man today, and probably most of you (and one can't blame you for it, because you haven't been taught differently) thinks that this protein is incorporated into the protein of the body, that the fat is transformed into the fat of the body and sugar into the sugar of the body. That is the view which is still given in literature today. It is not so at all. The most recent studies show that at the moment when the broken-down food substances are taken up, their further course is completely independent, proceeds completely independently. As our exact science says today, the food loses its individuality into the body. That protein which you take up in a piece of meat or a bean or in a grain of wheat cannot be recognized anymore as such, speaking strictly chemically, at the moment when it passes through the intestinal wall into the body. It disappears, and in turn other products can be discovered. What has today been discovered is exceedingly closely related to what Rudolf Steiner called the inner chemistry, when he talked about the abolition of the outer chemistry of nature and the development of counter-forces in man.

This can be recognized in what I will now quote to you from some of the current studies which were recently published in Chicago:[96] "In the processes of the food absorption out of the intestine into the body, the presently known physical-chemical laws are abolished, and the absorption of nourishment proceeds according to laws which are opposite to the presently known laws and are not yet understood."

What is involved here is that physical chemistry posits certain laws for the outer world about pressure, about movement from one concentration into another - but here the laws behave with the opposite signs. We can say that is all very nice, but why should that interest us? But I must tell you that once we really begin to understand these processes, they belong among the most fascinating things which one can discover about nature and about man; that here, through this study which is not at all influenced by anthroposophy, research into the life processes itself leads to it naturally: to the recognition of the truth of the transition from outer material conditions to inner conditions in man.

In this study, I personally find a process pointing to the future, raising the hope that even absolute materialism, if it does not speculate but only studies the phenomena, will one day be led to the lawfulness of spiritual activity. This is especially the case in this field of study, from which I will mention some examples.

It is shown here that the differences between proteins, carbohydrates and fats are abolished, and abolished in such a way that through liver activity (Rudolf Steiner uses the expression: "The liver is the organ which 'looks to' these metabolic processes) that now this liver activity attempts to regulate these processes. You see what goes on here. These substances are transformed by the

96. Source of reference unknown.

liver so that out of a protein can come a fat, out of a fat a sugar, and out of a sugar a protein, or vice versa. The newest biochemistry speaks of a "metabolic pool." Everything we take up actually disappears, and one substance gets transformed into another according to demand. The liver, the brain, the nervous system and the glands all work together. The important thing is that the matter which we take up into ourselves actually seems to be completely "transform-able," so that we must speak of a reservoir — as illustrated by tables — into which flows transformed outer material and out of which the body takes what it needs according to wisdom-filled laws. There would be complete harmony in ourselves if certain things did not happen which we will look at a little later.

Now we must ask ourselves: what does metabolism really mean? Here I can only say one thing: whoever has not studied this down to the smallest details may have heard the word metabolism - or whoever has read the lectures by Rudolf Steiner about the metabolic–limb man may have heard the word metabolism and probably thinks, when he hears "metabolism," of digestion and excretion, and maybe even of inhalation and exhalation. But actually, excuse me when I say this, he really knows nothing yet. Rudolf Steiner makes a medical remark about metabolism and points out that all substances in our body are completely renewed within seven years.[97] So if I had stood here on this platform seven years ago and someone had made a little mark anywhere on my body, and I stand here again today, you won't find the smallest remnant of such a mark. Instead, a completely different substance is here. This picture could be compared with the bed of a stream and the stream itself. The water in the stream is never the same; at every second it is different, while the bed of the stream remains. The river Rhine, or the Danube, has a certain persistence over a period of time. The water in the river is continually flowing. So it is also with our body. It is much too simplistic, however, to speak only of a renewing within seven years. After seven years we have arrived,

97. E.g. in the lesson from August 27, 1924, GA 270/3.

so to speak, at the end point, where one can be absolutely certain that nothing of the original substance remains anymore.

The transformation happens much more quickly. Think of a tooth perhaps, this one here. I mean a real one, of course! Everyone can feel a tooth and then follow a thought with me for a moment. This tooth contains calcium carbonate and calcium phosphate that formed as it renewed. Feel this tooth, and then say to yourselves: "In 240 days, all the calcium carbonate in this firm, solid tooth you are touching at this moment, all the calcium carbonate will be excreted, gone, and new calcium carbonate will have taken its place." And as long as the tooth renews its substance in 240 days, so long does it remain healthy and resistant. That is metabolism.

Another example: In the fatty tissues, fat is deposited. You can feel a small fat deposit here. There are also other parts of the body where you can very well feel these deposits. You should really try to picture this. Go ahead and feel one of those little rolls of fat! There you really have the feeling: this is a fat deposit. What you feel here between your fingers - that little roll of fat – 41% of it will be gone tomorrow evening at this same time where you felt it today. This fat has been transported back to the liver and will be transformed into other products. If the body for instance needs protein, fat or sugar, it will form them. If the body needs warmth, then it burns the fat; if it needs sugar, it manufactures sugar. If, for example, someone has diabetes, then the liver makes sugar out of the fat - and that makes diabetes. So 41% of this body fat is activated in one day, carried back to the liver and processed, and redeposited again in the same quantities. If it were not replaced, we would have an ideal treatment for obesity!

This fat transformation is truly amazing when you think how much activity and what dynamics are evident here. Forty-one percent in one day! Well, that this happens is just one part of metabolism, and this part of metabolism - which I have also studied scientifically - determines whether a person ages prematurely or remains young, or whether he gets sclerotic diseases such as arterial sclerosis, myocardial infarcts, coronary sclerosis, etc. The youth or aging of the body is determined by whether this fat transformation happens at the right time with the proper speed or not.

Then there is a critical point. I won't go into from pathological conditions such as gland disturbances etc., but in the relatively normal man there is a critical age, approximately the 35th year, when a man loses his youthful slenderness, and then, as evidence of the satisfied citizen – develops a little pot belly. This, you see, I say with purpose, the "pot belly of a satisfied citizen." Once the storms of youth are over; once the young person has lived out all his ideals; when this river flows into pre-formed banks; then this fat transformation slows down—this can be biochemically demonstrated—and different conditions arise. If this satisfied citizen gets transformed into a philistine, then the preconditions for sclerosis and hardening of all forms arise. In the metabolism of such a person, at twenty-five, twenty-eight, thirty years of age, one can actually see premature symptoms of aging. One can almost prophesy what will happen later.

I have a friend in Chicago. (He is, I believe, seventy-five years old and exceedingly active.) He used to say that he feels most human beings are already dead at thirty-five, but their corpses still keep running around.

The accumulation of these fat corpses in the body inhibits its dynamics and slows down the life process. Therein lies *one* of the problems of aging. Rudolf Steiner expresses this by saying that the fat in the body forms a wall, a wall against the spiritual. This should be understood physiologically and spiritually. I don't plan to discuss therapies for this condition; that would take too much time; but therapy could definitely help, were it to address nutrition as well as digestion, true enjoyment, as opposed to misleading false enjoyment, of food, and other psychological and spiritual issues. There is a school of scientists in Harcwood, Cambridge, that goes so far as to say that one should eat whatever one doesn't like, for then one wouldn't need to keep to a diet.

So much for fat metabolism. But there are other kinds of metabolism, for example mineral metabolism. Table salt is taken up directly into the body. One can track this ingested salt with isotopes, and within one minute find it in the whole body, out to the tips of the hair and the toes and into the outer skin, while calcium and magnesium salts, for example, are held back in the intestine. This is unimaginable to scientific thinking. There must be a circulation in the body of which we know absolutely nothing. This salt, which Rudolf Steiner calls the "salt phantom," spreads itself out inside the body within a minute; we don't know how. Within one minute the salt is distributed over the whole body, while the calcium and magnesium salts, for example, are held in the intestine and are only absorbed by the body when it wants them. They are never excreted out of the body; they remain. When the body decides—in this case it is not only the liver, but also the blood that decides—"Now I need calcium carbonate," then it will be absorbed from the intestine, out of which, in other circumstances, nothing could be absorbed. An unfathomable wisdom is at work here.

I have spoken of calcium. Calcium is also a constituent of the bones. We have the skeletal system, and a great portion of the bones consists of crystals of calcium carbonate and calcium phosphate. The metabolic transformations which lead to bone maintenance is so powerful that in each minute, the total calcium content of the blood crystallizes into the bones, and in that same minute a corresponding amount of calcium is dissolved out of the bones and returns to the blood. I repeat - because this is something that can lead to an imagination about the body system, about the skeleton, about death and resurrection of matter— in every minute, in all of you, the total calcium content of the blood crystallizes in your bones! Now it is an interesting fact that there are three layers in the bone. One of these layers is dead and another is so active that it is called the Life-sphere, or the Biosphere, by biochemists. And there is one layer that can crystallize as well as dissolve. Its cell structure consists of so-called giant cells which, if they were found in any other part of the body, would form the basis for cancer. But in the bone these cells are healthy because there they function with the ego-organization and the blood. Therefore these giant cells, which in the bones occasion crystallization and dissolution, are healthy.

In these processes we are taken completely beyond three-dimensional space. Once somebody took the trouble to determine the crystal surfaces of this mineral in us on the basis of microscopic studies (this mineral is apatite, a fluor-calcium-carbonate whose forms appear as a true crystal.) He found that in one gram of bone anywhere in the body, if all crystal surfaces which are formed there were placed next to one another, one would have approximately 100 square meters. If, however, the total crystal system of our bones were spread out, it would give a surface of about 15 acres – an ocean of crystals!

The processes which lead to crystallization and dissolution transcend three-dimensional space. The modern biochemist is forced to say this. Rudolf Steiner has already directed attention to these questions years ago. One learns really to respect this new research. Permit me to say it this way: if one has for many years been busy at the periphery of our movement, then there can be quite a few points of contact with this science. And if one then goes to some lecture or to a meeting where there may be three members and three hundred nonmembers, and there is an active member who cites that Rudolf Steiner said that the nutritional substances leave Space, then he makes himself look ridiculous, Yes, excuse me, he makes himself ridiculous because he says something about which he understands nothing. On the other side, however, one hears that the natural scientist says so, and now I quote directly: "If one looks at these processes and imagines," (says this scientist from Chicago) "that for every crystallization a point of light would flame up, and one would then look to the skeleton of man, then the skeleton would appear like a Christmas tree; yes, even much more, like a sparkling heaven of stars."

I must say, if someone who has come out of the absolute materialism of chemistry is forced to come to such an imagination, then I have a very high respect for that person, because he has found this out through devoted work and study. If we now, as Anthroposophists, want to meet such a man who is engaged in such difficult work, then we first have the responsibility to understand the processes at least as well as he, and have worked at least as hard as he.

Then a dialogue can result that can lead to the recognition of the spiritual, which can lead to the spreading of anthroposophy. And so it has happened. Then one is in the position to speak from knowledge, and does not need only to quote, I will not say what one doesn't understand, but rather, what one does not have as an inner experience. It is important that these physiological processes become inner experience.

Let us go further in this realm. We have another process, and this process is similarly of great significance for health and for the proper aging, so that in age one can remain young and stable. Illnesses occur in our body structure through Karma, through our own imperfections and mistakes or - as Christ said in his healings - in order to reveal the wisdom of the Divine. Illnesses are always teachers. For the biologist illnesses are teachers; pain is our best friend in this respect, because it calls us to an awakened consciousness. This must be the position, the view of a biologist.

We still have a further problem of metabolism, which is one of the most curious. Parts of the carbohydrate compounds which we have in protein, sugar and fat which we take up in our food and which are transformed as I have described are exhaled through the lung. Physiological experiments have determined that some protein components are not excreted in the body but are exhaled. So, by exhaling right in this hall, my very honored friends, you exhale a part of your lunch or your breakfast, since the physiological process has progressed to the point where a part of the carbon compounds are broken down and exhaled. In a certain sense that is actually a social problem, because thereby each one of us participates in the digestion of the other. I must say that I speak purely as a biologist when I say that it is a social problem. Rudolf Steiner points out[98] that especially such relations as sympathy and antipathy are based on such things. One person may have an exhalation of digested carbon compounds which is unpleasant to another. This sort of experience which we have of another can be registered as

98. G.A. 320 – *First Natural Scientific Course: Light Course.* See reference 47.

sympathy or antipathy. That's where human knowledge begins; one could even say, where the true love of man begins.

Well, we spoke about breathing. You see, we really learn to look differently at breathing, especially at exhaling. But processes also occur in inhalation. Recently it was discovered that we inhale not only with the lung and the nose; the eyes, for example, also inhale. It was discovered that during the day the eye, in the waking state, takes up oxygen. However, for the waking eye the oxygen does not come from the lung, but is inhaled directly through the white sclera. Only at night, in the closed sleeping eye, the process begins to be reversed, and oxygen inhalation does not take place, but rather, certain substances come from the blood and move to various parts of the eye, taking over the oxygen supply. When during the day the eye uses up oxygen in order to see, then in the darkness it replenishes that oxygen in the visual pigments.

These are very mysterious processes, to which Rudolf Steiner already referred years ago—to the breathing of the eye, that the eye inhales. It is quite unfortunate, when we look back over thirty-five years of scientific studies, that we have not discovered these things ourselves in our Anthroposophical science, and that we have to have the so-called outside world tell us point for point what Rudolf Steiner verified. It would be exceedingly satisfying for someone who has participated responsibly in this Anthroposophical natural research for years if we could point out: This work was carried out in our institutes. In this connection, Rudolf Steiner said: We must create phenomena where there are none, and certainly not speculate over the phenomena—but experiment. This would only be addressed to our natural scientists.

Now I have the task to point out something else. The nutrition which we take up is prepared in nature, and in this nature the preparation takes place in such a way that regardless of whether this food comes from the animal kingdom, in the final analysis it is still first prepared in the plant kingdom. In the green sap of the plant there is a process which is called photosynthesis, light synthesis, where the substances of the organs are built up. Through the interaction of light, warmth and physical substance, hydrogen, carbon dioxide, oxygen, nitrogen, the organic substances are synthesized into proteins, fats and sugars. It was discovered that in this photosynthesis of plants, to which we owe our food and physical existence, two processes take place: a darkness process and a light process. I don't know if these things are published yet. This darkness process leads to the formation of starch and sugar. Sugar is the product of the night activity of the plant. The release of warmth when brown sugar breaks down occurs by virtue of the dark warmth, i.e., the pure warmth element. What comes to expression in this sugar is scientifically called caloric energy, or warmth. Because warmth is liberated, light becomes free in the body. The light formation in the plants will occasion the formation of protein substances. Fats are formed in the plant as a kind of enhancement of the sugar process. When the sugar process makes a somersault and the sugar connects several compounds and then expels some water, the fatty acids are formed.

But protein is formed out of light. The substances which enable the plants to bind the light energies to matter so that protein can be built up are called enzymes. These mainly contain phosphor compounds: adenosine, tryptosine, etc., all substances in which phosphorus, and to a small extent magnesium, play a role. Phosphorus was already known to the alchemists as the light-bearer. Modern science speaks of a caloric value for the combustion of sugar to carbohydrates, which then give off the warmth energy to the body; but it does not yet speak of the light energies, which are given off when we digest proteins under the influence of certain enzymes. First, and this can be verified today, light is absorbed; then the light is liberated in digestion, and we receive light. When protein is digested in our body under the influence of warmth, almost the same enzyme participates. When we break down the protein, we receive light; light is liberated in the body, and this has a tremendously strong and illuminating effect. It is this which maintains life in the body, especially in the nerve substance, in the brain substance. It is taken into the brain susbstance in order to serve the processes of consciousness.

Enzyme: that is such a word. Rudolf Steiner says one could call money "money," or also "*vitzli-putzli*" or something in the social organism. So it is also with this word. When we speak about enzymes, we mean tremendous transformations and incredible speeds. These transformation reactions occur in a single living cell at the speed of 10,000 per minute. This, again, is metabolism. It is what our life is based upon, and as long as this transformation proceeds so rapidly, this means health and youthful vigor.

Now we can see that this light metabolism, which actually should come about in the protein digestion, in the activity of the sense organs and in the formation of consciousness in our brain - that this light metabolism in man, this phosphate enzyme transformation is considerably disturbed in man today. One could really see this if one looked at you by daylight as you came up the mountain; quite a few would be breathless, some of you would be tired. One could very well see in the whole demeanor of man how much light is liberated in his body, how much light is active. And one can also see this quite easily in nature, particularly in some years when the plants look truly tired. What a deficiency of light there is in nature today!

For years now I haven't been in Europe. Once I was gone for ten years, and then I returned at intervals. I still remember very well the light-permeated landscapes of my youth. In contrast to that, what one sees so strongly today if one has an eye for it is the deficiency of light, the physiological light deficiency in our atmosphere, the light deficiency in the plants which may be studied biochemically, and the ego–light deficiency in human beings.

The problem we confront here is that certain functions proceed in man today, in the years 1956, 1957, 1958, completely differently from the way they proceeded in the past. A grave question arises: Why? What is going on? It must first be said that the food, because of the way it is grown, due to selectivity and by forcing excessive quantitative production, can no longer completely carry through these light transformations, these hydrogen and oxygen transformations in their cells, and we receive a deficient protein. Throughout the last 30-50 years, all of humanity over all the earth has been receiving an increasingly deficient protein, whose constituent amino acids are not balanced anymore so that its nutritive value is reduced. Various protein combinations in our nutrition are continually weakened today.

If one eats noodles and spaghetti and potatoes, merely eating them will cause a deficiency of lysine and light in man. We can recognize and verify these phenomena in human excretions by a method which I have worked out recently on the basis of a very sketchy indication of Rudolf Steiner in which he suggested I should study the composition of human urine, since thereby he could come to certain conclusions about the spiritual conditions of friends and members. At that time, one did not know how to do this. Now we have a method which will allow us exactly to know the psychological as well as the physiological states of man and what disturbances are present.[99]

In tests on approximately 1700 healthy and ill patients, 90% actually no longer had a normal liver function. In studies in nature, of grains and proteins, it has become evident that there is a far-reaching decrease in protein combinations. Every biochemist who is working in this area racks his brain: What is normal?

It turns out that today in this field we can no longer determine what is normal. This is blurred since the incursion of radioactive fallout in nature; since the incursion of one-sided mineral fertilization, of insecticides, of new methods of conserving, and other methods, what grows on the earth today is no longer normal. We have no standard to compare it with.

A very clever scientist had the idea in 1937, during an expedition to the Antarctic, to leave cans of food behind. These were in the meantime enclosed by ice and covered with a layer of ice one meter thick and thereby protected from modern influences. The contents of these cans are then the only plant or food materials on the whole earth from which one can learn what was still normal in

---

99. See lectures to workmen in G.A. 312, March 24, 1920, *Spiritual Science and Medicine*, Rudolf Steiner Publishing Co., 1948; *Introducing Anthroposophical Medicine*, Steiner Books, 2009, at reference 48.

1937. Now these have been dug out and studied in order to find out what was normal twenty years ago. We are here confronting a cultural problem of enormous magnitude, because it is a matter of grasping and understanding the disturbances in protein quality, light metabolism and warmth metabolism of man, and, if possible, of healing it and preventing further deterioration. It turns out that these disturbances are connected with the quality of seeds. Dr. Rudolf Steiner pointed out that within our biodynamic movement the protein quality of seeds must seriously be brought into a closer connection with nature. Therefore, biodynamic seeds are being produced. I am now being absolutely objective and will tell you very objectively what does and what does not correspond to the established standard. I must say that whatever is biodynamic is good.

Something very surprising has come to our assistance. We have been able to determine that we have different kinds of protein in the seeds, and that the protein breaks down into amino acids. We have then identified these amino acids and have seen that they fluctuate from day to day, and that, for example, on the seventh day after sprouting a kernel of wheat of biodynamic origin, there was up to 42% protein, while in other plants there was at most 23%. We have been able to determine that it is possible to refine the protein quality of the seed.

I then spoke with our friend Gerhard Schmidt. He showed me a study. He heated biodynamic wheat for half an hour at a hundred degrees centigrade; to his surprise, after such rough treatment (heated to the temperature at which water begins to boil!) this wheat still sprouted; on the other hand, similarly treated kernels of artificially fertilized wheat did not sprout; they were dead. According to all you read in textbooks, protein should be coagulated at 100°C and the enzymes killed. In this biodynamic wheat which sprouted, neither was the protein coagulated, nor were the enzymes destroyed. This made a tremendous impression on me, and after I returned to the United States, I began to collect seeds of all kinds from all over the United States, biodynamic, artificially fertilized, non-fertilized, out of virgin soils, out of organically farmed but not biodynamically fertilized soils, etc. It was confirmed again and again that biodynamic seeds sprouted after the heat treatment; some of the others sprouted, but very few of the minerally fertilized seeds sprouted, and some of the strictly mineralized seeds did not sprout at all. Thus you have a kind of step-like loss of function. When I then determined the protein constituents, the amino acids, in those seeds, it was interesting that I found a varying balance: a natural balance in those that sprouted, and a non-balance in those that did not sprout. The results were such that I said to myself: "If this is how it is, maybe we can profit from it." So we planted the seedlings of those seeds that sprouted, raised new plants, and then harvested the new wheat in the summer. It turned out that this new wheat, which came from so brutally heat-treated kernels, was a completely new wheat. The first, original wheat was yellow-white, mealy, with 10% protein. The new wheat that we harvested this summer had an almost transparent, almost glass-like grain, and had 17-18% protein. By this selection, we obtained a nutritional wheat that, instead of the 10-11% of protein, had up to 18%. The result was a plant that was so nourishing that one could almost avoid eating meat, if one used this for food.

So this has actually come about. We are confronting a miracle in what happened here; namely, that an idea of Rudolf Steiner's has been realized: the search for a new protein quality, the transmission of nutritional values that we need so urgently: that here we have actually taken the plant back into its archetypal state. For it is indeed so that such wheat had 15-18% protein, and of a very good composition. This is a first step to the creation of a new food quality. But it is only a beginning. I presume that one day this grain can enter trade, but that will only be possible in about ten years.

Such a thought is very vitalizing – permit me a personal remark – so vitalizing that it actually creates new courage for life: one can be faced with a new goal and forgets that one has once been ill.

Now I come to a very, very serious problem. The natural conditions on the Earth are so radically changed by the advent of radioactive fallout that normal plants no longer exist. Radioactive iodine is spreading over the whole Earth and is being taken up by cows; something goes into the milk, something into the thyroid of the cow, and then into the thyroid of the calf even before birth, where it is a hundred times more active than in the thyroid of the mother, causing tremendous genetic damage, already today. The half-life of radioactive iodine is 146 days, and within these 146 days immeasurable damage has been done over the whole Earth to the genetic capacities in the thyroid process.

Yes, now comes the problem. We must face it with open eyes. It is said that fifteen hydrogen bombs and 150 atom bombs of type A, if exploded at one time, regardless of where in the world - equator, north or south pole - would make the Earth uninhabitable for ten thousand years. That's how long it would take for all that radioactivity to disappear again. Those are official numbers. Yes, honored friends, if that were so, it would still be simple. But the problem is not so simple, for in the so-called peaceful utilization of radioactivity and radioactive energy, this same amount of radioactivity is released into the air. According to the calculations I have seen, it would take 3000 years until we have exactly as much radioactivity in the atmosphere from peaceful use as if these fifteen and a hundred and fifty bombs were exploded at once. Hence, it is a process that has begun that already has an expected outcome, and this outcome – the impossibility for man to survive on the Earth – is within 3000 years. Even if one were to destroy all nuclear reactors, the danger would still exist that the Earth would not reach its goal. This is the situation we confront today.

This situation leads some people to think a bit. The thoughts that result can be quite literal. I would like to read to you something from the *Atomic Scientist*, a journal for atomic science in America, which speaks a very open and truthful language. I would like to read to you a few words from an article of the astronautical institution, i.e. space travel organization. It was written by James

B. Edson[100], the associate director of research in the U.S. Army, hence a very important personality. This Mr. Edson, who today as a scientist influences the American Army, says that one should prepare for space travel so that the conflicts of the Earth would not be fought on the Earth anymore, but rather on the Moon or on another planet, so that it would be possible to save the Earth. Now there are certain difficulties with that. [Laughter.]

Now see, one shouldn't laugh there; these are serious matters. Millions of dollars are expended for their study and to find ways to research them. This is a very, very serious matter because what is happening here is that the thinking of sub-nature is taking hold of our cosmos.

I translate literally: "It will be possible to develop a space medicine. Since it will not be possible to have oxygen out there to breathe, an artificial food must be developed which can be injected into the blood to make breathing as well as eating and drinking unnecessary. But one should permit man a little bit, so that he wouldn't lose his habits and can speak somewhat." In the research institutes today, they are working to find substances that can be injected into the blood to take the place of breathing and eating. For this, millions of dollars are expended.

The man who plans there on the General Staff is a man who plans for the future. One cannot say that the American General Staff is so clumsy with its plans! It has been calculated that if one could occupy the Moon, that would have two advantages. First, many ores could be found there that are rare on the Earth; one could start a good business there by building mines and exploiting the Moon. Many a businessman would gladly buy stocks for such a mine on the Moon. A wonderful speculation!

But on the other hand, says this Mr. Edson of the American General Staff, the foreign policies of the Americans and Russians are concerned about who will first occupy the Moon and use this

---

100. "Astronautics and the Future," in *Bulletin of the Atomic Scientists: A Magazine of Science and Public Affairs*, Chicago, Illinois, Volume XIV, Number 3, March 1958, pp. 102-105. See reference 49.

occupation to apply military pressure on the other countries. So, "what matters" - I am translating this as literally as possible - "is that it may perhaps be better that an international agreement could be made that the battles for world power were carried out on the Moon, so that not too much destruction would take place on Earth. The Earth must remain inhabitable. For a time, it will still be a matter of speculation to speak about this Moon fortification until it has been attained. However, if one does not want to risk wiping humanity completely off the Earth, such a battlefield on the Moon is the only way out, instead of a decision by battle here on Earth."

If one is so far enough advanced that the Moon can be conquered, then Mars can also be conquered; and then, maybe, if life can no longer continue on Earth, one could take the last survivors over to Mars and build up a new culture.

Yes, you see, my dear friends, that's how people think today. You may be outraged, or you may even find this a thinking of genius. But this is how they think, and these thoughts - knowing that in three thousand years this atomic decision will face mankind regardless of what happens - are a serious problem. These thoughts are a very, very serious problem. Now I must tell you something that I have only with difficulty decided to share with you, but it has come out of talks with Dr. Steiner. One does not know where, when, and how often one will still be able to get together.

I came here to Dornach as a young man in 1919, 1920, 1921, when I was an apprentice. As I did all the various activities, I strove at the time to bring a very specific thought, a very specific question, to Rudolf Steiner. The thought was this: Since present-day civilization leads to disintegration through the use of physical energies, i.e., electricity, magnetism and other energies – atomic energy was not yet discovered – since it is in the nature of these energies and their use in technology that they *can* only lead to destruction; would it not be necessary to introduce *an energy of life* into technology, a new energy containing the principle of constructiveness, of life, naturally eliciting in man such thoughts, feelings, will impulses that rather than continuing our technological destruction, disintegration and bombardment, we could learn to equilibrate, that we could learn to build up, to synthesize, to grow, to develop?

This was a question that I put to Rudolf Steiner: whether there was such an energy that could then emanate from the Goetheanum out into the world as an answer, as constructiveness, as an antidote to the destruction. Rudolf Steiner pointed out that such an energy could be studied in certain substance transformations in the human body. He pointed out that this energy in general is what we designate as the etheric formative force, the etheric body, the warmth ether, light ether, etc. I am now not referring to courses and lectures, but to his direct answer to this problem. My thought was to ask whether it would not be possible through the discovery and application of such energies to bring about a social technology and a social order. In answer, Rudolf Steiner suggested a few quite simple experiments, which I then did for him. Concerning the results of these experiments, he said that he had received an answer from the spiritual world, and the answer was: It is not yet time for this etheric energy to be made known and introduced. I was then obligated, according to Rudolf Steiner's instructions, to remain absolutely silent concerning this whole topic. But then I asked: Under what conditions would the spiritual world agree that this new energy could be studied, known, and eventually applied? Rudolf Steiner replied - and this is the reason I wanted to present at least this part of his answer, with the thought that perhaps there may not be another chance: One necessary condition to keep this energy from being misused is that a social order in the spirit of the Threefolding idea would have to happen, at least in a small region of the Earth; a consequent social order along spiritual lines would need to come about. The spiritual world would not permit these ether energies even to be discovered unless *this* happened.

The second condition, said Rudolf Steiner, was that certain spiritual leaders must be able to incarnate on Earth in order to take over the guidance of humanity; but that these guides are unable today to find bodies, because the present-day system of intellectual education does not make it possible to manifest through such a body; that there would be no possibility to manifest and that one must count with the possibility that these spiritual leaders may not be able to find bodies in this century unless Waldorf education becomes general. Only then, when such education enables certain spiritual leaders to incarnate who will then take over the guidance of humanity, and when a social order exists which guarantees against its misuse – then and only then could one continue working on this problem.[101]

With this, of course, the whole future was sealed for the time being.

This, my dear friends, is a book with seven seals. The answer that we could give as creatiors of a new energy which contains in itself only life-renewing, constructive and creative forces, the answer against atomic energy – we cannot give. This is a great responsibility that burdens us all in the Goetheanum and all of us who participate in this spiritual movement – that we have not attained the goal of which Rudolf Steiner spoke in this connection. A great responsibility, whether we might not at least take this goal seriously. A responsibility – that's all I can say about it.

Let me say it in my own way: we actually do not have all that much more time. Physical reproduction is fated to end in approximately 3,000 years since the physiological degeneration of the female body, as Rudolf Steiner said, will lead to the fact that no more physical children can be born. The storm warnings, the degeneration are already quite clear. Besides, radioactivity on Earth in 3,000 years will have increased to such an extent that abnormality will render the Earth uninhabitable.

---

101. On August 8, 1961, Pfeiffer announced in a lecture in Spring Valley about Mani, that R. Steiner told him that Mani would not incarnate in that century; he intended to do so in the next century provided he found a suitable body. Ordinary education offered no opportunity for his development; only Waldorf education. Under favorable conditions he would appear as a teacher of humanity and take over leadership in the fields of art and religion. He will act in the power of the Grail Mysteries and persuade the people to decide for themselves between good and evil. Pfeiffer added: Provided humanity does not destroy itself in an atomic war. See GA 264, p. 239 f.

So we can count on it that if no miracle happens in 3,000 years, this physical and mineral body that we carry around with us today will be useless for human beings. If no miracles happen. What, then, is the solution? The solution, I would like to say, is a simple one; yet it is not so simple. We could imagine the following. Until now I have attempted only to present facts. Now permit me to develop a picture for a moment, which is just a speculation. On the average, an ordinary man goes through an incarnation every 500 years at the currently increased tempo of reincarnation. That means six incarnations in 3,000 years. He will not incarnate in every century, as do the great spiritual leaders; this one cannot expect. But since all tempos are increased, it could well be that a great number of us will be incarnated every 500 years. Six more incarnations! In six more incarnations we must reach our goal. That was the speculation.

Now let us return to reality. Consider what this means: in six incarnations we should have developed so far that we would no longer need this mineral physical body, that we would become independent of what we have as a mineral body on Earth, that we would have a spirit-permeated physical body in which we could live so that we become independent of the catastrophe that will come over the Earth. That is one goal!

On the other hand there is the other goal: to develop the etheric energies that will prevent the catastrophe of technology. On the one hand, the goal that every single individual, through inner work, through the spiritualization of matter, through the metabolic processes, through sensory processes, through the ego activity, through the heart forces, through the etherization of blood in each man, transforms his physical body. This is a great task, and I can only say through what has been given to me by destiny that it is a task that I believe one can fulfill if only one wants to, and if one can learn to understand the natural and spiritual processes. Then the anthroposophy of Rudolf Steiner would be fulfilled; that Rudolf Steiner himself would head that small group of human beings who could save themselves, physically also, from the earthly catastrophe of the lower nature. Rudolf Steiner speaks of this remnant.

He says it would be only a very small group. But it is actually the fulfilment of this possibility through Rudolf Steiner and through our work toward which we strive, providing, absolutely, that one can hope such thoughts take hold in individual human souls and that all could work together to overcome subnatural matter. It is possible. One can definitely look into the future with hope. It is possible to enter on the path of knowledge with which Rudolf Steiner began, and to go on this path not sporadically, but very diligently.

In one of those conversations about this future energy and this etherization, Rudolf Steiner said to me, "If you only would meditate over the beginning of St. John's Gospel, and only study the book *Knowledge of Higher Worlds and its Attainment*, and would take it to heart, then you would be in the position to solve all these questions and to rewaken and recreate all of anthroposophy in yourself. It would then not even be necessary for you to read any one of my lectures." Why? Because, very simply, in the beginning of St. John's Gospel, the two archetypal creations are pointed out: the Word – the Logos, which creates divine world order also in matter and through which physical matter can be comprehended and transformed; and the Light, which shone in the Darkness, through which precisely one's self-transformation can be attained.

I must bring up something else, very briefly: another rearing up of the dragon and the subnature in our time in which I see much greater dangers for the spiritual in humanity than I see for the physical in atomic technology. This is described in the journal *Science*, in October of last year under the title, "The Invisible Word – or: No Thresholds Barred."[102] It describes that man can be influenced by sense impulses that are so brief that he cannot even perceive them. For example, an experiment was made in which a

102. DuShane, G. (editorial), "The Invisible Word, or: No Thresholds Barred," *Science*, Lancaster, Pa., Volume 126, Number 3276, October 11, 1957, p. 681. See also reply to this article by R. C. Wilcott, "LETTERS: Invisible Words – Invisible Evidence," *Science*, Lancaster, Pa., Volume 126, Number 3284, December 6, 1957, p.1202. See reference 50.

movie was shown, and because the eye cannot perceive impulses under 1/24th of a second, messages were written above the film in 1/24th-of-a-second intervals saying, “Get up! Go outside and buy…” or something similar. Now these people were observed as they sat there watching some story or other, and although they had never even thought of getting up to buy something outside, they did, in fact, get up and buy. These things are being worked with today. One can possibly be exposed to such things and have to deal with them and not even be aware of them, because they happen beneath the threshold of consciousness and there exercise their influence on people. The article states: “How simple would it be, if conscious activity of man could be completely bypassed, if with such prepared movies one could feed the region of the brain where will impulses and motives for action originate; then one could actually create a completely different humanity – a pliable, peaceful humanity; an animalized and slavish humanity.” What is the antidote? I cannot see it in anything else than in consciousness, in increased spiritual “I”-consciousness that recognizes that such applications of technological discoveries are immoral.

Curiously, this is the end of a cycle to which Rudolf Steiner pointed: if in the nutrition of man certain forces are not liberated for spirituality, that is when instead of moral thoughts, immoral thoughts can well up in man. Moral ideas, Rudolf Steiner says, can be regulated and enhanced through the release of light forces in the warmth-air organism; through the release of tone forces – the chemical ether – in the fluid organism; through the release of life seeds in the solid organism. But these are the processes I spoke about earlier in connection with nutrition, the forces which in man are liberated through an appropriate, balanced nutrition. These are not liberated in today’s degenerated nutrition of man. Theoretical ideas chill the warmth organism, paralyze the light organism, deaden sound and extinguish life.

Yes, this is what we also do in our nutrition today, and so you will understand that as Rudolf Steiner said, our lack or difficulty of success in anthroposophy with transforming spiritual impulses into deeds is a problem of nutrition. He pointed out to me, as I have written in the book *We Experienced Rudolf Steiner,*[103] that the problem of nutrition must first be solved before it is at all possible to affect spiritually the etheric impulses in man, to transform them into the reality of action. On the other hand, he indicated that in the middle of this century we will experience the darkest years of the century, and when the time arrives in which anthroposophy has become a way of life in all realms, people from all areas will come to us and ask for advice: "How should I do this or that in the world?"

These are our tasks. But humanity at present passes us by as long as we are not able to demonstrate and study practical aspects of life with precision; it develops faster. Our task is to speed up a little – with the same metabolic rapidity with which the blood shoots into bone crystals and new life emerges, completely every minute. Actually, as human beings, we should create our spiritual life anew every minute through spiritual activity. Then people would not pass us by, but we could begin, as students and helpers of Rudolf Steiner, to fulfill the work which he set for himself in the world. That should be a serious admonition for us all! Rudolf Steiner said that by 1965 one would see the dawning of a new age in the dark years of this century. Still seven years, my dear friends, are before us, in which we can catch up on what we have so far not achieved, so that we can also greet this new dawn.

---

103. See the corresponding passage here on p. 145. See also "New Directions in Agriculture" by Ehrenfried E. Pfeiffer, pp. 118-129 in "Rudolf Steiner:Recollections by Some of his Pupils," edited by Arnold Freeman and Charles Waterman, *The Golden Blade*, London, 1958, iv + 188 pages. This volume is a translation of *Wir Erlebten Rudolf Steiner: Erinnerungen seiner Schüler* [We Experienced Rudolf Steiner: Recollections by Some of his Pupils], edited by M. J. Krück von Poturzyn and published by the Verlag Freies Geistesleben, Stuttgart,1956, who retain the copyright. See reference 34.

On Experiencing the Christ

[The following notes, published here for the first time, were written down in German during the year 1959, under the title above. They were discovered in Pfeiffer's estate by Lexie Ahrens. At the beginning Pfeiffer wrote the following:

"To be read at a quiet time: sacred and not profane. Real experiences are dealt with here, nothing invented or imagined.

"An inner voice commanded me to write this down, after an experience at Easter, 1959.[104]

"Although written in the first person, it does not concern the personal 'I.' It concerns the SELF that in the highest moments of existence only shyly gleams through. A part of my Easter lecture at Threefold Farm,[105] contains another part of this experience and is a supplement to it."]

*

The experience of the Christ Essence is the center of all world and human events.

Merely listening to the learned description in the churches and so-called religions and praying accordingly leads to nothing, or at best to an intellectual–sentimental–conventional concept.

Can I *experience* the Christ?

I can, of course, have thoughts about it and even believe that I am closer to the "experience" when I know everything that Rudolf Steiner taught about the Christ Essence, its activity, its cosmic and earthly, human mission.

Though this, then, gives me a widened horizon and more real ideas and concepts and enables me, at least partially, to *think* Him, fundamentally I still have not *experienced* Him.

---

104. This experience occurred five hundred years after the important Easter experience of the great spirit-seeker Christian Rosenkreutz as described in *The Chymical Wedding*. See reference 51.

105. A transcript of this lecture is not available.

"In the future physicists and chemists will come and teach how the Christ has organized (*angeordnet*) matter."[106]

Just as there are physical forces of nature, so will HE as a new *force of nature* fashion matter... How and where can I find this force of nature: experience, perceive, be sensible of it and further aware of it?

It moved me deeply and repeatedly that in dreams and visions I saw the scene of the Crucifixion on Golgotha as though participating, as an eyewitness, looking on from above with a kind of birds-eye perspective; almost as if I was there and yet not physically present. ("Some stood from afar..."[107])

I saw the Crucified One, the soldier who offered the sponge with vinegar, Mary, John, the captain who became converted. I saw the vision of Catherine of Emmerich. (I also tried once to capture this scene in a colored sketch, because it was and is so intimate and immediately present to me.)

I also saw a much earlier scene, Jesus Christ on Mount Tabor, after His baptism, as he sent the tempter from him; saw, in detail like an eye-witness, the blue distance, the yellow desert, the white-grey-yellow limestone and the fertile plains.

I was moved, yet remained an onlooker.

In Rudolf Steiner's atelier in Dornach I saw the Statue and Group which he himself described with holy awe, and especially the painting in the small cupola and the west window, where rays from the hand of Christ penetrate the earth – Rudolf Steiner said about this window: "By the rays of the gold of Love that penetrate the Earth, Ahriman will be fettered and redeemed." I heard R.

---

106. R. Steiner writes in Lecture Three of *Spiritual Guidance of the Individual and Mankind* (G.A. 15) "...there will be in the future chemists and physicists who will not teach chemistry and physics as they are now taught under the influence of the backward Egypto-Chaldaeic spirits; but who will teach that: Matter is built up in the way in which the *Christ* gradually in the course of time ordained it!" See reference 52.

107. "Many women stood there and looked on from afar." according to Matthew 27: 35; similarly in Mark 15:40, and Luke 23:49.

Steiner explain: "This is the representative of humanity who holds the balance between the upper (Wisdom) and the lower (Matter, Love) forces, between Lucifer and Ahriman." And I heard Rudolf Steiner speak words of the Meditation:

> I will follow the path
> That releases the elements into activity,
> And leads me below to the Father
> Who sends illness to work out Karma,
> And leads me upward to the Spirit
> Who guides the erring soul to the attainment of Freedom.
> Christ leads downward and upward,
> Creating Spirit-Man in Earth-man in harmonious union.[108]

The intellectual and thought horizon extended itself, and I began to understand that the problem of balance, of equilibrium, unites natural and spiritual events, that it – wherever balance is created, out of chaos or contradictions – works as an active, creative force, in nature as well as in the inner man, in world evolution and human history, and I began to regard all natural and human events in this respect: Where is equilibrium established?

And I began to understand, at first in thought, then intuitively divining: this power in the human being, this force of nature, too, has part in the Christ; it is the *Garment* of Christ which was not divided at the Cross, because its nature is indivisible, indestructible. I began to understand the words: "I am the Life."

And I began to fathom the depth of: "Heaven and Earth shall pass away, but my words shall not pass away." I began to repeat the words and participate in the deeds. And yet I still saw the Garment only from the outside.

A few weeks after my 33rd birthday (which I spent on the ruins of Heliopolis and at the site where Mary found refuge with the Jesus-child), my Fate led me to the Jordan River in Palestine, to the

---

108. See Rudolf Steiner: *Pastoral Medicine*, G.A. 318, Anthroposophic Press, Hudson, New York, 1987. See reference 53.

place where according to legend the Baptism by John the Baptist took place.

This place is for me the most holy and unearthly place in the world. There still lives in the atmosphere, palpable, something which remembers, inexpressibly by words, the mood, color, air and water: the gateway to heaven was open, and the dove of purest spirituality became visible.

This was an experience of eternity; spiritual and yet physical, eternal, inextinguishable, spiritual and yet as if physically perceptible.

Even today, if I wish, I can be there, regardless of time and distance, breathing peace and purity, an eternal image in my soul, like the recollection of an eyewitness who has *experienced* it.

If I could paint, I could paint this as an experience; experienced as also the Dove, which appears in the Chalice at every genuinely conducted Transubstantiation; also within, on the Altar in the Heart.

Whoever experiences the Baptism in the Jordan, submerged in the water of the eternally flowing ether, feels permeated, enfolded, sheltered by this new natural and spiritual power.

And I know today that one only finds the Christ in one's self when one prepares one's etheric garment, when one envelops oneself in it, filling this garment from *within*, radiating outward.

And I was with the fishermen in the boat on the storm-tossed sea as the Christ walked on the water; shivers of excitement and awe ran through my body, so that I felt myself walking like Him on the water, towards Him.

I was with the Disciples on the shore, unseen, as the ETHERIC ONE stepped amongst them, and heard the words: "Fear not, *peace* be with you." Shivers of reverence and serenity touched my soul, and I heard the mighty voice, filled with cosmic love, full of the most intimate understanding and forgiveness. "Peace be with you." I saw Thomas, and with Thomas put my finger into the stigmata of the risen Christ, and saw the Etheric One eat the fish, whose substance dissolved into nothing, into spirit.

And I knew, and a voice spoke from within: This *is* the nature-force that transmutes dead matter into life.

I was in Gethsemane beneath the olive tree, the second place besides the ford across the Jordan in whose etheric aura this event is still inscribed today, and I heard the words: "Watch with Me," and I participated in His soul's struggle, "but not My will, but Thine be done."

It is as though under the impact of participation, soul and body break, and from every particle and fragment the voice resounded manifold with metallic tone: "In Christ death becomes life."

I know: This *is* the *truth*.

And yet – I still have not experienced the Christ. Though I have become a witness, like John, who said he was not the Light itself, but a witness of the Light.

Already as a child and throughout my whole life, in conversation, as lecturer, author, I always shrank from uttering the name "Christ." Nor have I done this through the years, just as I do not like to use the word "Love."

These are the holiest of words and should really only be spoken in the Temple Within, in the holiest moments, when the crescendo of mood and feelings allow the curtain before the altar to be drawn aside for an instant. And the altar must at once be covered again when one steps back into one's everyday mortal body.

When others came and related that they had experienced the Christ and described how perhaps they saw a radiant figure that somehow stepped into the room through the window, the wall, or the door, I always felt dubious: it's not like that. Only wishful thinking or wishful willing conjures up such an apparition, which the onlooker then names.

Or, too, when they spoke of feelings of universal love and redemption, this struck me as sentimental and false.

I must ask myself: am I too critical, intolerant, a heretic, heathen?

In the special quality of light in Nature which lets plants sprout out of the earth and fashions them, or in the delicate bond that is woven from one sentient soul to another, or in the feelings of empathy and sympathy that rise above the narrowness of one's own self and at least for moments frees the soul from the small "I," and the "Thou" comes into its own – yes, there is more of that Power present than in merely the reflection of a thought-dream or image.

*

The Christ was the Sun-spirit, and His body was the Sun, and His breath and thought were Light and Wisdom of the Sun. All life, including that of the physical world, can only be created through Light and lives as long as the Laws of Eternal Wisdom are revealed and activated in it .

To be the Sun means to radiate light in *all* directions of physical and spiritual space. The concept of "Sun-ray" (the ray of the physicist) is, however, an abstraction, not to say an untruth. For the essence of the Sun is the "*complete saturation with light.*" Instead of "ray:" "the weaving, flooding essence"[109] of the Sun would be a better description.

To be the *Sun* means: forever and ever to burn one's substance and in burning to generate light, to turn into light, and in turning into light eternally to open new sources of spiritual substance and to renew oneself .

Sun is inexhaustible.

Sun shines over all and for all equally, whether it is beheld and received or not.

Sun is itself, is eternal, has no end. The more it "shines," the more forces it develops to renew itself.

Sun sacrifices itself in every moment and brings forth new Sun without perceiving the sacrifice as "sacrifice."

Sun warms and shines and burns up the impure, the transitory. Whoever encounters it unprepared is blinded and burned = purified in the fire.

---

109. In the Mystery Drama *The Portal of Initiation*, Benedictus gives Thomasius the following meditation on light: "The light's *weaving being*, it shines through the depths of space…" See reference 54.

Sun can revive from the ashes of the purifying fire and cause new life to flare up.

Sun renews itself unceasingly.

Sun and love are one and the same, an indestructible unity.

Sun is Christ and Christ is Sun.

Sun lives without and Sun lives within.

Only with the *Sun within* can the external Sun in the universe, in the other human heart, in one's own and in another's, be recognized, grasped, understood, experienced.

Sun is all.

It is written: "Like the thief in the night, so comes the Christ into the soul," unnoticed – suddenly He is there = *Sun within*. It is written: "The Christ comes in the clouds" = in the starry mantle of the universe; in the soul that has expanded to the mantle of the universe, become the garment of the etheric state; which has gone beyond its own limits to be transformed into the Sun and as Sun become the dwelling-place of the Christ.

"Become like Suns," cried R. Steiner at the end of an address to the youth of the coming generation. Yes indeed – *become Suns*.

In your own inner self resides the power and the essence and radiates outwards.

However, the Christ is no longer on today's physical Sun. That is a fireball which will eventually burn out. The Christ has descended to Earth, has penetrated the depths of the Earth, has pervaded the earthly substance with His essence, thereby preparing it for dissolution, redemption, etherization, and shines through the Earth and from the Earth outward. The Christ has come to dwell in the hearts of human beings in order to transform them into Suns so that etherization may be accomplished. The Christ in nature, in thousands and myriads of human hearts. From one Sun, thousands and myriads of Suns are created - new, shining, warmth- and love-radiating heavenly bodies.

This is the secret of the Mystery of Golgotha.

Yes – ***I** have* experienced the Christ:

Not I – but the Christ in me.

The Johannine Brotherhood

[The following notes by Pfeiffer, in the German language, dated December 22, 1959, come from the papers of Lexie Ahrens. They bear the title *Gemeinschaft-Memorandum* (Community Memorandum), and refer to the individuality of John the Evangelist, who is connected with the later incarnation of Christian Rosenkreutz. The following, previously unpublished text is included not only because Pfeiffer felt an especially close connection to this individuality, but also because it shows how he thought at the end of his life about the Christian Community and the Anthroposophical Society.]

The spiritual needs filled by a religious cult are quite different from those filled, for example, by an esoteric or mystery cult, which is created through an action. With the religious cult the approach to the Divine is mediated by the priest, whereby the mood of the congregation can indeed be "uplifted," and the priest is merely the representative of God during the celebration of the act.

It is quite different for the mystery cult. There the student, after a long, careful preparation by an Initiate, is himself initiated, i.e. comes into the direct experience of Divinity, of the spiritual world, according to his degree of ripeness.

The highest fulfilment of the path and cult is the experience that the body is the temple of the Divine. On the altar of this temple – of the heart – the one to be initiated presents the sacrificial cup – the Grail – by self- purification through the etherization of the blood, through the transmutation of his earthly self into a Divine being (higher self), spirit self, etc. In this action the I itself becomes God, in the sense of "not I, but Christ in me."

In this sense one can understand the comment of R. Steiner that "who has correctly grasped anthroposophy" (i.e. practiced it personally) "does not need the Christian Community," since he is developing his consciousness-soul and can or should do within himself what the priest does acting for the congregation."[110]

110. See R. Steiner's remarks of December 30,1922, directly before the fire in the Goetheanum, in G.A. 219 (reference 55) and elsewhere.

He has become his own inner priest.

He can of course attend the Christian Community; for him it will mean something different from what it does for the so-called "believer." The believers rely on the authority of the priest; the Initiate, even in the preparatory stage, that is, the esoteric student "knows," does not need to believe, since he has access to direct experience, or at least is on the path. This way he avoids the danger of becoming dogmatic; a danger to which until now every church, including the Christian Community, has been exposed and succumbed. One can of course receive the Sacraments— baptism, marriage, extreme unction— or take part in them on behalf of one's children, wife, husband, relations: that is, to show human understanding for their otherness, and sharing— but one must experience God and spiritualize matter for oneself. No one else can do that for you.

Therefore, whether or not one needs a church service is a matter of the will, of the maturity of the individual I. A "dogmatic" church must of course be rejected by the I-conscious person.

The Christian Community is for those who do not yet experience the Spirit for themselves, are not yet able or willing to create anew their I-consciousness, i.e. for the intermediate stage. It points to the future: Johannine Christianity. But this discipleship "whom the Lord loved," of this disciple who lay on the breast – the heart – of the Christ and was appointed on Golgotha to be the son of the Divine World-Mother, Maria-Isis-Sophia, is the ultimate striving of every human being.

This manifestaion of the Spirit on the altar of the heart, where the sacrificial burning-up of matter and time take place out of which the new phoenix (of the alchemists) arises from the ashes; this creative deed that leads the I back to its spiritual origin and raises the human being to the next, coming hierarchy. This attainment is called on Earth the Holy Spirit.

Humanity can have as much of the Holy Spirit as they can create, each individual for himself.

Only one who, in deepest veneration, has stood before the potential majesty and greatness of this Holy Spirit arising from the breast, seen with his own eyes, felt with his own soul and has willed/created it with his entire being can truly grasp the cosmic widths and depths to which the soul is called.

Also in Rosicrucianism there is the task of transmuting the laboratory bench of nature, of the world and of one's own soul, the alchemy of the soul, into an altar. Outside anthroposophy there also exists this Johannine discipleship and community. No one ever speaks about this; never are its members on Earth physically recognized or denoted as such. Their preparation for this is certainly known on the outside. What is known exoterically about it and constitutes the beginning is also known in the sometimes jokingly put question of "the good deed for the day", i.e. a deed for which no external compulsion exists, no commitment, no karma, nothing. Then one does a free, good deed for someone else, or perhaps only a thought, a feeling. It is essential that one does not let the other know at all that one has done something good, i.e. that one remains unknown, expects, demands, receives no reward or recognition for it. This shall be practiced daily, this free deed for this day, every day. In this way forces of self-denial, of sacrifice are built up that could never cause harm.

When this has been practiced long enough (this is the true meaning of what one esoterically calls virtue, what is also meant when Christ says: "Let not the right hand know what the left hand is doing") — but no thought of creating, or wanting to create good karma in this way must ever arise, i.e., every gain or profit-motive is excluded; when this has been practiced long enough so that it becomes a daily matter of course, then one also begins to recognize another Johannine brother, becomes a Johannine brother and member of the Brotherhood.

Today this exists fully only in the Etheric. To lead towards this was the actual objective of Rudolf Steiner, of all Christian Initiates, of the Friend of God from the Higher Realm (the Master Jesus-Zarathustra), which is also why the first Goetheanum was to have been named "St. John's Building;" but Rudolf Steiner withdrew this name and replaced it with "Goetheanum," since he well knew that the time was not yet ripe. This esotericism has been lost in the Anthroposophical Society; therefore, only the kind of Johannine Brotherhood mentioned above is now possible. In the developing Brotherhood, among the Johannine brothers, there must be no "agreements" or "explanations" such as "I'm doing this; what are you doing?" on the physical level. What happens must be brought about in the most secret chamber of the heart, in the Holy of Holies, protected behind the curtain – let not the right hand know what the left hand is doing… and the Kingdom of Heaven will open for you: you will share in the fellowship of God.

In the next epoch (6)[111] some Johannine brothers will become known as spiritual leaders, and in the 7th period the Johannine Brotherhood will become known in public. It is the mission of St. John to guide the spiritualized Earth and humanity (quite a small number, as Rudolf Steiner said) into the next condition of the Earth.

---

111. This means the next great earth epoch that begins after the seventh post-Atlantean culture-epoch.

PART II

FROM PFEIFFER'S LETTERS

“Do We Pose the Right (…) Questions?”

(to Ita Wegman, 1924)

[The following letter by Pfeiffer to Ita Wegman was written at the turn of 1924/25. Compare also the article by Paul Scharff on p.217ff.]

Most respected dear Doctor!

In the course of the preparation for the working group on physiology I have been concerned with much that I would like to report to you with the request, should you have the opportunity and the inclination, that you correct any mistakes I have made, confirm what is correct and give indications for progress in these problems. For the most part we – Walter, Bockholt, Schickler, Roeschl [?] – have discussed these, and I will now sketch them.

On examining the chemical processes in the human being we found the following. One can actually find a kind of carbon cycle, indicating that carbon first occurs in the human being in a living, organic, combination, then dies away and appears again in a two-fold manner. On the one hand, the human being gets rid of the carbon which he apparently cannot use as the CO_2 of exhalation. Here the plant carries out in assimilation what the body cannot do. On the other hand the carbon becomes mineral-like and combines with salts: the skeleton is formed with its $CaCO_3$, where carbon is entirely mineralized. Now, because the mineral-crystalline condition is formed, immediately there arises in the physical state the basis for freedom.

But also in the mineral solid, life-ether can be active: it is active in the skeleton and revitalizes the $CaCO_3$ into living substance; bone marrow appears, in which from the depths of the mineral realm is formed the highest condition of physical matter: the carriers of the I-forces, the red blood corpuscles! Herr Doktor [Rudolf Steiner] once said that the Philosopher’s Stone consists of transparent carbon and signifies the transformation of the physical into spiritualized matter. The question now arises: Are we not in the process of forming the Philosopher’s Stone within ourselves by consciously grasping this process of blood formation coming from the mineral realm, combining it on the other hand with the exhalation of CO_2, and then – certainly in the far future – internalizing the blood circulation, including its outward exponents, so that we can allow the carbon cycle to take place completely within us, from the mineral state to warmth and back again?

And the other question arises: On the one hand there is the blood circulation transformed into the Philosopher's Stone; over this the Grail's Chalice descends, as it once received the blood of the Redeemer, now receiving as substance that which we fashion in our red blood – or as Herr Dr. once expressed it, in the Tree of Knowledge – and in the blue blood = the Tree of Life, which, however, for the present is still the Tree of Death, but which can become living through the Philosopher's Stone – this question stands burning before the soul: How do we relate to the Grail *today*, what does it mean for us; will its chalice of mercy open over us also, and how can we find it in a way suitable for our Anthroposophical striving? How do we put the right question to the "Parsifal-Fools" of the present? –

As I thought about the red and blue tree with its living tendency, something else occurred to me, but please just laugh at me if the following just seems fantastic.

These two blood-trees are also the pillars J[akim] and B[oas], as Herr Dr. said. Now it is written in the *Apocalypse Cycle:*[112] "For the Ancients, Moses appeared as the knowledge pillar and Elias as the other pillar: Life, which must become an impulse."

So I must think, then, that we bear within us in the red blood the Moses-stream: knowledge and wisdom, and in the blue blood the Elias-stream – Life.

And furthermore it follows: Plato was called an Athenian speaking Moses, since he carried the Moses-stream further. Thus we have in Moses-Plato – no doubt continued by Aristotle – the wisdom-stream of the great historical blood circulation. And Elias-John the Baptist was the blue blood of earthly humanity, which was condemned to death, but then by merging with John the Evan-

112. Nuremberg 1908, G.A. 104. See reference 56.

gelist and receiving the Christ can become the blood of Life. Through the Doktor [Rudolf Steiner] I now experience how he unites the Tree of Knowledge of history (Moses-Plato-stream) with the Tree of Life in history (Elias-John-stream). In this way actually the great *essence* of humanity of which we are only shadow-images (copies) is provided with the proper blood! The Doktor always says that anthroposophy shall not only remain knowledge, but become *Life*.

But what is this spiritual being whose blood circulation consists of historical streams of development, and where are its other parts? (I believe here also lies the possibility of coming to what Schickler speaks of wherein he rediscovers the Buddha-stream in physiology.)

I was also pleased when I found in an alchemical work the following sentence: Someone found true gold (= the higher ego-nature) on his journey to the wilderness of St. Michael. And it was a shining, transparent red (= Philosopher's Stone?).

Hopefully, what I have written is sufficiently understandable; I always find it very difficult to write down what I think and feel. But while I am still writing, may I present you with a further problem that arose in connection with the last lecture that Herr Dr. held,[113] namely, the connection of John the Baptist with John the Evangelist.

It appeared there that Elias = countenance of God (Jehovah) was earlier experienced in the activity of nature, in the wind and rain, etc., whereas John the Evangelist rises up from the lap of Christ, (metabolism – Dr. said once he is the raised-up metabolic nature – the spiritualized Cain-Hiram-stream) to the disciple who lies on the breast of the Lord. I perceive something in him that may be characterized like this: he is the heart of Christ. Elias, like a kind of Cosmic-Michaelic being of intelligence, is now more active in the priesthood (Abel-stream), so perfected that, as John the Baptist, he was able to baptize the Christ. He is actually more the

113. This refers to "The Last Address" of September 28,1924, contained in G.A. 238, at reference 57.

countenance of Christ – and now these two impulses are bound together. I can only express this as a comparison: It appears as something carried into the Mighty-Cosmic-Christ, what the one to be initiated experiences as an image of the formation of the lotus flowers when the center of the etheric streams moves from the head to the heart, as it is described in *Knowledge of the Higher Worlds*. Whether this is already prefigured in what takes place as Mystery between both the Johns.

But in all this stands Doktor as though he somehow unites everything in himself (also all these streams: Plato, Aristotle and John), partly incarnated, partly embodied or only spiritual, and this can be experienced as a mystery of the present. But may one, or even should one, be occupied with this or even consider it at all? May one even raise such questions? (Concerning the latter, naturally I have not spoken to anyone.)

Yes, this is the kind of thing that moves us. – The experiments with the frog's legs influenced by chemical reactions (you may remember that I spoke about them once in the clinic) have started and have already shown quite beautiful results, about which I would also like to report sometime. Meanwhile I send my heartfelt greetings and also ask you, if possible, to pass on my warmest greetings to Herr Dr.

Yours sincerely, Ehrenfried Pfeiffer.

Christian Rosenkreutz
and the Spiritual Function of the Heart

(to Gwenda Ormiston, December 8, 1950)

[The following notes are part of a letter that Pfeiffer wrote in English to Gwenda Ormiston (later Briggs, 1906-1997), a friend with whom he corresponded between 1950 and 1961. It consists of a supplement to the dissertation on the "fifth chamber of the heart" which Pfeiffer began a week later (see p. 129ff.), likewise his article on the St. John Brotherhood on p. 179ff.]

The question of the spiritual heart - I told you part of it. It is the fact that the material blood is transformed into ether; not everything, but a homoeopathic quantity. Out of this etherized substance once a new cosmos will be built, the one of which Christ could say that it will be his realm as he had to say on earth, "my kingdom is not of this world," but his true kingdom will be built from the substance which flows forth from the heart of man who is penetrated by the divine LOVE of Christ.

Once Rudolf Steiner said that in meditation about "my kingdom is not of this world" one can draw nearer the etheric Christ.

When I was endangered by Nazi and Gestapo in defending freedom of the Waldorf schools and anthroposophy, an inner experience told me that - as long as I would bear this in mind, "my kingdom is not of this world" – no such danger could ever reach and destroy me – and I learned this to be the truth.

Rosenkreutz is my guide who brought me and many others to R. Steiner. From here we move to a future period when Manes will take over and bring the social order of the practical application of Christian principles (we are far off still.) That will be in the next culture epoch.[114]

St. John, the the apocalyptic and gospel writer, the youth nearest to the heart of Christ – in fact THE apostle of the heart – will lead the last culture epoch of this earth state,[115] before the matter

114. Concerning the sixth great earth-epoch after the post-Atlantean age.
115 The seventh great earth-epoch is meant.

of this earth is dissolved and transformed into the ether, out of which the new next state (Jupiter) is then created.

John is the leader of this transformation. Towards him we all will develop.

Today already an unseen, not spoken about it, only in the spirit existing brotherhood begins to form. These brothers of St. John could be anybody, but they do not reveal themselves except on special command. They are not known even one to the other. They become brothers of St. John when they learn to do *one* good deed every day out of absolute spiritual freedom, with no urge, no reward, no obligation, no reason, no karma – that is, not caused by anything other but by the spontaneous creation out of their good will; no physical cause at all should then be behind it, no expectation of profit, reward or anything else. Just the desire to do *one* good deed a day (thought, feeling or will), small and modest though it may be.

(This, by the way, is what is meant when it says: By their deeds ye shall know them.)

The Rosicrucian Background of Edith Maryon

(to Lexie Ahrens, 1958)

[The following notes are from a letter that Pfeiffer wrote to Lexie Ahrens in English on October 22, 1958. See also Rex Raab, *Edith Maryon – Bildhauerin und Mitarbeiterin Rudolf Steiners* [Edith Maryon – Sculptress and Coworker of Rudolf Steiner], Dornach, 1993.]

...I met also the lady (some 78-80 years of age) who is the only surviving member of a traditional Rosicrucian order, living in London, with whom Rudolf Steiner had contacts, entirely unknown to the Anthroposophical. Society, an order which he briefly mentions as "another" Rosicrucian stream.[116] Out of this order which safeguards tradition (*Überlieferungen*) of the original cult Miss Maryon was detailed to help Rudolf Steiner. She became one of his closest coworkers, the one who carved the Christ Statue so that Rudolf Steiner could put on the final touches, that is she pre-carved it. She also saved his life once when he slipped and almost fell from the scaffold some 20 ft above ground. She was constantly present in his studio and took care of him when he worked in his studio (9 a.m.-12 p.m. and 3-7 p.m.). People really saw her but did not know her. When the first Goetheanum burned down, towards the morning when he was completely exhausted he went to her room and spent the rest of the night there. She got very ill from the shock and died six months later [one year and five months.][117] Before — she called me one morning before Rudolf Steiner would come to the studio and explained that it was her mission to protect the physical life of Rudolf Steiner and that she would pass on this mission to me and Dr. Wachsmuth. This however could not be

[116] This cannot be confirmed.

[117] Edith Maryon died on 2nd May 1924. See the obituary by R. Steiner of May 6, 1924 in G.A. 261 at reference 58. Steiner speaks there about how Maryon had been "at first a member of another esoteric group", which was connected with her membership in the Golden Dawn. See Raab, loc. cit., p. 62f at reference 59.

fulfilled (though we acted as bodyguard, on travelling, etc.) but at the time Ita Wegman entered and she told me "to stay out" because she would now take over. And thus the tragic karmic complications started of which our society suffered for so many years. There was, by the way, never any jealousy about Miss Maryon, neither by Wegman nor Marie Steiner. Her role was so well established that nobody ever touched it or thought bad about it. She was the only one who had the keys to Rudolf Steiner's studio for many years.

The Lady in London told me of the background out of which Maryon was sent to Rudolf Steiner. Rudolf Steiner gave this order some meditations and a kind of esoteric exercises which are entirely different from anything he gave to the Anthropops.[118] And nobody in the Society knows about it nor shall they ever know. So you keep them for yourself too. – There is more to it than I can tell.

---

118. In this connection it may be mentioned that the friend of Edith Maryon, the English doctor R. W. Felkin, played an important role. Felkin was the head of the Stella Matutina Order within the Golden Dawn. Steiner refers to him anonymously in Chap. 36 of *The Story of My Life*, G.A. 28. See reference 60.

R. Swinburne Clymer

(Passages from three letters to Lexie Ahrens)

[From time to time Pfeiffer returned to the quiet seclusion of Beverly Hall near Quakertown, Pennsylvania. Beverly Hall is still today the home of the *Fraternitas Rosae Crucis*; at that time Dr. R. Swinburne Clymer was the Supreme Grand Master. Here Pfeiffer recovered from his often excessive work load, studied Rosicrucian literature and had conversations with his friend and instructor, Clymer. None of his anthroposophical coworkers knew about this refuge; therefore so much the more important are these communications made to Lexie Ahrens by Pfeiffer, referring to his visits and to R. S. Clymer.

[From a letter dated May 29 to June 4, 1960.]

You ask, what I do in seclusion?

First day I am always just plain "flat" – but I can switch off the esoteric business and other pressures at once. I don't smoke, don't drink coffee, eat very little, so physical stimulants are removed. After the physical recovery – this time particularly needed, for the last months were just one big continuous stress to capacity – I begin to read, read – mainly literature on Rosicrucians and Alchemists, for this is the place with one of the most complete libraries on the subject. And this is the reason why I go here: to study the treasures of the Rosicrucian tradition, as they reached this country in about 1700 or maybe already in 1698. Then they have beautiful garden and water-lily pond (…)

These were days of great inner concentration. Nothing from the outer world was seen, no radio, newspaper, phone, mail, business of any kind. I read very little because I begin to discover a source of inner experience, which at least as far as reading knowledge of the spiritual is concerned, supersedes all that which can be read: by inner experience.

The quietness which is necessary does not exist in Spring Valley nor in Chester,[119] though there it would be better when alone. This here is a wonderful place with a park of rare trees, shrubs, hundreds of roses, ginko trees (of which I enclose a leaf), and you are to find that most beautiful poem of Goethe about it. If you don't, keep the leaf well guarded and I will write the poem when home; it is one I really love.

There are three ponds with the most beautiful lotus flowers and water-lilies, blossoming right now. It is dreamland, indeed.

So, there is not much to write – inner life from experiencing to the point one can tell about (via words and thoughts) is a long way. But I have learned one thing in recent years: in outer anthroposophy – where just lectures are repeated, more or less intellectually digested – one is far, far away from the *real experience* of the spirit. And the esoteric impulse of Rudolf Steiner has been understood by few only and practiced by even less.

The answer is in one self, in one's own Self, awakened, becoming Conscious (…)

From where the whole world springs
To where the whole world returns again
To be safely supported once more
From It, the Self, which knows all, comes all revelation.[120]

This meditation, which the Circle-Members[121] also have received, contains one of the most profound and powerful keys to open the door. Behind or in front of it, everyday life and the little

---

119. In New York State, Pfeiffer worked in his laboratory at the Threefold Community in Spring Valley, but spent weekends on his farm in Chester with his wife and children.

120. A different version, but in the Sanskrit word-order of this often-given mantram was made by R. Steiner (See G.A. 266/III) at reference 61, p.492.).

121. The "Jugendkreis" [Youth Circle] founded in 1922, the unofficial "Society" without statutes, to whom R. Steiner gave a special meditation. (See G.A. 266/III at reference 61). Pfeiffer was a member of this circle.

ego sink into being-less nothing and insignificance. I would wish for you too that the liberated butterfly may ascend to the ego-light and leave the sheath [*Hülle*] behind.

With love, Your Ehrenfried.

[From a letter of June 24, (St. John's) 1960:]

The days near Quakertown are over. Very restful and peaceful; I lived entirely withdrawn from the crowd, devoted to the higher world and my own better self.

The crowd was very heterogeneous and not too well put together – some serious, some rather vulgar dabbling in occultism, a few "oldtimers" who had eaten the cat and felt "above" the multitude, and a few nice, decent, modest souls, who were here last year, too. The ones I liked most from previous occasions, alas, were not here.

It is not that I would say I dwelled at other new high peaks. After that experience in California (I found now *who* it was)[122] there is probably no other peak except to meet Christ himself, face to face in his full appearance - but the experience perpetuates itself, so that many details become clear, are modeled on sharp contours. It is like scales fall off the eye, [*Schuppen],* cataracts are removed. Once being able now to look into the real realities, everything past appears in such different light – all this has created a feeling of perfect peace and at ease, but not so that it radiates into the outside.

By a sheer coincidence I discovered the background and one decisive reincarnation of R. S. Clymer and understand the whole, peculiar method and setup and dynamics and direction of his

---

122. In May, 1960 Pfeiffer met a personality whom he identified as one of the Apostles and with whom he carried on deeply moving conversations, inter alia concerning the new spiritual-physical body or about the "etheric protein." "The secrets unveiled to me were extraordinary (…) To become acquainted with someone who was at the Mystery of Golgotha and reported it as an eye-witness", he wrote in a letter to Lexie Ahrens of May 24, 1960.

movement. I also understand why he did not answer all my questions re rose croix. (and he couldn't.) He derives from the Knights Templar stream, being one of the templars who were tortured. These are the most straight-forward, strict, righteous and honest people, but because of their past, repellent and suspicious. It takes a while until they gain confidence and open up. When I saw this clear before me, I pinned him down, to the name, so that he could only confirm.

Because of this honesty he feels to collect and maintain the other occult movements too – for instance Rosicrucian tradition; but here he substitutes. Now this is not the wheel of the Rose Cross and M. J. [Master Jesus] but some juxtaposition of alternating impulses. Some of these older "Knights" we had also in the Anthr. Society, actually personalities who knew nothing about the Clymer stream but had contact with the same origin in England and Germany and were part of the old F-M [ritual "class" arranged by R. Steiner]. Esotericists, some who then influenced very much the social task of Rudolf Steiner (three-folding), for instance, Count Lerchenfeld[123] and karmically connected personalities. Now these European and American exponents of the Knights Templar movement never met in the physical world in this century, and this is one real great tragedy. How different would have been the entire development of both movements if both would have met and culminated in Rudolf Steiner. How real tragic.

To get the details straightened out, I will now study history of the Templar times.

That rose-croix question I have, he (Clymer) cannot answer. In fact as matters stand today I would seem to be the only one to answer, but then I feel that I should withhold the answer until somebody comes who understands and utters the "fateful" question, i.e. the right word.

---

123. Count Otto Lerchenfeld in 1917 asked R. Steiner about the possibility for a peaceful solution for the Central Powers. As a result R. Steiner developed for the first time the idea of the Threefold Social Organism.

Destiny was very, very kind to me in that it allowed me to meet some of the greatest face to face (naturally this also includes Rudolf Steiner). To see, also, the initiation sites in Egypt, Italy, Spain, France, Germany (Externsteine and Swantewit, Rügen), to see Tintagel, the good and the evil, the Mexican [sites of initiation] and in the distance and under water to see the Temple of Atlantis, the greatest art treasures, and finally, to let the blinkers and scales to fall from the eyes: to open the door to the inner Temple and – not in abstract speculation – truly enter and experience. I remind you of the last words in Rudolf Steiner's First [Class]: understood, etc., grasped, experienced,[124] etc. A great blessing indeed (…)

[From a letter of July 17, 1960:]

As is my habit, when I get interested in something, I try to exhaust the subject from every possible angle and learn about it from every possible source. Since I do not [have] to prepare a lecture instantly as was the case this spring, with U.S. Lincoln, Emerson, etc., I can do this at leisure. But what I learn belongs, of course, to the American spiritual background, second to none.

The sudden revelation that Clymer was a Knight Templar in France – the knowledge about his predecessors [in the Rosicrucian Order] Lincoln, Washington, etc., played a role here, how this group came into being, contacted occult society leftovers in France especially, the interplay of dark and light forces, hence and now, all this weaves into an even more complete picture; history is in reality comparable to a tapestry woven from many colored threads, with pictures clear and defined emanating from the web: the creation of the western world…

(…) Clymer is a singularly honest Templar who seeks to grasp and maintain the tradition in an honest way (…)

Indeed I can now see all these connections clearly, very clearly (…), but fundamentally I have been left a thankless task: neither did I succeed in reconciling Wegman and Frau Steiner nei-

124 Part of a mantric phrase from the 16th Class Lesson, G.A. 270/II. See reference 62.

ther could I either reconcile or endure their followers (Stein, Kolisko including Zbinden, Englert) nor can I bring Clymer together with Rudolf Steiner, since Clymer in spite of his greatness is caught up in traditions. In all this lies the struggle of the awakening of the Consciousness Soul.

In the Temple of Hatshepsut

[The following passage – from a letter to Lexie Ahrens of July 21, 1960 – points to a backward glance into an Egyptian incarnation confirmed by Rudolf Steiner]

...Today I see this whole tableau of a life before me. The pieces of this life begin to form a pattern. There can be only a feeling of extreme gratefulness. There is, of course, also that knowing that I have not quite accomplished what I should.

But I stand before the innermost altar – and see the light emanating from the cup on the altar and feel the transformation; it is not a wish or desire, but now I see the altar and the inner temple, in great awe. Strange too, but just now they showed that movie of the art and treasures of Egypt and they showed the temple of the queen Hatshepsut near Thebes – which I visited in 1932 too, after returning from Jerusalem... when I *saw* the places of the experience I had, in 1924, which showed me in that temple, standing on the stairs and seeing Roeschl[125] below me – the experience which I told Roeschl, and she told Rudolf Steiner and Rudolf Steiner confirmed. So in these days a cycle of thousands of years is completed. It was not happenstance, that you were there just that moment to see Roeschl and Florence,[126] for you belong to this cycle too.

We were together in Egypt, in Heliopolis, where Manes taught and the Grail was instituted and Moses got his mission – and Hatshepsut was there and got the architect, who then built the temple near Thebes for her. At that time, John the Apostle was at Heliopolis, too, to whom we looked up, to whom we shall belong.

---

125. Maria Roeschl (1890-1969) classical scholar, esoteric pupil of R. Steiner, involved with the first Waldorf School in Stuttgart. Roeschl was the teacher of Lexie Ahrens at Hawkwood College, near Gloucester.
126. Lexie Ahrens undertook a journey to Florence with her sister, in the summer of 1960, after meeting Maria Roeschl and Ernst Lehrs in Schleswig-Holstein.

It is great to read about the mysteries, it is greater to live in them and experience them. This whole of life is a mystery in itself. Nobody but you knows of these things which go on in my soul. Roeschl felt part of it, Sabarth by the way too felt something, which guided her to become my helper.

There is great peace at this moment, while I write these lines…

Music – The Unfulfilled Aspiration

[The personality with whom Pfeiffer had probably the longest continuous correspondence, between 1938 and 1961 was his former secretary and then independent collaborator in the crystallization work, Lisa von Herwarth. She was also the one who regularly provided Pfeiffer with news from Europe, for which he was very grateful. Von Herwarth wrote him a letter in July 1959 during a Sicilian trip, in which she mentioned her love of Wagner's music. The following passage comes from Pfeiffer's letter in reply of July 31, 1959.]

I'm not 100% with you on one point; I used to be deeply affected by Wagner's music, now there are still some motifs which resound in my head, the woodland birds motif from *Siegfried*, "*Schläfst Du, Kurneval*?" ["Are you sleeping, Kurneval?"] from *Tristan und Isolde*, the swan song [in] *Lohengrin*, this and that [in] *Parsifal*, however *Die Götterdämmerung* ["Twilight of the Gods"] seems to me really barbaric, too much Merlin in it. The spiritualization of the elemental leads to a purity even of the musical experience about which Wagner did have some views, though in general he kept very much in the elemental-astral, i.e. he takes too long, for my temperament, until he struggles through to the spiritual-devachanic.

In the light-filled transfiguration, [in the] devachanic ocean waves and devachanic, light-filled continents I see, or rather hear, the future of Mystery Music.

Music is the unfilled aspiration of my soul; in this life, when I was a child it was thought I would become a musical prodigy and I was sent to the conservatory against my will until it just could not go on (I suppose I was 16 then.) Knowledge of the chem[ical] ether in physical matter replaced that as my objective. In a future life, this recognition of the chem. ether may well break through in an enhanced form as tone ether in light and air. Just as today we have a laboratory, we could then have an orchestra as a work team and could create genuine new Mystery Music. As I said, when I was in Sicily in 1953, all of nature resounded and sang in the spheres of air and light.

What we do and have accomplished today is but a mere imperfect fragment over against what lives as aspiration and objective. Merely an unfinished— not even a symphony.

My destiny had led me to many scenes of earlier lives on Earth. Today, after all the inner and outer struggles, I am done with the past. Today I no longer think or feel about journeys into the past, but into the future: in the realm of music, in the realm of mankind.

PART III

PERSONAL MEMORIES OF EHRENFRIED PFEIFFER

Personal Memories of Ehrenfried Pfeiffer

(Lexie Ahrens)

[Lexie Ahrens gave the first impetus for this book. At our request for a written sketch of her life we publish her memories of Pfeiffer below.]

I was born in Hamburg on September 9, 1927, and baptized with the names Elisabeth Alexandra Bjönness. My mother was German, my father Norwegian. We moved to Oslo in 1942. There, at age fifteen, attended weekly lectures of Curt Englert. I've had a connection with anthroposophy since then. Between 1950-52, I was in England training as aWaldorf teacher at Hawkwood College where my most important mentors were Roeschl and Lehrs. In 1952 I moved to Spring Valley where I taught the first grade at Green Meadow School. I met Ehrenfried Pfeiffer there, who called on me and wanted to know my plans. The class was discontinued; the school was not restarted until some years later. In 1953 I married Tino Ahrens – a physicist for many years, and professor at Georgia Tech in Atlanta, whom I had met in Germany when I was twelve years old. We had two sons: Hanno (1954) and Cristofer (1956). In 1959 we divorced and I moved with my sons to Phoenixville, Pennsylvania where I taught at the then Kimberton Farm School (today Kimberton Waldorf School). Pfeiffer had visited me in Atlanta, causing me to see the necessity for a divorce. We maintained a correspondence. Pfeiffer came as often as possible to Phoenixville on visits. Whenever possible I traveled to New York City to attend his classes. In 1965, I moved to Sacramento, California, with two couples of teachers, in order to revive the local Waldorf school which was in the process of closing (today an anthroposophical center). In 1976, I opened the "Grand Piano Coffee House" on Haight Street in San Francisco. Through 1985 there were altogether more than a million visitors at the "Grand Piano"! People gathered who were interested in Waldorf-pedagogy and anthroposophy to explore the possibility of establishing a Waldorf school in San Francisco. (A San Francisco Waldorf school opened in 1978; today there are three kindergartens and eleven classes.)

After the sale of the "Grand Piano," I worked with AIDS patients for years.

In 1993 I moved to Bucks County, Pennsylvania in order to help found a Waldorf kindergarten there. On my arrival there were neither teachers nor a site to be found. Through letters from Pfeiffer and no doubt, also through his influence, our attention was drawn to Beverly Hall (Pfeiffer had walked here forty years before) where we rented school rooms and grounds. In the autumn of 1999 a First Grade could be opened there also.

In 1947 I became a member of the General Anthroposophical Society in Oslo. After fifty years I resigned from the G.A.S. Among other reasons, for two decades it had become increasingly difficult for me to identify with the Anthroposophical Society. "My mentors were and are Dr. Maria, Dr. Ernst Lehrs and Dr. Ehrenfried Pfeiffer. Their sincerity, their dedication, their social awareness and their honest esoteric striving are the lights after which I strive," I stated in my letter of resignation.

At present [1999] I work privately with parents. As soon as trust develops, people come with astounding questions; a few children have memories of reincarnation. The spiritual climate of the area is varied and interesting, besides Rosicrucians, Quakers, followers of Zinzendorf and others (though not altogether favourable) for the spreading of spiritual science.

*

In 1999, there can hardly be anyone who still experienced Rudolf Steiner personally.[127] Soon there will hardly be anyone anymore who knew people who knew Steiner personally. And finally no one will know anyone anymore who knew such individuals. Perhaps it is good if this "generation succession" is interrupted. The younger and young people will then have to find esoteric

---

127. On June 3, 1998, Siegfried Pickert was able to celebrate his 100th birthday in complete fitness. Pickert belongs, along with Albert Strohschein, Franz Löffler and Werner Pache to the original curative pedagogues trained by Steiner.

guides and follow their paths in the sense of Spiritual Science without personal models or prompting images. Freedom in the sense of Steiner means inner freedom, freedom of thought. No group-consciousness, no uncritical admiration, or blind attachment. This is how I see the onset of the next millennium.

But I have been asked to write briefly about my mentor Ehrenfried Pfeiffer. I belong to the generation that considers itself lucky to have had personalities like Ernst Lehrs and Maria Roeschl as teachers for two years in England; later in the USA. Then Pfeiffer. In 1957, I lived in Atlanta, Georgia. One day a letter came from Pfeiffer, with whom I had become acquainted in Spring Valley during1952/53 when I taught the first class at the Green Meadow School.

Pfeiffer wrote that he would be in Atlanta at such and such a time, on his way to Gainsville, Georgia, to see the "chicken king", whose name escapes me, where he had been called. The latter had heard of Pfeiffer's work and told him that from several thousand chickens processed daily, he wanted everything without exception be utilized, including "chicken shit." For the following months Pfeiffer was in Gainsville several times. In his laboratory in Spring Valley he developed a preparation which transformed the chicken manure into a practically sweet-smelling compost. Pfeiffer and the "chicken king" were delighted. Large sheds were built, plans devised for a large enterprise. When everything was ready, the sheds burned down; they were not insured, and the "chicken king" gave up on the whole affair.

Years later Pfeiffer was frequently in Oakland, California. A large construction was built there for processing trash. The rubbish came on great conveyor-belts; above them magnets were erected to extract all the tins and other metal. Then the refuse would be treated with preparations until it formed a good organic compost. Again, nothing came of it; flames destroyed this undertaking also.

Before the Second World War, Pfeiffer lived and worked in Holland. It had become clear to him that wheat no longer had the life-forces to nourish mankind. With several coworkers he successfully bred a new wheat. Some fields were already reserved for cultivating the seed. Then the war broke out, while Pfeiffer himself, with his family, were already in the USA. The wheat cultivated in Holland was destroyed by war battles, except for a few ears that later found their way to the USA.

In 1941/42 Pfeiffer became very ill; he developed a galloping consumption. He spent these years in a hospital and finally overcame the illness. However, one lung did not heal. During his time in the hospital Pfeiffer had many impressive spiritual visions, which he drew in the most delicate colors with crayons. Many of these drawings he later painted in water-colors or chalk. Each drawing can become the occasion for deep meditation.

I do not want to be too personal, but the connection between Pfeiffer and myself reached far back into the past. He once made a drawing of Ephesus and remarked: "That's how it was." Concerning the end of this millennium he said once that the population of the earth in this century has increased so much (today six billion; in 1961, when Pfeiffer died, about four billion; in 1918, 1.8 billion) because it is like on a train where formerly lunch would be served only at certain fixed times. After a while a waiter would go through the train and call out: "Second serving! Last call for the second serving!" In this century, all souls that are united with the earth (including the ego-less) would incarnate because such manifold opportunities would not present themselves either before or afterwards. Besides, after the year 2000 it will become much more difficult to incarnate; that would require a particularly strong individual. There is much talk today that early anthroposophists, and also Steiner himself, are now reincarnated. Steiner himself speaks about it in his karma-lectures: "We will be on earth again at the end of the century."[128] I will certainly not question this, but would

128. See, i.a., *Karmic Relationships, Vols IV and VI* (G.A. 238 and 240) Rudolf Steiner Press, 1971. R. Steiner made a quite direct remark concerning himself at Stratford-on-Avon in 1922. A diary entry by W. J. Stein reads, "Heydebrand [a teacher – colleague at the Stuttgart Waldorf School] said: 'In Stratford in 1922 Dr. Steiner said he would return in 80 years' time, in America.' " See references 63 and 64.

only mention that Pfeiffer said to me that he would not be on the earth again at the turn of the millennium.[129]

He told me also that the date of his birthday,19 February 1899, fell on the day that Kali Yuga had come to an end.[130] Pfeiffer expected much from himself, expected much from his coworkers, and certainly it was not always easy to get on with him. He en-

---

129. In his very last lecture, "On Threshold Experiences," on September 10, 1961 in Spring Valley, six weeks before his death, Pfeiffer made the following statement: "As far as we are here, as I look at some people here, they will be here at the end of the century. And others won't. Dr. Steiner has painted the picture that the end of the century will be the decisive moment for all humanity. In many religions, in many esoterically trained groups we learn the same thing: It will be a decisive moment. It may be a personal whim, but I would like to be there. I would not want to be in heaven if the Earth goes to pot. I would want to be here if the Earth goes the good way, takes the good turn. I would like to be a witness to that which goes on. I would like to exercise the powers of that much Ego consciousness that I have acquired. – You may say: 'this is your dream,' but I think it is a dream that a true Anthroposophist can develop. I am dead sure that this is a dream that Dr. Steiner developed, the conscious dream that we should be able as human beings to learn that much that we should participate, no matter under what conditions, in the decisive moments that turn the Earth up or down." (*Ehrenfried Pfeiffer – Notes and Lectures, Compendium II*, Spring Valley 1991, p. 101 – reference 17.)
130. This information is confirmed by Elisabeth Vreede: "In a conversation at home with Fräulein H. Janssen von Raay about the great significance of the work of Dr. Ehrenfried Pfeiffer, the following was said by Dr. Elisabeth Vreede: that the last day of Kali Yuga had been February 19, 1899 (the birthday of Ehrenfried Pfeiffer)." See T. Jurriaanse, *Aktualität und heilende Kraft des Grundsteinspruches* [The significance and healing power of the Foundation stone verse] in *Was in der Anthroposophischen Gesellschaft vorgeht* [What is Happening in the Anthroposophical Society], September 7, 1980, p. 147 – reference 65]. The pubisher owes the note about this indication of Dr. Vreede to Herr Emanuel Zeylmans van Emmichoven. In Blavatsky's *Secret Doctrine,* there is an indirect and approximate confirmation: Blavatsky dates the beginning of Kali Yuga on *February 16*, albeit in the year 3102 B.C. See reference 66.

joyed his food, smoked like a chimney although he had only one lung and he was constantly threatened with a leg-embolism. Patience was not one of his strengths. There is no doubt that one was dealing with a quite extraordinary individuality. It is incomprehensible to many that he added his signature to the letter of conflict directed against Ita Wegman and others.[131] He explained to me that he had promised Rudolf Steiner to support Marie Steiner to the end.

Pfeiffer suffered from loneliness. He meant much to many, but had scarcely any people from his narrow karmic circle around him. On the other hand he came in contact with the most varied circles within agriculture and natural science.[132]

He lived a life filled with great discoveries, disappointments, and a lack of recognition; but also a life full of deep spiritual insights and experiences — a powerful prelude to the realization of impulses fructified by spiritual science in the not too distant future.

---

131. Refers to the so-called *Denkschrift über Angelegenheiten der Anthroposophischen Gesellschaft in den Jahren 1925 bis 1935* [Memorandum about the affairs of the Anthroposophical Society in the Years 1925 to 1935]. This very contentious letter of contributed substantially to the expulsion of Ita Wegman and Elisabeth Vreede from the Committee of the Society, along with a line of valued coworkers of R. Steiner. David Clement explained to the publisher that Pfeiffer on a visit to England after the war described it as a mistake that he had signed the memorandum. See reference 3.

132. The Hahnemann Hospital of Philadelphia awarded him an honorary doctorate.

Ehrenfried Pfeiffer and the Future

(by Paul W. Scharff, M.D.)

Ehrenfried Pfeiffer was born on 19th February 1899. Kali Yuga came to an end at the time of his birth. Five thousand years of spiritual darkening and darkness came to an end in the year that he was born. One can think that he helped usher in this new age of light.

For many, a birthday is an occasion to contemplate the spiritual world out of which the human soul and spirit is born. Not so for Ehrenfried as I contemplate his life. It is the future to which I feel I must turn in writing this preface. To this end I have to turn to his *DEATH DAY*.

On November 30, 1961, Ehrenfried Pfeiffer crossed over into the spiritual world as a result of a severe heart attack. For years he had been hampered in his work for the earth and mankind in one way or another, by health problems or by opponents. At the time of his death he was looking to a rising sun, in his work. This new sun in his life came to him in the form of a request from the Korean government to introduce composting in that country in order to transform "night soil", that is human excreta, into a usable material for agricultural practices. This "night soil" was a bane to the land and people of that country. To begin work to find a way to transform this poisonous material, this gave a foundation for him to find a new direction in life and live on.

A second support to live on was his work with a new strain of heat-resistant wheat with a very high protein content. Humanity of the future would need a high protein content in their diet, protein derived from a plant source. He saw totally new possibilities with his heat-resistant strain of wheat. With these new possibilities in his 62nd year of life his life on earth came to end.

Those who have known Ehrenfried Pfeiffer have often said that he was a true Rosicrucian. Any one who looks into Rudolf Steiner's writings will find that there are not so many true Rosicrucians, even if the spiritual path given in relation to anthroposophy is called a Johannian-, Rosicrucian-, Christian Path. As can be found in the lectures given by Ehrenfried Pfeiffer, he took the different spiritual streams and shared his researches for years with members of the Threefold Community. It is quite usual in this day, that visitors to the Threefold Community sense its unusual atmosphere, its unusual aura as it were. He gave hundreds, if not several thousand lectures over the course of his life time, and many were given in the Threefold Community. For twenty-seven years he gave the opening lecture at the Summer Conference held in the name of the School of Spiritual Science. Few countries in the world will have had such an able representative of anthropo-sophy work for its furtherance as here in the United States. He quite loved America, but of course not in a nationalistic way. He loved the openness of the souls who live here, and he loved the potential for the future.

His was an attempt to work for a responsible future for this country in relation to the world. It was quite easy to sense with almost every lecture, whether in a more closed circumstance or more public, that he was a human being with extraordinary depth. Some liked this, but others were very much put off by it. Those who were farmers in the Biodynamic Movement loved his way, as he could live into the soul of the farmer with much ease as he approached the end of his life.

However, with all this said he remained quite an unknown in the world at large, a very typical Rosicrucian trait. He sought specific relationships, particularly when dealing with public officials. He continually sought for souls of stature and of depth. One such soul that he found and met was Swinburne Clymer. Clymer was a physician, and a fairly well known occultist who worked devotedly within the Rosicrucian Movement. He held himself to be a true Rosicrucian as it were. Ehrenfried in meeting him felt that he was in fact one of the more genuine souls in the world who could say that he or she was a Rosicrucian. However, with this said, he tried to make it quite clear to me as we had conversations about such matters that he, Pfeiffer, had his reservations about the purely Rosicrucian element in Clymer's work. There was no question that Pfeiffer wanted that one is faithful to Rudolf Steiner when it comes to a spiritual path. He, Pfeiffer, also made it clear that he was a very close friend of Clymer's. This friendship with Clymer is of the greatest import, and at the same time it is important to see that this friendship did not interfere in any way with Ehrenfried's sense of faithfulness to Rudolf Steiner. Why do I point to this? It is simply the case that one cannot "*SERVE TWO MASTERS*" when it comes to a spiritual path. Not only was Pfeiffer clear about this, but Clymer was, as well. When I conversed with Clymer after Pfeiffer's death, this was what Clymer addressed with a conviction that could move mountains. This faithfulness to a spiritual guide, friend, teacher, is all important, as it builds the threads needed in our day to make the needed steps to the spiritual world. This is not a matter of authority, blind faith or following dogma, but a matter of brotherly love and cooperation which involves the life of one's own organism and one's soul. This I believe one can find by study of the great leaders of mankind, the Great Initiates. Pfeiffer joined with Clymer to further the Rosicrucian work in our times.

It is on this basis that Ehrenfried Pfeiffer came to work with Clymer at the end of life. Each one of these two men were individuals through and through, and it was their individual work which each could share with the other. It was then this individual, Swinburne Clymer, who could help allay the loneliness of Ehrenfried Pfeiffer.

The loneliness of Ehrenfried was more than evident, as I have shared again and again, to numerous individuals. I often went to meet with him, hoping to share some of my concerns. I usually left with much that he had to share, after sitting before one of the most lonely souls I have yet met. In what he had to say, much of the history and struggles of Rudolf Steiner, the Anthroposophical Movement and the School of Michael was poured out. In retrospect, in looking back over the last 38 years I am amazed how much he shared; that has only slowly emerged as the history of what has happened out of the life and work of Rudolf Steiner. This content was totally alive in the soul of this human being, and with relatively few could Ehrenfried share this content. This content was shared with Swinburne Clymer, who felt he could not recognize Rudolf Steiner as a legitimate Rosicrucian because of purely administrative considerations, but seemed to have less trouble in terms of spiritual content.

A very deep impression was left on my own soul in meeting with Swinburne Clymer, after Ehrenfried had entered the spiritual world. For one it was very possible to sense immediately that this was a very unusual individual, and in no way could he be judged from his writings. Secondly it was more than evident that he had an unusual respect and love for Ehrenfried Pfeiffer. Though standing in different streams, they could have a deep regard if not love for one another. When we spoke together, he noted Ehrenfried's loneliness. He also noted that it was actually a pity that more within the Anthroposophical Movement did not recognize Ehrenfried Pfeiffer. From his perspective he felt that his friend Ehrenfried Pfeiffer had managed a self-unfolding for the good of mankind which surpassed anyone that he knew on the American continent and anyone he was familiar with in the circles where he worked during the course of this century. I found this to be most interesting and important coming from a friend who obviously was walking in a different river bed, but knew that at one point all waters can flow together. What I have attempted to articulate is that for me, this soul of Ehrenfried Pfeiffer lived continually in the future, though lonely through the loss of his teacher and guide at an early age. At the same time this individual attained a spiritual path, a lonely path, but ultimately found a friend who walked a different path. They both could share and work together. Both were concerned for the future of humanity and this earthly world. For Ehrenfried Pfeiffer, there was no question regarding the Michaelic-Johannine-Rosicrucian impulse for the future.

Such a picture of the future still stands livingly before my eyes. It was June 24, 1960. I was busy in our small garden behind our house, which now is part of the Fellowship Community in Chestnut Ridge (formerly Spring Valley), New York. The air was clear. The sun was ascending into its zenith. The sky was as blue as one can imagine, and all was quiet. The quiet and the depth of that late morning was unusual, with the birds singing on wing, and with the gentle music of the breeze occasionally passing through the nearby woods. All seemed fresh and beautiful as on the day of Creation. I was busy weeding in a bean patch whose height was close to three feet, and the plants were laden with beans. It could have been thought that Nature was contemplating Her own creation of the previous months. The Spring and early Summer were unusual that year. As I worked along, I was suddenly jolted when someone spoke to me from behind. It was Ehrenfried Pfeiffer. He said he had been standing there watching me while I worked. We then came into conversation. Our exchange took the direction of the season, the unusual summer's day, and the fact that the earth on this day appeared to be renewed. As we spoke, the bean patch seemed to become more a patch of elemental beings, the birds more like some spiritual beings playing instruments and the plants living beings which were responding to the life inherent in the light. A creative symphony appeared to lie around us as we conversed.

Two days later Ehrenfried Pfeiffer gave a usual Sunday morning lecture,[133] where he took the occasion to speak of new elemental beings in nature and the need for a new understanding of physical existence. For him the physical world was not as dead as it might appear to some. His concern was to show that life is an actuality which can become manifest under specific laboratory conditions. The conditions for such a manifestation he had created with his "*sensitive crystallization*" which he had been using as a research tool for many years. Others were finding their way to his work, and he was obviously pleased about this. His was a search for an expression of etheric forces, life forces or formative forces. His teacher, Rudolf Steiner, had pointed him in this direction.

---

133. St. John's Day lecture, June 26 1960, *Compendium II*, Mercury Press, 1991. See reference 67.

Pfeiffer's Crystallization Work and Its Role in the Origin of the Book *Fundamentals of Therapy: an Extension of the Art of Healing through Spiritual Knowledge*

Paul W. Scharff, M.D.

[The following contribution by Paul Scharff gives an insight into an important fact connected with Pfeiffer's crystallization work and draws attention to his hitherto still largely unnoticed share in the origin of the book written by Rudolf Steiner in collaboration with Ita Wegman: *Fundamentals of Therapy: an Extension of the Art of Healing through Spiritual Knowledge.* Scharff's notes of May 6, 1995 were abridged for publication.]

Ehrenfried Pfeiffer introduced me to the crystallization method and taught me to read the crystallization images. We talked about the method and its application every day. I was impressed by the fact that he had absolutely no interest in using the method to prove or test anything. It was to serve purely for the cultivation of a perception of "form" and to awaken a new, scientifically based faculty of cognition. The process as a whole was to serve to develop in certain people the faculty of perception of the etheric world. What also impressed me was that in reading the crystallization images, one observed the so-called deviations from a basic archetypal image: the archetypal image Pfeiffer used was the scene of the Crucifixion with three crosses. The central cross was the one on which the crucified Christ hung; right and left of it were the crosses with the two criminals. In the archetypal picture, these two criminals were regarded as human beings in whom Lucifer and Ahriman worked. This image stood in the background when observing the deviations in the crystallizations. If the crystallization method itself was strange, still more so was using the Mystery of Golgotha to read the crystallization images. In this way the sick person can be seen in the light of the activity of Lucifer and Ahriman, the Great Healer standing in the middle.

We often talked about the development of anthroposophically oriented medicine as well. Pfeiffer told of the meetings with Rudolf Steiner and Ita Wegman at the time when the book *Fundamentals of Therapy* was coming into being. Rudolf Steiner would discuss a section of the book with Ita Wegman. After one, two or maybe even more days, Ita Wegman would come back with the results of the conversation. She had carried the content through sleep several times. Rudolf Steiner and Ita Wegman then reviewed the topic she had worked on by virtue of his questions. There came a moment when questions of *chemistry* were discussed in detail. It was at this point that Rudolf Steiner asked the young Ehrenfried Pfeiffer to join them. Pfeiffer said that Ita Wegman appeared at first to be rather bothered by his presence.

As is well known, Pfeiffer had been recommended by Rudolf Steiner to study Chemistry. And Pfeiffer, as we know, took up the suggestion. That was why, since he was concerned with the latest developments in this field, he was drawn into these discussions. It is further evidence of how much Rudolf Steiner could work with immediate actuality.

Pfeiffer reported that Rudolf Steiner's main interest at these meetings was in the development of a clinical biochemistry. Anyone familiar with chemistry knows that such a trend would not be adopted in academic research for another thirty years. In the meetings with Ehrenfried Pfeiffer and Ita Wegman, Rudolf Steiner thus anticipated this development.

So the book that was coming into being was to contain a path to a modern biochemistry as well; a path on which a new living biochemistry could be developed with regard to the diseased human being. The human being was to be considered even from the point of view of the transmutation of substance. This required a fundamental *knowledge* of substance. This was, and is, not the only concern of the book in question, of course. Nevertheless, in view of a future, more Rosicrucian chemistry, this point should not go unnoticed.

A Conversation with Pfeiffer about the Night of the Fire

Paul W. Scharff, M.D.

[The following notes from Paul Scharff were written down on August 16, 1993, and circulated among friends. They have been slightly edited for this publication with the consent of the author. Scharff writes at the beginning of the article:

"In 1959 my family and I moved to Spring Valley. We were interested...in particular in associating with Ehrenfried Pfeiffer with his laboratory, medical and Bio-dynamic Agricultural work. In the case of Ehrenfried Pfeiffer, my contact dates back to 1936 when he visited our farm in Lorain, Ohio. I was a young boy at the time – six years old. My memory of him is vague, but the import of his visit is well embedded in memory. It was in 1953 that I first had a conscious, mature meeting with Ehrenfried Pfeiffer. To begin with, I had contact with him intermittently and then frequently after our move in 1959. Soon after our family's arrival, we had almost weekly meetings. I had exchanges with him while I continued my post graduate work in internal medicine and psychiatry. It was during one of the weekly meetings that a very important exchange took place, and this I will record for sharing. The reason is that I think this particular exchange throws light on the destiny of Rudolf Steiner and Ehrenfried Pfeiffer, and as well gives a little insight into the suffering of Rudolf Steiner at the time of the burning of the first Goetheanum."]

In my first conversations with Ehrenfried in 1953, I was encouraged by him to give lectures and talks on human physiology and organology. Rudolf Steiner had repeatedly stated to him, nay even complained, that anthroposophists know too little about the make up of the human being, particularly the physical and physiological make up. Rudolf Steiner related that a development of esoteric life for a deeper anthroposophy required a significant knowledge of the human organism. Needed was a new organology.

Ehrenfried Pfeiffer held that Rudolf Steiner's founding of the Michael School was a most significant step in the history of mankind, since Aristotle had failed at this task in Greek times. Next to the placing of the Threefold Social Order in mankind's development, the founding of the School was a close second accomplishment. For the unfolding of this School, a deeper, non-intellectual anthroposophy was needed. He repeatedly bid me to fight against intellectual anthroposophy, join him in this task and further knowledges concerning man's physical and life organization.

Ehrenfried Pfeiffer liked to speak about the "Workmen's Lectures,"[134] the lectures of Rudolf Steiner to the workmen busy at the first Goetheanum. These lectures were given to those who carried questions in such a way that Rudolf Steiner could share in a much less intellectual fashion. Ehrenfried held these lectures as exemplary of anthroposophical development and presentation needed by so many in mankind. He said that Rudolf Steiner had said that he had to give these lectures only to workmen because of the social circumstances of the working class in that day and because the workmen were open so that he could speak about material things in the light of the spirit. Rudolf Steiner invited Ehrenfried to these lectures, though today I still hear that Ehrenfried was an intruder by being present at these lectures. I gather there may have been some objections to his presence, which I have been told was not in the midst of the audience, but more hidden. If he had been asked to keep a bit out of sight by his beloved Rudolf Steiner, this I do not know. I do know, however, that Ehrenfried had a destiny which could easily raise the ire of some of those around him, as well as make immediate heart-felt connections with others. Ehrenfried repeatedly explained to me that Rudolf Steiner felt that the content he shared with the workmen should become content for many Anthroposophists. As Rudolf Steiner explained in those workmen lectures, if the human make up is not known, soul-spirit as well as bodily make up, the needs of human beings cannot be perceived, and thereby a foundation for proper social action cannot be laid.

In conversations with Ehrenfried, I often posed questions about Rudolf Steiner. He shared freely, but usually encouraged me to step out and begin speaking about anthroposophy. Of course, he,

---

134. G.A. 347-354. See references 68-75.

Ehrenfried, had begun at an early age, encouraged by Rudolf Steiner. One day, in the spring of 1959, during one of our exchanges, he again was pressing that I speak out. I responded by saying that he could easily say what he does because he had had Rudolf Steiner at this side. I explained that for my part, I felt I had to be able to stand alone and independently. This would take many years for me (and it has.) But because Ehrenfried pressed, I asked him if he had really differed with Rudolf Steiner. Had he stood up to Rudolf Steiner at a time of real difference? He had often shared how close he felt to Rudolf Steiner and how much of a "father-like" being Rudolf Steiner had been for him. Thus I knew that such a differing would not be easy.

Ehrenfried responded easily and quickly. Yes, he had had a real difference. So I asked if he could share this difference, the occasion of the difference. Ehrenfried seemed almost eager to do so.

He began by sharing that the foundation for the "difference" began at the time when Rudolf Steiner first visited Dornach. At that time, 1912, he walked the hill at Dornach and the valley of the Hermitage in Arlesheim. The sequence, as I recall, was that Rudolf Steiner walked the hill in Dornach. He retired for the night. During the night, he had great struggles as he foresaw the burning of the Goetheanum. This Rudolf Steiner had shared with Ehrenfried. Following the troubled night, Rudolf Steiner walked the Hermitage and then made the decision to go ahead on the Dornach hill despite the foreboding foresight. When Rudolf Steiner shared this with Ehrenfried, I do not know.

When the time of the fire arrived, as we know, Rudolf Steiner was very much in the midst of the circumstance. Ehrenfried related that he was also present – very much with an eye to the activities and whereabouts of Rudolf Steiner. He, as well as a group of other younger members, had formed a watch-guard around Rudolf Steiner. Some time during the night – my impression is after the height of the flames – Rudolf Steiner disappeared from the scene. Ehrenfried Pfeiffer said he began looking for him and finally located him in a room not far from the fire. I have often thought that this was a room in the Schreinerei. However, some older knowing Anthroposophists have assured me that this was not the case. It was only with the books by J. E. Zeylmans van Emmichoven that I could consider the room to be in the house of Frau Finckh, the recorder of Rudolf Steiner's lectures.[135]

As Ehrenfried unfolded this story, the circumstances became so alive that the immediate surroundings fell away, and I felt as if I stood in the midst of the events being shared.

Ehrenfried said he entered a room where Rudolf Steiner was. I do not recall whether Rudolf Steiner was standing or sitting. However, Ehrenfried said he found a human being crushed, sunken and totally alone. He felt his heart go out to his beloved teacher and at that moment recognized the reality of their relationship. Rudolf Steiner shared that he could not go on. With that statement Ehrenfried was shaken to the core. He said he braced himself and addressed Rudolf Steiner to the effect that he had to go on and that he, Ehrenfried, would do everything in his power to see that there would be no interruption in the flow of events and the further unfolding of the Society and the School.

Ehrenfried has on previous occasions shared his participation in meetings in Dornach. He said there were 18 attendees at these meetings. These meetings occurred at the end of the second decade of this century, when Rudolf Steiner shared his great concern for the loss of the esoteric within the anthroposophical work. Esoteric activity was at the heart and core of Ehrenfried's strivings, and he always felt united with his teacher in these strivings.

Thus it was that the young pupil stood before his beloved teacher at the time of great trial, darkness and need. Since this was no ordinary pupil, the pupil offered help. In a similar circumstance some years earlier, of much less import, Ehrenfried Pfeiffer had ordered a glass of sparkling water for Rudolf Steiner when he first heard Rudolf Steiner giving a talk to the workmen in a beer gar-

---

135. In the statement of Lisa von Herwarth, another coworker of Pfeiffer's in the Dornach years, she referred to the second Eurythmy house at Ruttiweg 32 (disclosed by Pfeiffer to her personally.)

den. Rudolf Steiner was speaking in behalf of the Threefold Commonwealth movement to a group of workers in Stuttgart. All the listeners had, as I recall, something to drink, but not Rudolf Steiner – on this hot day. Thus Ehrenfried acted, as was his nature throughout life. He ordered something to drink for Rudolf Steiner. This circumstance at a beer garden was a preparation for the moment of greatest need. Here the active, will-filled, heart-warmed pupil directed his life and desire to serve his teacher.

Ehrenfried left the "room" to attend to what needed to follow. I gather that his outer efforts were visible to almost no one, as he repeatedly shared that his words went unheard. We do know, however, that Rudolf Steiner did continue without halt. What role Ehrenfried played in the outer events that followed, I do not know. However, I do know that for Ehrenfried Pfeiffer, this was a decisive moment, and I suspect the same for Rudolf Steiner as well as for the Society and the School.

From this sharing I could glean how close Ehrenfried felt to the work and efforts of Rudolf Steiner to form a Society for the unfolding of a School for the sake of mankind's future.

Though it is now over thirty years since I was told of these events, the mood and aura of the telling and the immediacy of the burning seem to stand as if all had occurred quite recently. The seventy years, at this writing, appear as if yesterday. I share as I think this event tells something about the individual Rudolf Steiner, whom so many love and are grateful to. It also tells about a faithful pupil who irritated many, but who in a lifetime did much to help the Society and the School. In the work of the School he was a very quiet worker, always trying to lay a foundation in the reality of nature, where an esoteric striving has to find its footing.

The Background to the Plot for Poisoning Rudolf Steiner on January 1, 1924

[This report has recently been received (1999), from someone who prefers not to be named. Compare also the article *Von den okkulten Hintergründen der Zerstörung des ersten Goetheanums und des Vergiftungsanschlages auf Rudolf Steiner* [The Occult Background to the Destruction of the First Goetheanum and the Poison-Plot on Rudolf Steiner], *Der Europäer* [The European], *Jg.* [Year] *1, Nr.* [No.] *5, März* [March] *1997*, p. 6f., on webpage: *http://www.perseus.ch/PDF-Dateien/Brandvergiftung.pdf*.

Cf. also Pfeiffer's description on p. 91ff.]

Toward the end of the 50s, when after recovering from a serious illness Ehrenfried Pfeiffer once again came to Arlesheim and Dornach, I was called to an internal meeting in the *Grundsteinsaal* [Foundation Stone Hall] of the Goetheanum. There were only a few present - approximately thirty to forty people. Pfeiffer wished to communicate what had concerned him during his illness and what he still wanted to entrust to a few people; before this he could not leave this Earth. What he said, if I may summarize it, was like a "general confession" of his whole life and striving. From this, the following detail: one reason for his going to America was to contact those with authentic knowledge about mechanical occultism. One such person he found fairly quickly. A trusting relationship developed. One day they discussed various phases in the life of Rudolf Steiner. His poisoning at the tea party after the Christmas Conference (January 1, 1924) was also mentioned. There followed a surprising and dramatic statement by Pfeiffer's confidant. He said: "Please forgive me, I must say something, alas, which will greatly shock you and could separate us again, although I would deeply regret this: *I* was the one charged with poisoning Rudolf Steiner! This poisoning, however was not intended to be fatal, but to bring Rudolf Steiner into a condition in which he would no longer control his high occult faculties so that they would practically be extinguished. One would then be able to point to Rudolf Steiner and say: 'See? When you strive for an occult schooling in his sense, as he describes it, for example, in *Knowledge of the Higher Worlds and Its Attainment*, then you will end up like this.' " —Ehrenfried Pfeiffer did not say whether or not he continued his connection with this macabre occultist. He only indicated that Rudolf Steiner overcame this poisoning attempt with the aid of spiritual forces.[136] The brothers of the left hand did not succeed.[137]

---

136. The following verbal statement by Guenther Wachsmuth to W. J. Stein on October 8, 1924 throws a surprising additional light on this until now unknown, disclosure by Pfeiffer: "Dr. Wachsmuth thought that the Doctor was poisoned at the tea party. It was an oriental poison that affects the etheric body and causes a crisis every Wednesday. Karmically it meant for him further Initiation." (See *Der Europäer* [The European,] *Jg.1* [First Year,] No.5, *März* [March] 1997, p. 7, at reference 29.)

137. "Brothers of the Left Hand" describes those who use their occult knowledge in destructive ways.

APPENDIX

Sir Albert Howard Memorial
(1873-1947)

Sir Albert Howard's Deed for Science

Dr. Ehrenfried E. Pfeiffer[138]

[Dr. Pfeiffer, Rudolf Steiner's pupil, was responsible for the introduction of the Biodynamic system of organic farming.]

Sir Albert Howard's life work has only just begun. It is the highest tribute one can make to a man if one can say that his aims, his thought, his work begin only at his death and will survive his physical death, granting him a spiritual survival. Sir Albert is one of whom one can thus speak. The importance of his thought is established not only for agriculture but it also leads into the realms of nutrition and health. And it is here that future generations will take up the work in order to complete what he has begun.

Sir Albert (this is the way one would address him in England according to his title of knighthood) started out from an intimate study of soil fertility. At a time when not the least thought of soil conservation existed and the term "erosion" had not yet been formed (even though erosion had existed all over the earth for hundreds of years) he began to worry about the poor state of agricultural soils, the decline of their fertility and the decline of crops, despite the fact that agricultural methods seemed to improve and more and more fertilizers were applied. At the same period when mineral fertilizers held the highest rank, his attention was directed to the very core of soils – the role which humus plays in their maintenance and improvement. It is true that the humus concept was not new. There was, to refer only to one, the humus theory of

---

138. "Sir Albert Howard Memorial Issue", *Organic Gardening Magazine*, Emmaus, Pa., Vol. 13, No. 8, September 1948. See webpage: http://journeytoforever.org/farm_library/howard_memorial.html. See reference 78. Sixty years later on October 1, 2008, HRH The Prince of Wales delivers the Sir Albert Howard Memorial Lecture. See webpage: http://www.princeofwales.gov.uk/speechesandarticles/hrh_delivers_the_sir_albert_howard_memorial_lecture_471496085.html. HRH's video lecture may be viewed on The Royal Channel on YouTube at: http://www.youtube.com/watch?v=5dadwzpIbfo

the German agriculturist Thaer, current early in the 19th century, long before Liebig.[139]

But Liebig had given the agricultural concept a turn towards the mineral theory, in fact, towards the very one-sided concept that only a few major elements are needed for plant growth, namely, nitrogen, potassium, and phosphate. The application of these three elements brought about a revolution in farming; an increase of crops was observed. As a consequence, agricultural science and practice still believe today that "this is it." Many other factors were neglected during the next hundred years as a result of Liebig's discovery. One can objectively state that it led to the excessive use of soils and brought increases of crops at the expense of other factors in soil, all the other elements, including trace elements, the important biocatalysts, and organic matter. World agriculture, deceived by the NPK theory, demanded more from soils than they could give and a general depletion cycle began. More fertilizer had to be applied in order to maintain the new crop levels until the breakdown of soils set in. "To hold the soil" by all means became the urgent demand. Mankind was living on the capital of soils rather than on what they could offer in a natural way.

It was here, decades ago, at the high tide of the mineral theory, that Sir Albert Howard, as a Cassandra, with courageous words and writing, based on observation and experience, began to stem the tide and call attention to the fallacies of a one-sided agriculture. Had his call been listened to thirty years ago, then a U.S. Soil Conservation Service might not have been necessary, or have been founded fifteen years earlier than it actually was. It is this foresight which scientists could treasure highly in studying Sir Albert's life work.

Sir Albert had to walk the rough and thorny path of every prophet and pioneer, overlooked, viewed with pitying silence, attacked from the side of the then current beliefs and customs – a lone man for many years. Even his enemies have to admire the will

139. The German chemist Justus von Liebig (1803-1873) pioneered the use of chemical fertilizers.

power and enthusiasm with which he propagated his gospel of soil fertility as an organic concept in spite of all obstacles. Time and future developments and discoveries upheld him though and he could, at least during the last decade of his life, look with satisfaction upon the fact that the organic movement grew in momentum and depth.

A few years before the outbreak of World War II a symposium of scientists and practical farmers took place, called together upon the initiative of Lord Lymington (now the Earl of Portsmouth). "Famine in England," a book by Viscount Lymington (published in 1938), picturing in urgent words the future of English agriculture, which came only too true, was just in preparation. Lord Northbourne in "Look to the Land" seconded the organic idea. Captain Wilson, the successful farmer and gardener from Lincolnshire, whose products stole all the prizes at agriculture exhibits, was also there. Many outstanding personalities were present. Sir Robert McCarrison (see Notes, below), the apostle of health based on better nutrition from living soils, was there, too.

The purpose of the symposium was to bring together and merge into one great endeavor all the different organic points of view and movements. It was felt that differences of opinion in the organic field could be bridged over, in fact, were healthy and a stimulus for the creation of future research and cooperation rather than opposition and stubborn disagreement. Field tests, laboratory experiments and health studies were decided upon. The need to extend soil studies into the analysis of products, their health and nutrition values, in short, a broad program of future research was instituted. Many valuable experiences and observations were constituted. Such a spirit of cooperation, mutual stimulation and enthusiasm to give momentum to the organic cause reigned there as the writer has rarely experienced at any other scientific conference. The meeting radiated a truly creative atmosphere. It was at this meeting that the writer, as the representative of the Biodynamic Movement (see Notes, below), met Sir Albert Howard for the first time, although he had followed his ideas with the greatest interest before. In fact, one purpose of the conference was to bring the organic idea of Sir Albert Howard and the biodynamic method into peaceful cooperation. Mutual experiments were discussed, thoughts exchanged and results agreed upon. This acquaintance was continued with several visits of Sir Albert to the writer's former biodynamic farm in Holland, where he inspected and acknowledged the results of the biodynamic endeavor.

A personal memory of the first impression made by Sir Albert's personality may perhaps be mentioned here. When the writer entered the livingroom of Lord Lymington's beautiful home a lively discussion was already in full swing. Sir Albert was "enthroned" on the davenport and the writer was seated beside him. He was very impressive with his large head, which might be called a "Jupiter head" by a phrenologist, as he sat there animatedly propounding the organic gospel. There was immediate contact in basic ideas, in our approach to the needs of soil and health. Past experience provided a foundation for ideas for future research. Sir Albert had a slightly singing voice and spoke always with warmth and life. Never an abstract theory was voiced but everything sprang from a long and rich life experience. One had the feeling, one can trust this man, his whole personality is devoted to his cause. He has nothing for sale but his arguments are sound for they are founded on reality. The writer always wondered why Sir Albert, with his solid background, appeared at times to be so much on the defensive, particularly toward "professional" scientists and officials. This would not have been necessary since the organic movement even at that time, ten years ago, already had substance enough to wait until the others came around. When we rose from our seats to continue a lively discussion standing and walking about, the writer experienced a real surprise. Sir Albert was what one calls a "sitting giant" with a large head and trunk, but short legs. When he stood up he seemed to diminish in stature. He had this peculiar physical characteristic in common with Goethe.

The research program outlined at the symposium is still valid: to study soils treated with and without organic fertilizer; to follow up the health value of products thus raised; to study the influence of organic and mineral soils with a view to the resistance of plants to disease; to study the health and resistance of cattle and other animals fed with the different types of products thus raised; to introduce the organic idea as a basis for human health and diet. Doctors and dietitians, nowadays, unaware of the organic approach, prescribe diets. They speak, for instance, of vitamins, of orange juice, lemons, etc. etc. as daily supplements necessary for health. Such a program as outlined above if truly taken up by experiment stations could deliver data of the most surprising nature and lead eventually to an entirely different aspect of the problem of health. We have heard much of preventive medicine in recent years. Sir Albert Howard's importance was that he sought to catch the trouble at its very source, namely the soil from which our food comes. Here indeed is the source of health, not merely later when we eat the fruits of the earth. All questions of the preservation of farm products in such a way that the original nutritive level is maintained are involved too.

Were we to follow the organic concept such embarrassing situations as that described to the writer recently by a chemist could not occur. This chemist had analyzed tomatoes and carrots and found not a trace of vitamins. One should grasp what that really means. A doctor tells a patient to eat carrots, tomatoes, or other vegetables and fruits for his health. The patient buys such products – but they are worthless. He believes he has done the right thing and wonders why the diet does not help, finally he blames the poor doctor. However, it is certain that the doctor was at fault, if he did not consider the origin of the products he prescribed. Ignorance of the organic idea excuses him no longer since Sir Albert Howard's organic movement and the sister movement of Rudolf Steiner's biodynamics have paved the way. We must become conscious of all the questions involved, otherwise mankind will "starve" in spite of eating. "Hidden Hunger" has since become a familiar concept but it should be enlarged so as to embrace the organic field as well.

An interesting panorama is revealed to us when we start to study composting processes. Bacteriological processes of different kinds, breakdown processes and up-building, humus forming processes are going on. For thousands of years these composting methods have been instinctively applied by the Chinese, by the natives of India (here Sir Albert made his basic observations). They took place at random, but now they have developed into a science. What goes on can be called by proper names, and what is active can be identified. These processes can now be consciously followed and directed. Composting has become a science, yes, even an art. If man loses out with the soil he can only blame his own ignorance of organic matters. Future research institutions will add all the tests and proofs which Sir Albert Howard needed so much and the absence of which forced him still to be on the defensive, even though he could point to empirical findings.

The soil itself is now considered a living being. It dies when it is abused and mineralized. It is sustained when organic methods are practiced. A new soil science has begun – that of humus as the basic matter. If humus is in the minimum, all other improvements will be costly and in the long run condemned to inefficacy. The law of the minimum has been broadened so that it now embraces not only a purely mineral, dead concept, but a wider, living concept too. It is this enlarged horizon in agriculture which forms one of Howard's most important contributions to science. Sir Albert has thousands of followers in the practical realms of farming and gardening. The day is near when professional scientists will furnish proof of the enlightenment they received from him for research and the betterment of our basic conditions for health. Then his eternal entelechy will live forever in a future more prosperous and healthier mankind.

Notes

Sir Robert McCarrison

Nutrition and Health, by Sir Robert McCarrison – McCarrison's Cantor Lectures, to the Royal Society of Arts in 1936, Faber and Faber, London, 1953. A full outline of McCarrison's groundbreaking work in India with national diets and how closely they were reflected in patterns of health and disease. With photographs. Full text online at the Small Farms Library at: http://journeytoforever.org/farm_library/McC/McCToC.html.

Nutrition in Health and Disease by Sir Robert McCarrison, British Medical Journal – Full text of a speech opening discussion in the Section of Nutrition at the Annual Meeting of the British Medical Association, Oxford, 1936. See text at webpage: http://journeytoforever.org/farm_library/medtest/medtest_mccarrison1.html.

Studies in Deficiency Disease, Introduction, by Sir Robert McCarrison, Oxford Medical Publications, Henry Frowde and Hodder & Stoughton, London, 1921. See text at webpage:http://journeytoforever.org/farm_library/medtest/medtest_mccarrison2.html.

Diseases of Faulty Nutrition by Sir Robert McCarrison, Transactions of the Far Eastern Association of Tropical Medicine, 1927. See text at webpage: http://journeytoforever.org/farm_library/medtest/medtest_mccarrison3.html.

Nutrition & Soil Fertility – Full text of speeches by Sir Robert McCarrison and Sir Albert Howard at a meeting at the Town Hall, Crewe, on March 22, 1939, in support of the Medical Testament of the Local Medical and Panel Committees of the County Palatine of

Chester. From Supplement to “The New English Weekly,” April 6th, 1939. See text at webpage: http://journeytoforever.org/farm_library/medtest/medtest_speeches.html#mccarrison.

Sir Robert McCarrison’s contribution to the *Medical Testament – Nutrition, Soil Fertility, and the National Health*, published by the 31 doctors of the Cheshire Panel Committee in England in 1939. See text at webpage: http://journeytoforever.org/farm_library/medtest/medtest.html#mcc.

McCarrison bibliography – References to the “Medical Testament”. See text at: http://journeytoforever.org/farm_library/medtest/medtest_refs2.html.

Biodynamic Farming and Gardening Association (BDA) Home Page – “Based on a series of lectures given by Austrian philosopher Rudolf Steiner in 1924, Biodynamics is a method of agriculture which seeks to actively work with the health-giving forces of nature. It is the oldest non-chemical agricultural movement, predating the organic agriculture movement by some 20 years and has now spread throughout the world.” Biodynamics is very impressive, in its wholism, its results, and its science. See website: http://www.biodynamics.com/.

REFERENCES

References

1. Theo Paijmans, *Free Energy Pioneer: John Worrell Keely*, IllumiNet Press, Lilburn, GA, USA, 1998.

2. Selawry, Alla, *Ehrenfried Pfeiffer - Pionier Spiritueller Forschung und Praxis, Begegnungen und Briefwechsel – Ein Beitrag zu seiner Biographie*, Philosophisch-Anthroposophischer Verlag Am Goetheanum, Dornach/Switzerland, 1987. English edition *Ehrenfried Pfeiffer: Pioneer of Spiritual Research and Practice*, Translated by Joe Reuter and edited by Gerald Karnow, M.D., Mercury Press, Spring Valley, New York, 1992.

3. Bessenich, Carl et al., *Denkschrift über die Angelegenheiten der Anthroposophischen Gesellschaft in den Jahren 1925 bis 1935* [Memorandum concerning the affairs of the Anthroposophical Society in the years 1925 until 1935], *als Manuskript gedruckt nur fürMitglieder der Anthroposophischen Gesellschaft und diesen vorgelegt von Dr. C. Bessenich et al.* [a manuscript printed only for members of the Anthroposophical Society and offered to them by Dr. C. Bessenich et al.] Dornach, *Schweiz* [Switzerland] 1935, 154p. Reprinted in English as *Memorandum of Some Events in the Anthroposophical Society during the Years 1925-1935* by C. Bessenich et al., translated from the German, Dornach Switzerland. Privately printed, 1935.

4. Steiner, Marie, *Briefe und Dokumente* [Letters and Documents,] *Rudolf Steiner Nachlassverwaltung* [Administration of the Estate of Rudolf Steiner,] Dornach, 1981.

5. Steiner, Dr. Rudolf and Wegman, Dr. Ita, *Grundlegendes für eine Erweiterung der Heilkunst: Nach Geisteswissenschaftlichen Erkenntnissen* [Fundamentals for an Extension of the Art of Healing: Following Spiritual-Scientific Knowledge], G.A. 27, Rudolf Steiner Verlag, Dornach/Schweiz, 5.

Auflage, [Rudolf Steiner Publishing Company, Dornach/Switzerland, fifth edition] 1977; English translation: *Fundamentals of Therapy*: *An Extension of the Art of Healing through Spiritual Knowledge*, authorized translation from the German, Anthroposophical Publishing Co., London, 1925; authorized translation by George Kaufmann, M.A., Anthroposophic Press, New York and Anthroposophical Publishing Co., London, 1938. Translated by George Adams, M.A., Rudolf Steiner Press, London, third edition (revised) 1967; *Fundamentals of Therapy: An Extension of the Art of Healing through Spiritual Knowledge,* Translated by E. A. Frommer and J. M. Josephson, Rudolf Steiner Press, London, fourth edition (new translation) 1983; *Extending Practical Medicine: Fundamental Principles based on the Science of the Spirit*, translated by A. R. Meuss, FIL, MTA, Rudolf Steiner Press, London, 1996; *Fundamentals of Therapy: An Extension of the Art of Healing through Spiritual-Scientific Knowledge*, English and German Text, translation by Christa van Tellingen, M.D., Mercury Press, Spring Valley, New York, 1999.

6. Pfeiffer, Ehrenfried, *On Rudolf Steiner's Mystery Dramas,* four lectures by Ehrenfried Pfeiffer Nov/Dec 1948, Mercury Press, Spring Valley New York, 1988.

7. Steiner, Rudolf, *The Challenge of the Times*, G.A. 186, The Anthroposophic Press, Inc., Spring Valley, New York, 1941. See lecture III, "The Mechanistic, Eugenic and Hygienic Aspects of the Future," December 1, 1918, pp 70-118.

8. *Der Strader-Apparat, Modell – Skizzen – Berichte* [The Strader Apparatus, model -sketches – reports], in *Beiträge zur Rudolf Steiner Gesamtausgabe* [Supplements to the Collected Edition of Rudolf Steiner], Dornach, No. 107, *Michaeli* [Michaelmas] 1991.

9. Clymer, R. Swinburne, "Grail," in *The Great Work: The Council of Three,* Philosophical Publishing Company, Quakertown, Pennsylvania, 1961, p. 121f.

10. Podak, Christoph O.,*"Zur Geschichte und Soziologie der anthroposophischen Forschunginstitute in den 20er Jahren,"* [History and Sociology of the Anthroposophical Research Institutes in the Twenties,] *Der Europäer* [The European,] *Jg. 3* [3rd yr.,] No. 9/10, Juli/August 1999, pp. 30-36. See webpage:
http:/www.perseus.ch/PDF-Dateien/forschunginstitute.pdf.
English translation from the original German by Paul Carline: "Towards a History and Sociology of the Anthroposophical Research Institutes in the 1920s," *Archetype: Newsletter Articles Supplement*, Science Group of the Anthroposophical Society in Great Britain, London, Issue 5, September 1999, pp. 48-60; reprinted in *The Schiller File: Paul Eugen Schiller,* supplement to the *Collected Edition of Rudolf Steiner Beiträge* [contributions] no. 122, "Scientific Research Suggested by Dr. Rudolf Steiner," translated by Henry Goulden. Henry Goulden Books, Delabole Cornwall, 2007, pp. 113-127.
Webpage:http:/www.science.anth.org.uk/history.html.

11. Selawry, Alla and Oleg Selawry, *Die Kupferchlorid-Kristallisation in Naturwissenschaft und Medizin, mit elner Einführung in die kristallographischen Grundlagen von A. Neuhaus* [Copper-Chroride Crystallization in Natural Science and Medicine, with an Introduction into Crystallographic Principles by A. Neuhaus,] Gustav Fischer Verlag, Stuttgart, 1957.

12. Pfeiffer, E. E., *The Spiritual Leadership of Mankind: Notes from Lectures Given in 1947.* Mercury Press, Spring Valley, NY, 1985. See lecture V, "Rudolf Steiner," August 17, 1947, pp. 53-67.

13. Steiner, Rudolf, *The Occult Movement in the Nineteenth Century and its Relation to Modern Culture,* GA 254, ten lectures given in Dornach October 10-25, 1915. Translated by D.S. Osmond. Rudolf Steiner Press, London, first English edition 1973. See Lecture X, October 25, pp. 166-190. Joan M. Thompson, Rudolf Steiner Press, London, 1992. See the Introduction by Rudi Lissau, August, 991, pp.vii-xv. Available at webpage:
http://wn.rsarchive.org/Lectures/KarmUntru2/KarUn2_intro.html.

14. Steiner, Rudolf, *The Karma of Untruthfulness,* vol. 2, GA 174. Twelve lectures given in Dornach from January 1-30, 1917, translated by Johanna Collis, edited by Joan M. Thompson, Rudolf Steiner Press, London, 1992. See the Introduction by Rudi Lissau, August, 1991, pp. vii-xv.
Available at webpage:
http:/wn.rsarchive.org/Lectures/KarmUngtru2/KarUn2_intro./html.

15. Lissau, Rudi, *Ein Vorwort zur englischen Ausgabe von "Das Karma der Unwahrhaftigkeit"* [An Introduction to the English edition of *The Karma of Untruthfulness*] *Was in der Anthroposophischen Gesellschaft vorgeht: Nachrichten für deren Mitglieder* [What is Happening in the Anthroposophical Society: Newssheet for Members], *Nr.* [No.] 11, 15. *März* [March] 1992, p. 57-60. *Allgemeine Anthroposophische Gesellschaft* [General Anthroposophical Society], CH-4143 Dornach, *Schweiz* [Switzerland]), 69. *Jahrgang* [Year,] No. 11, März [March] 1992, pp. 57-60.

16. Steiner, Rudolf, *The Inner Aspect of the Social Question*, G.A. 193, Three lectures given in Zürich, Switzerland February 4, 11 and March 9, 1919. Translated by Charles Davy from shorthand reports unrevised by the lecturer, Anthroposophical Publishing Company, London, first printed 1950;

Rudolf Steiner Press, London, second Impression 1974. See Lecture II, February 11, 1919, pp 23-46. Available at webpage:
http://wn.rsarchive.org/Lectures/19190211p01.html.

17. Pfeiffer, Ehrenfried, "On Threshold Experience," unedited notes of a lecture given at Threefold Farm on 10 September 1961, in *Notes and Lectures, Compendium II*, Mercury Press, Spring Valley, NY, 1991, pp. 92-103.

18. Steiner, Rudolf, *Supersensible Influences in the History of Mankind, With Special Reference to Cult In Ancient Egypt And In Later Times*, G.A. 216, Six lectures given by Rudolf Steiner in Dornach, Switzerland from September 22, 1922, to October 1, 1922, translated by D. S. Osmond from shorthand reports unrevised by the lecturer. Thanks are due to Owen Barfield for his help in the translation of Lecture VI, Rudolf Steiner Publishing Co., London, 1956. See Lecture I September 22, 1922, pp. (1)8-(11). See webpage:
http://wn.rsarchive.org/Lectures/SuperInfluence/19220922p01.html.

19. Goethe, Johann Wolfgang von, *Faust*, a drama by Goethe and Schiller's *Song of the Bell*, translated by Lord Francis Leveson Gower and John Murray, London, 1823. See "Midnight," pp. 28-45. *Faust: A Tragedy*, translated in the original meters by Bayard Taylor with explanatory notes, Frederick Warne & Co., London, c. 1880. See Part I, Scene I, Night (Faust's Monologue,) pp. 17-25. *Faust:, Parts I and II* in Everyman's Library v. 335. Goethe's *Faust, Parts I & II.* Translated with Introduction by Albert G. Latham. J.M. Dent & Sons, Ltd., London; E.P. Dutton & Co., New York. First published in this edition 1908; reprinted 1910, 1912, 1914, 1919; reset 1925; reprinted 1926, 1928, 1930,1935. (See "First Part of the Tragedy: Goethe's *Faust,* translated by John Anster, L.L.D."), The People's Library Cassell & Co.,Ltd.,

London & New York, Toronto & Melbourne MCMIX [1909,] "The Tragedy of Faust, First Part, Scene I: Night (Faust's Monologue,)" pp. 33-44; *Faust* by Goethe, from the German by John Anster, illustrated by Harry Clarke, Harrap Illustrated Classics, Harrap Ltd., London, 1985. *Faust,* with illustrations by Harry Clarke, translated into English in the original meters by Ayard Taylor, Arden Book Co., n.d., "First Part of the Tragedy, Scene I; Night" (Faust's monologue,) pp. 47-56. In pdf format from:
http://www.archive.org/download/faustgoethe00goetiala/faustgoethe00goetiala.pdf;

"*Faust*: The First Part of the Tragedy, translated with an introduction and notes by David Constantine with a preface by A.S. Byatt, Penguin Classics, Penguin Books, Ltd., London, 2005. See "The First Part of the Tragedy: Night," verse 512, pp. 21-29.

20. Nietzsche, Friedrich Wilhelm, *Also Sprach Zarathustra* [Thus Spake Zarathustra], published between 1883-1885 in four parts. See bilingual German-English translation of *Teil* [Part] 1, Kapitel [Chapter] XVIII. "*Von alten und jungen Weiblein"* [Old and Young Women] on webpage at:
http://www.hamilton.net.au/nietzsche/zarathustra/zara028.html.

21. Steiner, Rudolf, "*Neugestaltung des sozialen Organismus"* [New Formation of the Social Organism*], Rudolf Steiner Gesamtausgabe Vorträge, Vorträge über das Soziale Leben und die Dreigliederung des Sozialen Organismus* [Collected Edition of Rudolf Steiner's Lectures, Lectures on the Social Life and the Threefolding of the Social Organism], GA 330/331. Fourteen public lectures held in Stuttgart between April 22 and July 30, 1919,] *Verlag der Rudolf Steiner-Nachlassverwaltung* [Publishing House of the Estate of Rudolf Steiner], *Dornach/Schweiz* [Dornach/Switzerland], *1.*

Auflage Gesamtausgabe Dornach [1st Collected Edition Dornach] 1963. Of these 14 lectures only four have been translated into English, as follows: Lecture II, "Esoteric Introduction to an Exoteric Treatment of the Social Problem," Stuttgart, April 23, 1919, Typescript R58 (II), Rudolf Steiner House Library, London, 32 pages; also published as "Proletarian Demands and How to Put Them Into Practice: A Lecture to the Employees of the Waldorf-Astoria Factory," Stuttgart, April 23, 1919 in *Education as a Force for Social Change*. Translated by Robert F. Lathe and Nancy Parsons Whittaker, *Foundations of Waldorf Education* [IV], Anthroposophic Press, Hudson, NY, 1997, Part II *Backgrounds of Waldorf Education*, pp 105-124 + Notes, pp 223-224; Lecture VIII. "The Impulse Towards the Threefold Order: No Utopia, But the Practical Demand of the Hour," Address given by Dr. Rudolf Steiner at a meeting of the League for the Threefold Social Order, Stuttgart, May 31, 1919 in *The Threefold Order of the Body Social: Addresses and Articles by Dr. Rudolf Steiner,* Study Series I. Translated by E. Bowen-Wedgwood and issued as manuscript for members of the Anthroposophical Society by permission of Mme. Marie Steiner, c1933, Part 2, pp 18-41; Lecture XI. "The Tasks of Schools and the Threefold Social Organism: A Lecture to the Union of Young Teachers," Stuttgart, June 19, 1919 in *Education as a Force for Social Change*. Translated by Robert F. Lathe and Nancy Parsons Whittaker, *Foundations of Waldorf Education* [IV], Anthroposophic Press, Hudson, NY, 1997, Part II, Backgrounds of Waldorf Education, pp 185-218 + Notes, p 232; Lecture XIII, "The Supersensible Being of Man And the Evolution of Mankind: Observations and Results of Spiritual Science," a lecture by Rudolf Steiner given in Stuttgart on July 11, 1919. Translated by Pauline Wehrle and published in *The Anthroposophical Review*, London, Volume 2, No. 3, Autumn 1980, pp 15-25. See also Steiner, Rudolf, *Betriebsräte und Sozialisierung: Diskussionabende mit den Arbeiterausschüssen der großen Betriebe Stuttgarts* [Work Councils and

Socialization: Discussion evenings with the worker committees of the large enterprises of Stuttgart], GA 331, *Einleitende Worte, Diskussionsbeiträge und Schlußworte auf neun Versammlungen in Stuttgart vom 8. Mai bis 23. Juli 1919 und ein dokumentarischer Anhang* [Introductory words, discussion contributions and conclusions on nine meetings in Stuttgart from May 8 to July 23, 1919 and a documentary Appendix], *Rudolf Steiner Verlag* [Rudolf Steiner Publishing House], *Dornach/Schweiz* [Dornach/Switzerland], 1989

22. Steiner, Rudolf, Ph.D.(Vienna), *The Philosophy of Freedom: A Modern Philosophy of Life Developed by Scientific Methods*, G.A. 4, authorized translation by Mr. & Mrs. R. F. Alfred Hoernlé. Authorized translation edited by H. Collison, G. P. Putnam's Sons, London and New York, 1916; *The Philosophy of Spiritual Activity: A Modern Philosophy of Life Developed by Scientific Methods*, being an enlarged and revised edition of *The Philosophy of Freedom,* together with the original thesis on *Truth and Science.* Authorized translation by Professor & Mrs. R. F. Alfred Hoernlé, edited by H. Collison, G. P. Putnam's Sons, London & New York, second edition revised and enlarged, 1922; *The Philosophy of Spiritual Activity [Freedom]: Fundamentals of a Modern World Conception*, fourth edition, based on the original authorized translation by Prof. and Mrs. R. F. Alfred Hoernlé newly revised and amended by Hermann Poppelbaum, Ph.D., The Rudolf Steiner Publishing Co., London, and Anthroposophic Press, New York, fourth edition revised, 1939; sixth edition, based on the original authorized translation by Prof. and Mrs. R. F. Alfred Hoernlé, revised and amended by Hermann Poppelbaum, Ph.D., The Rudolf Steiner Publishing Co., London. Sixth edition, 1949; *The Philosophy of Spiritual Activity: Fundamentals of a Modern View of the World – Results of Introspective Observations According to the Method of Natural Science*, translated from the German by Rita Stebbing, Introduction by Hugo S. Bergman, Ph.D., edited, and with notes

by Paul M. Allen, Rudolf Steiner Publications, Inc., West Nyack, New York, First Edition, 1963. *The Philosophy of Spiritual Activity: Basic Features of a Modern World View: Results of Soul Observation Arrived at by the Scientific Method*, translated by William Lindeman, Anthroposophic Press, 1986. *The Philosophy of Spiritual Activity: A Philosophy of Freedom: The Basic Elements of a Modern World View – Results of Observing the Human Soul According to the Methods of Natural Science.* Revised translation by Rita Stebbing, Rudolf Steiner Press. Revised edition, 1992.

23. Steiner, Rudolf, *The Way of Initiation, or How to Attain Knowledge of the Higher Worlds*, with a foreword by Annie Besant and some biographical notes of the author by Edouard Schuré, G.A. 10, translated by Max Gysi. First impression December 1908; Second impression May 1909, Theosophical Publishing Society, London, 1909; *Initiation and Its Results: A Sequel to "The Way of Initiation".* Authorized translation from the German by Clifford Bax. First edition, November 1909; second and revised edition with a new preface by the author, Theosophical Publishing Society, London, April 1910; *The Way of Initiation, or How to Attain Knowledge of the Higher Worlds*, translated from the German by Max Gysi with some biographical notes of the author by Edouard Schuré. First Americanized edition, Macoy Publishing and Masonic Supply Co., New York, U.S.A., 1910; *Knowledge of the Higher Worlds and Its Attainment: A Revised and Enlarged Edition of "The Way of Initiation" with "Initiation and its Results."* Authorized English translation by G. Metaxa, edited by H. Collison, G. P. Putnam's Sons, London & New York. Revised edition first published August, 1923; *Knowledge of the Higher Worlds and its Attainment.* Authorized English translation by G. Metaxa, edited by Harry Collison M. A. (Oxen), by Health Research, Mokelumne Hill, CA, reprinted 1964; *Knowledge of the Higher Worlds: How Is It Achieved?* Revised translation by D. S. Osmond and C. Davy,

Rudolf Steiner Press, London; Sixth edition revised by D. S. Osmond and C. Davy, 1969, reprinted (paperback) 1973, 1976, 1985, 1989, 1993; *Knowledge of the Higher Worlds: How Is It Achieved?* Translation revised by D. S. Osmond and C. Davy, facsimile of the sixth revised edition of 1969, Rudolf Steiner Press, Forest Row, 2004.

24. Steiner, Rudolf, *An Outline of Occult Science*, G.A. 13. Authorized translation from the fourth edition, Editor Max Gysi, Theosophical Publishing Society, London 1914 and Rand McNally & Company, Chicago, 1914; authorized translation from the fourth edition (Newly Revised), Anthroposophic Press Publishers New York, 1922; *Occult Science – An Outline.* Translated by George and Mary Adams; new translation by George and Mary Adams 1962/1963, Rudolf Steiner Press, London, 1963; Reprinted 1969; reprinted 1979; *An Outline of Esoteric Science: Classics in Anthroposophy.* Translated by Catherine E. Creeger, Anthroposophic Press, Hudson, NY, 1997. Downloadable in pdf format from: http://www.hermetics.org/pdf/steiner/Rudolf_Steiner-An_Outline_of_Occult_Science.pdf.

25. Steiner, Rudolf, *The Spiritual Guidance of Mankind*, G.A. 15, the authorized English translation edited by H. Collison, Anthroposophical Society, London, n.d.; *Spiritual Guidance of Man and Humanity*, Three Lectures by Rudolf Steiner, authorized English translation by Henry B. Monges, Anthroposophic Press, Inc., New York, first edition 1950; *The Spiritual Guidance of Man and Humanity*, authorized English translation edited by Henry B. Monges, Anthroposophic Press, Inc., New York, Second Edition, 1970; *The Spiritual Guidance of Man*, edited by Henry B. Monges, The Anthroposophic Press, Spring Valley, New York, third printing 1976; *The Spiritual Guidance of the Individual and Humanity: Some Results of Spiritual-Scientific Research into Human History and Development,* Translated by Samuel Desch,

Classics in Anthroposophy, Anthroposophic Press, Inc., Hudson, New York, 1992.

26. Pfeiffer, Ehrenfried, *Rudolf Steiner als Schöpfer einer neuen Bühnen-beleuchtungskunst* [Rudolf Steiner as Creator of a New Art of Stage Lighting], *Das Goetheanum: Wochenschrift für Anthroposophie* [The Goetheanum: Weekly Journal for Anthroposophy], Dornach, *19. Jahrgang* [19th Year], Nr. 10, *3 März* [March 3] 1940, pp. 75-76; *Bühnenbeleuchtung zur Eurythmie* [Stage Lighting for Eurythmy], published by Georg Wurmehl, Dornach 1969. Reprinted (in German only) in Rudolf Steiner's *Farbenerkenntnis* [Color Recognition], GA 291a, as *Eurythmie-Beleuchtung* [Eurythmy Lighting], *S.* [pp.] 385-394; "Eurythmy Lighting at the Time of Rudolf Steiner," a talk by Ehrenfried Pfeiffer at the Goetheanum 22 February 1955, typescript copy translated from the German by MHW [Michael Wilson] on January 29, 1979, retyped and slightly clarified by Peter H Reeve June 4, 2008. Typescript held in the Library of Rudolf Steiner House, London.

27. Goethe, Johann Wolfgang von, *Goethe's Reineke Fox, West-Eastern Divan*, and *Achilleid*, translated in the original meters by Alexander Rogers, Bohn's Standard Library, George Bell and Sons, London, 1890, pp 195-339. See VIII. *Zuleika Nâmah*; or, Book of Zuleika., pp 269, 302-303; *Goethe's West-Eastern Divan in Twelve Books*, translated by Edward Dowden, J. M. Dent & Sons Ltd., London and Toronto, *MCMXIV* [1914], pp 97, 142-143. See VIII. *Suleika Nameh* [Book of Zuleika] LI; *West-Östlicher Divan* [West-Eastern Divan,] rendered into English by J. Whaley, Oswald Wolff (Publishers) Ltd., London, 1974. See *Suleika Nameh, Buch Suleika* [Book of Suleika], pp 112, 164-167; "Poems of the West and East: West-Eastern Divan – West-Östlicher Divan", *Germanic Studies in America* No. LXVIII (68), bilingual edition of the complete poems, verse translation by

John Whaley, with an Introduction by Katharina Mommsen, Peter Lang AG, European Academic Publishers, Berne 1998. See *Suleika Nameh, Book of Suleika – Buch Suleika* [Book of Sueika], pp 24, 344-345.

28. Steiner, Rudolf, *Das Schicksalsjahr 1923 in der Geschichte der Anthroposophischen Gesellschaft: Vom Goetheanumbrand zur Weihnachtstagung* [The Fateful Year of 1923 in the History of the Anthroposophical Society: From the Geotheanum Fire to the Christmas Conference,] *Ansprachen – Versammlungen – Dokumente Januar bis Dezember* [Addresses – Meetings – Documents January to December] 1923, GA 259, Rudolf Steiner *Verlag* [Publishing House,] Dornach/*Schweiz* [Switzerland,] *I. Auflage* [1st Edition] *Gesamtausgabe* [Collected Edition,] Donach, 1991.

29. Meyer, Thomas, *Von den okkulten Hintergründen der Zerstörung des ersten Goetheanums und des Vergiftungsanschlages auf Rudolf Steiner: Zwei bisher unveröffentlichte Aufzeichnungen* [The Occult Background to the Destruction of the First Goetheanum and the Poison-Plot on Rudolf Steiner: Two unpublished recordings,] *Der Europäer* [The European], *Jg.* [Year] 1, No. 5, *März* [March] 1997, S. 6f., downloadable in pdf format from:
http://www.perseus.ch/PDF-Dateien/Brandvergiftung.pdf.

30. Steiner, Rudolf, *The Origins of Natural Science,* Nine lectures delivered in Dornach December 24 to 28, 1922 and January 1 to 6, 1923, GA 326. Translated from the German text by Mari St. Goar and edited by Norman Macbeth, with an Introduction by Owen Barfield. Anthroposophic Press, Spring Valley, NY and Rudolf Steiner Press, London, 985. See Lecture VI, January 1, 1923, pp. 72-83 + Notes 52-58, pp. 142-143. See also webpage:

http://wn.rsarchive.org/Lectures/Places/Dornach/19230101p01.html

Note: *The Origins of Natural Science* only contains nine lectures and ends on January 6, 1923. However, there should have been ten lectures in this cycle. The last lecture was given on January 7, 1923, but was published as Lecture III in G.A. 220. Two lectures were given on January 7, 1923; the one in G.A. 220 belongs to *The Origins of Narural Science.* There is an English translation of this lecture entitled *The Widening of Man's Perception.* See tgoescruot trabskatuib Ubdex Bi, Z 89 held in the Library of Rdolf Steiner House, London.

31. Steiner, Rudolf, The *Story of My Life*, G.A. 28, authorized translation edited by H. Collison, With an Afterword by Marie Steiner with autographs and four portraits of Rudolf Steiner. Anthroposophical Publishing Co., London; Anthroposophic Press, New York, 1928; *The Course of My Life*, Revised translation by the authorized translator Olin D. Wannamaker, Anthroposophic Press, New York, 1951*; Rudolf Steiner: An Autobiography*, translated from the German by Rita Stebbing, Edited with a Foreword, Reference Notes and Chronological Outline by Paul M. Allen, Afterword by The Reverend Peter Roth, O.B.E., Rudolf Steiner Publications, Blauvelt, New York. First Edition, 1977; Steinerbooks, Affiliate of Multimedia Publishing Corp., New York, N.Y.; Second Edition, 1980; Steinerbooks, a division of Garber Communications, Inc., Blauvelt, New York, Second Printing, 1991. *Autobiography: Chapters in the Course of my Life: 1861-1907 Rudolf Steiner*. Original translation from the German by Rita Stebbing, Notes and Chronology by Paul M. Allen. Anthroposophic Press, Hudson, NY, 1999.

32. Steiner, Rudolf, *Briefe* [Letters], *Band* [Volume] I 1881-1890, G.A. 38, *Rudolf Steiner Verlag* [Rudolf Steiner Pub-

lishing House], *Dornach/Schweiz* [Dornach/Switzerland], *1. Auflage* [1st edition] *Briefe* [Letters] I: 1881-1891 *mit Vortrag Berlin 3. Februar 1913 und "Credo"* [with lecture Berlin February 3, 1913 and "Credo"] Dornach 1948*; 2. Auflage* [2nd edition] Dornach 1955*; 3., veränderte und erweiterte Auflage* [3rd, revised and enlarged edition] *Briefe* [Letters] I: 1881-1890 *Gesamtausgabe* [Collected Edition] Dornach 1985.

33. Steiner, Rudolf, *Briefe* [Letters], *Band* [Volume] II: 1890-1925, G.A. 39, *Rudolf Steiner Verlag* [Rudolf Steiner Publishing House], *Dornach/Schweiz* [Dornach/Switzerland], *1. Auflage* [1st edition] *Briefe* [Letters] II: 1892-1902 *mit Vortrag Dornach, 27. Oktober 1918* [with lecture Dornach, October 27, 1918] Dornach 1953; *2., veränderte und erweiterte Auflage* [second, revised and enlarged edition] *Briefe* [Letters] II: 1890-1925 *Gesamtausgabe* [Collected Edition] Dornach 1987.

34. Pfeiffer, Ehrenfried E., "New Directions in Agriculture" in *Rudolf Steiner: Recollections by Some of his Pupils,* edited by Arnold Freeman and Charles Waterman, *The Golden Blade*, London, 1958, iv + 188 pages, pp. 118-129. This volume is a translation of *Wir erlebten Rudolf Steiner* [We Experienced Rudolf Steiner.] edited by M. J. Krück von Poturzyn and published by the Verlag Freies Geisesleben, Stuttgart, who retain the copyright.

35. Steiner, Rudolf, *Über Fichtes "Wissenschaftslehre" Fragment eines Manuskriptes* (1879) [On Fichte's "Science of Knowledge" Fragment of a Manuscript (1879)], *Beiträge zur Rudolf Steiner Gesamtausgabe* [Supplements to the Collected Edition of Rudolf Steiner], *Veröffentlichungen aus dem Archiv der Rudolf Steiner-Nachlassverwaltung* [Publications from the Archives of the Adminstration of the Estate of Ru-

dolf Steiner], *Heft* [Issue] Nr. 30 Dornach, *Sommer* [Summer] 1970, *S.* [pp.] 28ff

36. Pfeiffer, Ehrenfried, "A Soliloquy," in *Notes and Lectures, Compendium I*, Mercury Press, Spring Valley, NY, 1991, pp. 1-4.

37. Steiner, Rudolf, *The Etherization of the Blood: The Participation of the Etheric Christ in Human Evolution,* G/A. 130. A lecture given at Basel October 1, 1911, from a shorthand report unrevised by the author. Esoteric Studies VIII, Rudolf Steiner Publishing Co., London and Anthroposophic Press, New York, 1935; revised 1943; translated by M. Cotterell, Rudolf Steiner Publishing Co., London, third edition 1955. *The Etherization of the Blood: The Entry of the Etheric Christ into the Evolution of the Earth* from a lecture given at Basel October 1, 1911. Translated by Arnold Freeman and D. S. Osmond from a shorthand report unrevised by the author. Rudolf Steiner Press, London, fourth edition 1971 (new translation). Reprinted 1980, 1985. See webpage: http://wn.rsarchive.org/Lectures/Places/Basel/19111001p01.html: "The Etherization of the Blood," Basel, October 1, 1911 in *Esoteric Christianity and the Mission of Christian Rosenkeutz: Twenty-three Lectures Given between September 17, 1911 and December 19, 1012*, Rudolf Steiner Press, London, 2000. See Lecture 6, pp.70-92 + Notes 39, p. 319; "The Etherization of the Blood," Basel, October 1, 1911 in *The Reappearance of Christ in the Etheric: Selected Lectures*, Steiner Books, MA, 203, Lecture IX, pp. 122-145. See webpage:
http://wn.rsarchive.org/Religion/ReapChrist/19111001p02.html
or downloadable in pdf format from:
http://www.steinerbooks.org/research/archive/the_etherization_of_the_blood/the_etherization_of_the_blood.pdf.

38. Steiner, Rudolf, Ph.D., *An Occult Physiology*, G.A. 128, eight lectures by Rudolf Steiner, Ph.D., Prague, March 20-28, 1911. Authorized translation edited by H. Collison, printed for members of the School of Spiritual Science, Goetheanum, Class I., H. Collison, London, 1932; Anthroposophic Press, New York, 1932. See Lecture 2, "The Human Duality," March 21, 1911, pp. 13-27, authorized translation from a shorthand report unrevised by the lecturer, Rudolf Steiner Publishing Co., London, revised edition, 1951. See Lecture II, "Human Duality," March 21, 1911, pp 26, 29-48; Rudolf Steiner Press, London, third edition, revised 1983. See Lecture II, "Human Duality," March 21, 1911, pp 27-49, Rudolf Steiner Press, Forest Row, East Sussex, 2005. See also webpage:
http://wn.rsarchive.org/Lectures/19110321p01.html.

39. Steiner, Rudolf, *Spiritual Science and Medicine*, G.A. 312, Rudolf Steiner Publishing Co., London, first published 1948; *Spiritual Science and Medicine*, twenty lectures given in Dornach from March 21-April 9, 1920, translated from shorthand reports unrevised by the lecturer, Rudolf Steiner Press, London, second impression 1975; *Spiritual Science and Medicine*, Steinerbooks (A division of Garber Communications, Inc.), Blauvelt, New York, first American revised edition 1989. See Lecture II, pp 24-36. See also webpage: http://wn.rsarchive.org/Lectures/SpiSciMed/19200322p01.html. *Introducing Anthroposophical Medicine*, March 21-April 9, 1920 lectures, Dornach, Switzerland, translated by Catherine E. Creeger, Introduction by Dr. Steven M. Johnson, *Foundations of Anthroposophical Medicine Volume 1*, Anthroposophic Press, Hudson, NY, 1999. See Lecture 2., March 22, 1920, pp 19-33.

40. Steiner, Rudolf, *From Mammoths to Mediums...Answers to Questions*, G.A. 350, sixteen discussions with workers at

the Goetheanum in Dornach between May 30 and September 22, 1923, Rudolf Steiner Press, London, 2000.

41. Steiner, Rudolf, *Curative Education*: *A Course of Lectures* by Rudolf Steiner given at Dornach, Switzerland, June 25 to July 7, 1924, G.A. 317. Translated by Mary Adams, with a Foreword by Fried Geuter, Vol. I *General Principles*, shorthand report unrevised by the lecturer, all rights reserved, printed for private circulation for the use of students, Clent, Stourbridge, Worcestershire, 1954; Vol. II *Individual Cases*. See the eleventh lecture, July 6, 1924, pp XI/1-XI/13; *Curative Education*, twelve lectures for doctors and curative teachers given in Dornach from June 25 to July 7, 1924. Translated by Mary Adams from shorthand reports, unrevised by the lecturer. First printed in 1972 from an earlier duplicated edition, revised. Rudolf Steiner Press, London, 1972; reprinted 1981; reprinted, with additional material, Rudolf Steiner Press, Bristol, 1993. See the eleventh lecture, July 6, 1924, pp 187-204. See also webpage: http://wn.rsarchive.org/Medicine/19240706p01.html.

42. Steiner, Rudolf, *From the History and Contents of the First Section of the Esoteric School 1904-1914: Letters, Documents, and Lectures*, G.A. 264, Edited by Hella Wiesberger. Translated by John Wood, Anthroposophical Press, Hudson, N.Y., 1998. See Rudolf Steiner's letter to Günther Wagner dated December 24, 1903 in Part I: *An Account of the Founding of the First Section of the Esoteric School and Some of the Material Used 1904-1914, Letters to Esoteric Pupils with Exercises, pp 43, 51-53, 127.*

43. Steiner, Rudolf, *The Effect of Occult Development upon the Bodies and the Self of Man*. First published privately in English, G.A. 145; *The Effect of Occult Development upon the Self and the Sheaths of Man, A Course of Ten Lectures*, The Hague, March 20-29, 1913, Rudolf Steiner Publishing

Co., London, and Anthroposophic Press, New York, second edition, 1945. See Lecture I, pp 7, 15-20; *The Effects of Spiritual Development*, a cycle of ten lectures given at The Hague from March 20-29, 1913, translated by A. H. Parker from shorthand reports unrevised by the lecturer, Rudolf Steiner Press, London, third edition (new translation) 1978. See Lecture One, pp 7, 14-18. See webpage reference:
http://wn.rsarchive.org/sumries.txt;bytes=111338-111939;

The Effects of Esoteric Development, ten lectures at The Hague, March 20-29, 1913 and the address given at the first general meeting of the Anthroposophical Society, Berlin, February 3, 1913. Translation revised by Jann Gates based on the third edition, Anthroposophic Press, Hudson, NY, 1997. See Lecture 1, pp 29, 38-42.

44. Steiner, Rudolf, *Man in the Light of Occultism, Theosophy and Philosophy*, ten lectures given by Rudolf Steiner in Christiania (Oslo), June, 1912. (shorthand report unrevised by the lecturer), Rudolf Steiner Publishing Co., W.C.I; Anthroposophic Press, New York, 1945. See Lecture VI, Christiania, June 8, 1912, pp 100, 115-118; ten lectures given in Christiania (Oslo), June 2-12, 1912, translated from shorthand reports unrevised by the lecturer, Rudolf Steiner Press, London, second English edition 1964. See Lecture VI, Christiania, June 8, 1912, pp 100, 115-118.

45. Steiner, Rudolf, *Agriculture: A Course of Eight Lectures* by Rudolf Steiner, Ph.D., G.A. 327, given at Koberwitz, Silesia, June 7-16, 1924. English translation by George Adams, M.A., translated from shorthand reports unrevised by the lecturer. Preface by Ehrenfried Pfeiffer, M.D.(Hon.), Bio-Dynamic Association, Rudolf Steiner House, London, revised edition 1958; reprinted with minor corrections 1972; *Spiritual Foundations for the Renewal of Agriculture*. A course of lectures held at Koberwitz, Silesia, June 7 to June 16, 1924,

translated from the German by Catherine E. Creeger and Malcolm Gardner. Edited by Malcolm Gardner, Bio-Dynamic Farming and Gardening Association Inc., Kimberton, PA, 1993; *Agriculture Course: The Birth of the Biodynamic Method*. Eight lectures given in Koberwitz, Silesia, between June 7 and 16, 1924. Translated by George Adams, Rudolf Steiner Press, Forest Row, East Sussex, 2004. See also the translation based upon the notes of Lilly Kolisko at webpage: http://www.garudabd.org/Agriccourse/contents.html.

46. Steiner, Rudolf, *From Elephants to Einstein…Answers to Questions*. Ten discussions with workers at the Goetheanum in Dornach between January 7 and February 27, 1924, G.A. 352, English by A. R. Meuss, FIL, MTA, Rudolf Steiner Press, London, 1998. See 9: Discussion of February 23, 1924, Anabolism and Catabolism in the Human Organism. Significance of Secretions, pp 143-163.

47. Steiner, Rudolf, *First Scientific Lecture-Course: Light-Course*, Given at Stuttgart by Rudolf Steiner, Ph.D., Ten Lectures, 23 December 1919 to 3 January 1920, shorthand report unrevised by the lecturer, G.A. 320, authorized translation by George Adams M.A. from the 1925 edition of the original issued by the Natural Science Section of the Goetheanum, Dornach, Switzerland, with a Foreword by Dr. Guenther Wachsmuth, Volume I. Lectures 1-5, English edition issued by the Goethean Science Foundation, Clent near Stourbridge, Worcs., England, on behalf of the College of Teachers, Michael Hall, Forest Row, Sussex, printed for private circulation for the use of students, reprinted for Steiner Schools Fellowship, Michael Hall, Forest Row, East Sussex, England, 1977; ibid, Volume II. Lectures 6-10. Available on-line at:
http://wn.rsarchive.org/Lectures/LightCrse/LitCrs_index.html
; 'Light: First Scientific Lecture-Course (Light-Course)', by Rudolf Steiner, Ph.D., ten lectures given at Stuttgart 23 December 1919 to 3 January 1920, with a Foreword by Dr.

Guenther Wachsmuth, shorthand report unrevised by the lecturer, authorized translation by George Adams, M.A., first published in English in 1977 by the Goethean Science Foundation, Clent, Stourbridge, Worcs., U.K., Reprinted in one volume in 1987 by Steiner Schools Fellowship Publications, Michael Hall, Forest Row, East Sussex, 1987; 'The Light Course. First Course in Natural Science: Light, Color, Sound – Mass, Electricity, Magnetism', ten lectures on physics delivered in Stuttgart, December 23, 1919-January, 1920, Translated with a foreword by Raoul Cansino, Foundations of Waldorf Education [XXII], Anthroposophic Press, Great Barrington, MA, 2001. Downloadable in pdf format from: http://steinerbooks.org/research/archive/light_course/light_course.pdf.

48. Steiner, Rudolf, *Spiritual Science and Medicine*, G.A. 312, Rudolf Steiner Publishing Co., London, first published 1948. See webpage: http://wn.rsarchive.org/Lectures/SpiSciMed/19200324p01.html. *Spiritual Science and Medicine*, twenty lectures given in Dornach from 21 March to 9 April, 1920, translated from shorthand reports unrevised by the lecturer, Rudolf Steiner Press, London, second impression 1975; *Spiritual Science and Medicine*, Steinerbooks (a division of Garber Communications, Inc.), Blauvelt, New York, first American revised edition 1989. See Lecture IV, pp. 131-143; "Introducing Anthroposophical Medicine", March 21-April 9, 1920 lectures, Dornach, Switzerland. Translated by Catherine E. Creeger, Introduction by Dr. Steven M. Johnson, *Foundations of Anthroposophical Medicine Volume 1*, Anthroposophic Press, Hudson, NY, 1999. See Lecture 4, March 24, 1920, pp. 50-65.

49. Edson, James B., "Astronautics and the Future," *Bulletin of the Atomic Scientists: A Magazine of Science and Public*

Affairs, Chicago, IL, v. XIV, no.3, March 1958, pp. 102-105 See webpage:
http://books.google.com/books?id=WAkAAAAAMBAJ&sourcegbs_all_issues_r@cad=2.

50. DuShane, G. (editorial), “The Invisible Word, or No Thresholds Barred,” *Science,* Lancaster, Pa., vol. 126, no. 3276, October 11, 1957, p. 681. See also reply to this article by R. C. Wilcott, “Letters: Invisible Words – Invisible Evidence,” *Science*, Lancaster, Pa., vol. 126, no. 3284, December 6, 1957, p. 1202.

51. Pfeiffer, E. E., *The Chymical Wedding of Christian Rosenkreutz: A Commentary*. Notes of eight lectures given by Dr. E. E. Pfeiffer from January to May, 1947, at the Threefold Farm, Spring Valley, New York. Transcribed by Fred and Alice Heckel, published by Mercury Press, Spring Valley, N.Y., 45 pages; *The Chymical Wedding of Christian Rosenkreutz: A Commentary by E. E. Pfeiffer*. Notes on eight lectures by Ehrenfried Pfeiffer given at Threefold Farm, Spring Valley January - May, 1947, Mercury Press, Spring Valley, New York, slightly revised edition of the earlier edition 1984, 63 pages.

52. Steiner, Rudolf, *The Spiritual Guidance of Mankind*, G.A. 15, the authorized English translation, edited by H. Collison, Anthroposophical Society, London, 1921. See Lecture III., pp. 66-100, or webpage:

http://wn.rsarchive.org/Books/GA015/English/ASGB1921/GA015_c03.html; *Spiritual Guidance of Man and Humanity: Three Lectures by Rudolf Steiner,* authorized English translation by Henry B. Monges, Anthroposophic Press, Inc., New York, first edition 1950. See Lecture III, pp. 51-78; *The Spiritual Guidance of Man and Humanity*, authorized English translation edited by Henry B. Monges, Anthroposophic

Press, Inc., New York, second edition, 1970. See Lecture III, pp. 51-78, or webpage: http://wn.rsarchive.org/Books/GA015/English/AP1970/GA015_c03.html; *The Spiritual Guidance of Man*, edited by Henry B. Monges, The Anthroposophic Press, Spring Valley, New York, third printing 1976.; fourth printing 1983. See Lecture III, pp. 51-78, or webpage: http://wn.rsarchive.org/Books/GA015/English/AP1976/GA015_c03.html; *The Spiritual Guidance of the Individual and Humanity: Some Results of Spiritual-Scientific Research into Human History and Development*. Translated by Samuel Desch, *Classics in Anthroposophy*, Anthroposophic Press, Inc., Hudson, New York, 1991; 1992. See Lecture Three, pp51-76 or webpage: http://wn.rsarchive.org/Books/GA015/English/AP1992/GA015_c03.html.

53. Steiner, Rudolf, *Pastoral Medicine: The Collegial Working of Doctors and Priests*, G.A. 318. Eleven lectures delivered in Dornach in September of 1924. Translated from the German by Gladys Hahn. Anthroposophic Press, Inc., Hudson, New York, 1987.

54. Steiner, Rudolf, *Four Mystery Plays,* G.A. 14. Translated and edited with the author's permission by H. Collison, M.A. Oxon, S.M.K. Gandell, M.A. Oxon and R.T. Gladstone, M.A. *The Portal of Initiation (A Rosicrucian Mystery,) The Soul's Probation.* Vol. I; *The Guardian of the Threshold The Soul's Awakening,* Vol. II, Anthroposophical Publishing Co., London Second Edition, 1925. *The Portal of Initiation: A Rosicrucian Mystery; The Soul's Probation: A Life Tableau in Dramatic Scenes as Sequel to "The Portal of Initiation" through Rudolf Steiner; The Guardian of the Threshold; The Soul's Awakening: Soul Events in Dramatic Scenes by Rudolf Steiner*. Translated by Ruth and Hans Pusch, Steiner Book Centre, Toronto, Canada. First edition in English of this translation 1973; *Four Mystery Dramas,* Steiner Book Cen-

tre, Inc., North Vancouver, Canada, second printing 1978; *The Four Mystery Plays*. Translated from the German with Introduction by Adam Bittleston, Rudolf Steiner Press, London. First published in English in this translation 1982. *Four Mystery Dramas*. Translated by Ruth and Hans Pusch, Rudolf Steiner Press, London, reprint 1997.

55. Steiner, Dr. Rudolf, *The Movement for Religious Renewal: The Christian Community*, G.A. 219. A lecture given in the Goetheanum at Dornach, December 30, 1922, authorized translation by H. Collison, London, n.d. See pp. 3-23. Also in *Man and the World of Stars: The Spiritual Communion of Mankind*. Twelve lectures delivered at Dornach, November-December, 1922. Translation by D. S. Osmond, Anthroposophic Press, Inc., New York, 1963; second printing 1982. See *The Spiritual Communion of Mankind*, Lecture IV. "The Relation of the Movement for Religious Renewal to the Anthroposophical Movement," Dornach, December 30, 1922, pp. 156-171. See also webpage:
http://wn.rsarchive.org/Lectures/RelMov_index.html;

Steiner, Rudolf and Benesch, Friedrich, *Reverse Ritual*: *Spiritual Knowledge Is True Communion* with an Introduction by Christopher Schaefer, Floris Books, Edinburgh, 2001. See Part I: *Spiritual Communion of Humanity,* Five lectures by Rudolf Steiner, Chapter IV: "The Relation of the Movement for Religious Renewal to the Anthroposophical Movement," Dornach, December 30, 1922, pp. 43-58 for R. Steiner's remarks of 30 December 1922, directly before the fire in the Goetheanum.

56. Steiner, Rudolf, *The Apocalypse Of St. John*, Twelve lectures with an introductory lecture given in Nuremberg, June 17-30, 1908, G.A. 104,translation from shorthand reports unrevised by the lecturer. Edition revised 1958 by M. Cotterell, introductory lecture published in English translation for the

first time, Anthroposophical Publishing Company, London, 1958. *The Apocalypse Of St. John*: *Lectures on the Book of Revelation*, a cycle of twelve lectures given at Nuremberg from 17 to 30 June 1908, translated from shorthand reports unrevised by the lecturer, Rudolf Steiner Press, London, fourth edition (further revised by J. Collis), 1977.

57. Steiner, Rudolf, *The Last Address Given by Rudolf Steiner* at Dornach, on Michaelmas Eve, 1924, G.A. 238, Translated by George Adams with a preface by Alfred Heidenreich, translated from a shorthand report unrevised by the lecturer, Rudolf Steiner Press, London, first English edition 1967.

58. Steiner, Rudolf, *Unsere Toten: Ansprachen, Gedenkworte und Meditationssprüche 1912-1924* [Our Dead: Addresses, Commemorations and Meditations 1912-1924], *mit zwei Vorträgen, gehalten in Kassel am 9. und 10. Mai 1914* [with two lectures, held in Kassel on May 9 and 10, 1914]; *Das Hereinragen der geistigen Welt in die physische* [the violent entry of the spiritual world into the physical], G.A. 261, *Verlag der Rudolf Steiner-Nachlassverwaltung* [Publishing House of the Administration of the Estate of Rudolf Steiner], Dornach/Schweiz [Dornach/Switzerland], 1. Auflage in dieser Zusammenstellung, Gesamtausgabe [first edition in this compilation, collected edition] Dornach 1963. See obituary: *Ansprache bei der Kremation von Edith Maryon Basel, 6. Mai 1924* [Address at the Cremation of Edith Maryon, Basel, May 6, 1924], pp. 308-316.

59. Raab, Rex, "*Edith Maryon – Bildhauerin und Mitarbeiterin Rudolf Steiners – Eine Biographie mit zahlreichen Abbildungen und Dokumenten*" [Edith Maryon - Sculptress and Assistant of Rudolf Steiner – A Biography with Numerous Illustrations and Documents], *Pioniere der Anthroposophie Band* [Pioneers of Anthroposophy Volume XI], *Philoso-*

phisch-Anthroposophischer Verlag am Goetheanum [Philosophical-Anthroposophical Publishing House at the Goetheanum], Dornach, Switzerland, 1993.

60. Steiner, Rudolf, *The Story of My Life*, G.A. 28, Authorized translation edited by H. Collison, with an Afterword by Marie Steiner with autographs and four portraits of Rudolf Steiner, Anthroposophical Publishing Co., London; Anthroposophic Press, New York, 1928. See Chapter XXXVI, pp. 325-329 or webpage:
http://wn.rsarchive.org/Books/GA028/TSoML/GA028_c36.html; *The Course of My Life*, Revised translation by the authorized translator Olin D. Wannamaker, Anthroposophic Press, New York, 1951. See Chapter XXXVI, pp. 340-344; *Rudolf Steiner, An Autobiography*, translated from the German by Rita Stebbing, edited with a Foreword, Reference Notes and Chronological Outline by Paul M. Allen, Afterword by The Reverend Peter Roth, O.B.E., Rudolf Steiner Publications, Blauvelt, New York, first edition 1977. See Chapter XXXVI, 1903-1906: Berlin Paris, pp. 389-394; Steinerbooks (affiliate of Multimedia Publishing Corp.) New York, N.Y., second edition 1980; Steinerbooks (A division of Garber Communications, Inc.,), Blauvelt, New York, Second printing 1991; *Autobiography: Chapters in the Course of My Life: 1861-1907 Rudolf Steiner*, Original translation from the German by Rita Stebbing, Notes and Chronology by Paul M. Allen, Anthroposophic Press, Hudson, NY, 1999. See Part Three: "Must I Remain Unable to Speak?" Berlin, 1897-1907, Chapter 68, pp. 289-293.

61. Steiner, Rudolf, *Aus den Inhalten der esoterischen Stunden: Gedächtnisaufzeichnungen von Teilnehmem und Meditationstexte nach Niederschriften Rudolf Steiners* [From the Contents of the Esoteric Lessons: Recollections by the Participants and Texts for Meditation from Notes by Rudolf Steiner], G.A. 266/III, *Band* [Volume] III: 1913 *und* [and]

1914, 1920 – 1923, *Rudolf Steiner Verlag* [Rudolf Steiner Publishing House], *Dornach / Schweiz* [Dornach, Switzerland], *1. Auflage, Gesamtausgabe* [First edition, Collected Edition] Dornach, 1998. Downloadble in pdf format from: http://bdn-steiner.ru/cat/ga/266_3.pdf.

62. Steiner, Rudolf, *Esoteric Lessons for the First Class of the School for Spiritual Science at the Goetheanum*, G.A. 270/II, Anthroposophical Society in Gt. Britian, London, 1994. See part of a mantric phrase from the 16th Class Lesson, pp. 113-129.

63. Steiner, Rudolf, *Karmic Relationships: Esoteric Studies, Vol. IV*, ten lectures given at Dornach, Switzerland, between September 5 and 23, 1924 from shorthand reports unrevised by the lecturer, G.A. 238, translation of lectures II-X by George Adams; of Lecture I by D. S. Osmond and C. Davy, Anthroposophical Publishing Company, London, First published 1957; second edition 1983 (amended in accordance with the revised German edition of 1965), Rudolf Steiner Press, London, 1983; *Karmic Relationships: Esoteric Studies, Vol. IV*, eleven lectures given at Dornach, Switzerland, between September 5 and 24, 1924. Translated by George Adams, D. S. Osmond and C. Davy. Reprinted 1997, with the addition of *The Last Address,* Rudolf Steiner Press, London, 1997.

64. Steiner, Rudolf, *Karmic Relationships: Esoteric Studies*, Vol. VI, nine lectures given in Berne, Zürich, Stuttgart and Arnheim between January 25 and July 20, 1924. Translated from shorthand reports unrevised by the lecturer, G.A. 240, translation and revision of Lectures I to VI by D. S. O. and E. H. G. and of Lectures VII to IX by D. S. O. and M. K., Rudolf Steiner Press, London, first edition 1971.

65. Jurriaanse, Tom, "*Aktualität und heilende Kraft des Grundsteinspruches*" [The Significance and Healing Power of the Foundation Stone Verse], in *Was in der Anthroposophischen Gesellschaft vorgeht: Nachrichten für Mitglieder* [What is Happening in the Anthroposophical Society: News for Members], Dornach, *Schweiz* [Switzerland], *57*. Jahrgang [57th Year] No. 36, September 7, 1980, pp. 147-149. *Schluss folgt* [conclusion follows] and No. 37, September 14, 1980, *Schluss* [conclusion], pp. 151-153.

66. Blavatsky, H.P., *The Seret Doctrine: The Synthesis of Science, Religion and Philosophy,* Volume I: "Cosmogenesis," Volume II: "Anthropogenesis," The Theosophical Publishing House Ltd., published 1888; second edition 1888; third edition 1893; reprinted 1902, 1905, 1908, 1911, 1913, 1918, 1921, 1928; Volume III and Indices published 1897, reprinted 1910, 1913, 1918, 1921, 1928. See Vol. I, Part III, Addenda, Section XVI: "The Zodiac and Its Antiquity," pp. 710-730; *The Secret Doctrine: The Synthesis of Science, Religion and Philosophy,* Vol. 1, "Cosmogenesis" Part 1; vol. 2, "Cosmogenesis" Parts 2 and 3; vol. 3, "Anthropogenesis" Part 1; Vol. 4 & 5, "Anthropogenesis" Parts 2 and 3; Vol. 6, Index and Glossary; fourth (Adyar) edition, Theosophical Publishing House, Adyar, India, 1938. See vol. 2, Part 3, Addenda, Section 16, "The Zodiac And Its Antiquity," pp. 373-392. See also webpage:
http://www.theosociety.org/pasadena/sd/sd1-3-17.htm.

67. Pfeiffer, Ehrenfried, "St. John's Day Lecture." A lecture by Dr. E. Pfeiffer (unrevised) at Threefold Farm, Spring Valley, NY, June 26, 1960, in Ehrenfried Pfeiffer: *Notes and Lectures, Compendium II*, Mercury Press, Spring Valley, NY, 1991, pp. 56-63.

68. Steiner, Rudolf, *Die Erkenntnis des Menschenwesens nach Leib, Seele und Geist: Über frühe Erdzustände* [Knowl-

edge of the Human Being Relating to Body, Soul and Spirit] *Band* [Volume] 1, G.A. 347, *Zehn Vorträge gehalten vor den Arbeitern am Goetheanumbau* [Ten lectures given to the workers at the Goetheanum building] *in Dornach vom 2. August bis 30. September 1922*, [in Dornach from August 2 until September 30, 1922.] Rudolf Steiner Verlag Dornach/Schweiz, *1. Auflage in dieser Zusammenstellung.* Gesamtausgabe [first edition in this form, Collected Edition] Dornach, 1976; *2. Auflage (photomechanischer Nachdruck) Gesamtausgabe* [second edition (photo-mechanical reproduction) Collected Edition] Dornach, 1985. See webpage: http://www.rudolfsteinerweb.com/GA_Detail.php?GA=347.

69. Steiner, Rudolf, *Über Gesundheit und Krankheit: Grundlagen einer geisteswissenschaftlichen Sinneslehre* [Health and Illness: Fundamentals of a Spiritual-Scientific Approach] *Band* [Volume] 2, G.A. 348, *Achtzehn Vorträge gehalten vor den Arbeitern am Goetheanumbau in Dornach vom 19. Oktober 1922 bis 10. Februar 1923* [eighteen lectures given to the workers at the Goetheanum building from October 19, 1922 until February 10, 1923,] Rudolf Steiner Verlag, Dornach /Schweiz, *1. Auflage Gesamtausgabe* [first edition of the Collected Edition,] Dornach, 1959*; 2., neu durchgesehene und mit den Stenogrammen verglichene Auflage, Gesamtausgabe* [second newly revised edition compared with the shorthand notes, Collected Edition] Dornach, 1976.

70. Steiner, Rudolf, *Vom Leben des Menschen und der Erde: Zehn Vorträge* [The Life of Man and the Earth: Ten lectures;] *Über das Wesen des Christentums*: *Vier Vorträge gehalten vor den Arbeitern am Goetheanumbau in Dornach vom 17. Februar bis 9. Mai 1923*, [The Nature of Christianity: Four Lectures Given to the Workers at the Goetheanum Building from February 17 until May 9, 1923,] *Band* [Volume] 3, G.A. 349, *Verlag der Rudolf Steiner-Nachlassverwaltung* [Publishing House of the Administration of the Estate of Rudolf

Steiner] Dornach/Schweiz, *1. Auflage in dieser Zusammenstellung* [first edition in this form] Dornach 1961*; Vom Leben des Menschen und der Erde: Über das Wesen des Christentums: Dreizehn Vorträge gehalten vor den Arbeitern am Goetheanumbau in Dornach* vom 17. Februar bis 9. Mai 1923 [The Life of Man and the Earth: Thirteen Lectures Given to the Workers at the Geotheanum Building from 17 February to 9 May 1923], Rudolf Steiner Verlag, Dornach/Schweiz, 2. neu durchgesehene und mit den Stenogrammen verglichene Auflage, Gesamtausgabe [second edition newly revised and compared with the shorthand notes] Dornach, 1980. See webpage:
http://www.rudolfsteinerweb.com/GA_Detail.php?GA=349.

71. Steiner, Rudolf, *Rhythmen im Kosmos und im Menschenwesen Wie kommt man zum Schauen der geistigen Welt? Vom Wirken des Ätherischen und Astralischen im Menschen und in der Erde. Sieben Vorträge.* [Rhythms in the Cosmos and the Human Being: How Does One Come to Observe in the Spiritual World? The Working of the Etheric and Astral in the Human Being and in the Earth: Seven Lectures;] *Ursprung und Bedeutung der Kulte Ernährungsfragen: Sechzehn Vorträge gehalten vor den Arbeitern am Goetheanumbau vom 30. Mai bis 22. September 1923* [Origin and Meaning of the Food Cults: Sixteen Lectures Given to the Workers at the Goetheanum Building from May 30 to September 22, 1923] *Band* [Volume] 4, G.A. 350, Dornach, *Verlag der Rudolf Steiner-Nachlassverwaltung* [Publishing House of the Administration of the Estate of Rudolf Steiner] Dornach/Schweiz, 1962. See webpage:
http://www.rudolfsteinerweb.com/GA_Detail.php?GA=350.

72. Steiner, Rudolf, *Mensch und Welt: Das Wirken des Geistes in der Natur: Über die Bienen. Band* [Volume] 5, G.A. 351, *Fünfzehn Vorträge gehalten vor den Arbeitern am Goetheanumbau in Dornach vom 8. Oktober bis 22. Dezem-*

ber 1923 [Fifteen Lectures Given to the Workers at the Goetheanum Building in Dornach from October 8 to December 22, 1923,] *Verlag der Rudolf Steiner-Nachlassverwaltung* [Publishing House of the Administration of the Estate of Rudolf Steiner] Dornach/Schweiz, *1. Auflage in dieser Zusammenstellung* [first edition in this form], *Gesamtausgabe* [Collected Edition] Dornach, 1965. See webpage: http://www.rudolfsteinerweb.com/GA_Detail.php?GA=351.

73. Steiner, Rudolf, *Natur und Mensch in geisteswissenschaftlicher Betrachtung* [Nature and Man Seen From a Spiritual-Scientific Point of View] *Band* [Volume] 6, G.A. 352, Zehn Vorträge gehalten vor den Arbeitern am Goetheanumbau in [Ten lectures Dornach vom 7. Januar bis 27. Februar 1924, Verlag der Rudolf Steiner-Nachlassverwaltung [Publishing House of the Administration of the Estate of Rudolf Steiner] Dornach/Schweiz, 1. Auflage [first edition] Dornach 1950 *unter dem Titel* [under the title] *Geisteswissenschaftliche Erkenntnisse über Natur und Mensch* [Spiriitual-Scientific Knowledge About Nature and Man*] 2. Auflage Gesamtausgabe* [Second Collected Edition] Dornach. 1967. See webpage:

http://www.rudolfsteinerweb.com/GA_Detail.php?GA=352.

74. Steiner, Rudolf, *Die Geschichte der Menschheit und die Weltenschauungen der Kulturvölker, Band* [History of Humanity and World Conceptions of Earlier Cultures, Volume] 7,] G.A. 353, *Siebzehn Vorträge gehalten für die Arbeiter am Goetheanumbau in Dornach vom 1. März bis 25. Juni 1924, Verlag der Rudolf Steiner-Nachlassverwaltung Dornach/Schweiz, 1. Auflage in dieser Zusammenstellung, Verlag der Rudolf Steiner Nachlassverwaltung Dornach/Schweiz, 1968; 2. Auflage, neu durchgesehen und mit den Stenogrammen verglichen, Gesamtausgabe, Rudolf Steiner Verlag, Dornach/Schweiz, 1988.* [Seventeen lectures given to the

workers at the Goetheanum building from March 1 to June 25, 1924, Publishing House of the Administration of the Estate of Rudolf Steiner, first edition in this form, Dornach/Switzerland,1968; 2nd newly revised edition, compared with the shorthand notes, Rudolf Steiner Publishing House, Dornach/Switzerland, 1988.] See webpage:
http://www.rudolfsteinerweb.com/GA_Detail.php?GA=353.

75. Steiner, Rudolf, *Die Schöpfung der Welt und des Menschen: Über Welt- und Menschenentstehung und den Gang der Kulturentwickelung der Menschheit, Ernährungs-fragen, Erdenleben und Sternenwirken: Vierzehn Vorträge gehalten vor den Arbeitern am Goetheanumbau in Dornach vom 30. Juni bis 24. September 1924, Verlag der Rudolf Steiner-Nachlassverwaltung, Dornach/Schweiz, 1. Auflage in dieser Zusammenstellung, Gesamtausgabe, Band 8, G.A. 354* [The Creation of the World and Man: On World and Human Origins and the Course of Cultural Development of Mankind. Questions on Nutrition, Earth Life and Cosmic Influences: Fourteen Lectures given to the workers at the Goetheanum building in Dornach from June 30 to September 24, 1924. Publishing House of the Administration of the Estate of Rudolf Steiner, Dornach/Switzerland. first edition in this form, Collected Edition, vol. 8, G.A. 354, Dornach, 1969.] See webpage:
http://www.rudolfsteinerweb.com/GA_Detail.php?GA=354.

76. Pfeiffer, Ehrenfried E., "Sir Albert Howard's Deed for Science," *Organic Gardening Magazine,* Emmaus, PA., vol. 13, No. 8 September, 1948. (Sir Albert Howard Memorial Issue.) See also webpage:
http://journeytoforever.org/farm_library/howard_memorial.html.

Bibliography

1. Pfeiffer, Ehrenfried, *Formative Forces in Crystallization.* A condensed and revised translation of the author's works *Kristalle* [Crystals] and *Studium von Formkräften an Kristallisationen* [Studies of Formative Forces in Crystallizations] with 98 illustrations, Rudolf Steiner Publishing Co., London, & Anthroposophic Press, New York, 1936.

2. Pfeiffer, Ehrenfried, *Sensitive Crystallization Processes: A Demonstration of Formative Forces in the Blood,* with five drawings in the text and 36 plates containing 105 photographic reproductions. Authorized translation from the German text by Henry B. Monges. *Verlag Emil Weises Buchhandlung* [Emil Weises Publisher and Bookstore] (Karl Eynmann), Dresden, 1936. 66p.; *Sensitive Crystallization Processes: A Demonstration of Formative Forces in the Blood,* with four drawings in the text and 26 plates containing 78 photographic reproductions. Authorized translation from the German text by Henry B. Monges 1936, revised by Erika Sabarth and Henry N. Williams, M.D., Anthroposophic Press, Spring Valley, New York, second printing 1975, ii + 59p.

3. Pfeiffer, Ehrenfried, *Chromatography Applied to Quality Testing*. Bio-Dynamic Literature, Wyoming, R.I., 1984. 47p. with 8 foldout pages of 56 full-color chromatograms (soils #1-#12, vitamins & enzymes #13-#24 and grain & flour #1-#32.) See webpages: http://www.biodynamics.com/ catalog/chromatography-applied-to-quality-testing-pfeiffer or http://www.florisbooks.co.uk/books/9780938250210.

4. Pfeiffer, Ehrenfried, *Heart Lectures.* Mercury Press, Spring Valley, NY, 1982. Lecture given on December 17, 1950 may be downloaded from webpage:

http://www.anthroposophia.org/PDF/Heart_Lecture.pdf. See also webpage: http://gurbirsingh.com/Pfeiffer.aspx

5. Goethe, Johann Wolfgang von, *The Fairy Tale of the Green Snake and the Beautiful Lily.* Translated by Thomas Carlyle with an Introduction by Paul Allen. Rudolf Steiner Publications, Blauvelt, NY, 1979; Floris Books, Edinburgh, 1979; Garber Communications, Inc., Blauvelt, NY. Second Printing 1991; *Goethe's Fairy ale of the Green Snake and the Beautiful Lily,* Translated by Donald MacLean, with a commentary by Adam McLean. Magnum Opus Hermetic Sourceworks series #14, Phanes Press, Grand Rapids, MI, 1993; *The Fairy Tale of the Green Snake and the Beautiful Lily,* translated by Thomas Carlyle, illustrated by David Newbatt with an Introduction by Tom Raines, Wynstones Press, Stourbridge, UK, first edition 2006.

6. Goethe, Johann Wolfgang von, "Die Metamorphose der Pflanzen" [The Metmorphosis of Plants] in *Johann Wolfgang Goethe: Selected Poems.* Edited by Christopher Middleton with translations by Michael Hamburger, David Luke, Christopher Middleton, John Frederick Nims and Vernon Walkins, Goethe Edition vol. 1. Suhrkamp/Insel Publishers Inc., Boston, 1983, Part III: "'Klassik' and the Turn of the Century," pp. 154-159 + Notes pp. 291-294; *Goethe: Selected Verse,* with an Introduction and prose translations by David Luke, The Penguin Poets, Penguin Books, Harmondsworth, UK. First published 1965; Reprinted 969, 1972. Part II: The Classical Goethe (1786-1800,) pp. 147-151.

7. Prasâd, Râma: *Nature's Finer Forces: The Science of Breath and the Philosophy of the Tattvas*, Theosophical Publishing Society, London, second and revised edition 1894. Available online at webpage: http://www.hermetics.org/prasad.html); The Society of Metaphysicians Ltd, Hastings, East Sussex, Reprint April 1986. See website: http://www.metaphysicians.org.uk/; Samata Books, Chennai, India, Reprint December 1998. See website: http://www.samatabooks.com/; R A Kessinger Publishing Com-

pany, Whitefish, Montana, U.S.A., Reprint March 1997. See website: http://www.kessingerpub.com; Health Research Books, Pomeroy, WA, Reprint February 2003. See website: http://www.healthresearchbooks.com/; facsimile of third and revised edition 1897 available from Sacred Science Library, Idyllwild, California. See website: http://www.sacredscience.com.

8. Pfeiffer, Dr. Ehrenfried, *Sub-nature and Super-nature in the Physiology of Plant and Man: The True Basis of Nutrition.* Authorized translation by G.F. Karnow, M. D., of the Lecture *Unternatur und Übernatur in der Physiologie der Pflanze und des Menschen: die wahre Grundlage der Ernährung* given in Dornach October 10, 1958, Mercury Press, Spring Valley, NY, 1981.

9. Steiner, Rudolf, "The Chemical Wedding of Christian Rosenkreuz," translation of a three-part essay by Rudolf Steiner, published in *Das Reich* [The Empire], Munich, October, 1917 to April, 1918. Typescript translation Index No. Z 452 held in the Library of Rudolf Steiner House, London. See also the translation, "The Chymical Wedding of Christian Rosenkreutz" by Carlo Pietzner in *A Christian Rosenkreutz Anthology,* Compiled and Edited by Paul M. Allen in collaboration with Carlo Pietzner, Rudolf Steiner Publications, Blauvelt, NY. First Edition 1968, pp. 19-59 + Editorial and Reference Notes p. 635; revised third edition 1981, pp. 19-50 + Editorial and Reference Notes p. 577, Garber Books, 2000.

10. Steiner, Rudolf, *Gedenkworte für Charlotte Ferreri und Edith Maryon* [Memorial Addresses for Charlotte Ferreri and Edith Maryon], Dornach, May 3, 1924, in *Unsere Toten: Ansprachen, Gedenkworte und Meditationssprüche* [Our Dead: Addresses, Commemorations and Meditations] 1912-1924; *mit zwei Vorträgen, gehalten in Kssel am 9. Und 10. Mai 1914* [with two lectures held in Kassel on May 9 and 10, 1914,] *Das Hereinragen der geistigenWelt in die physische* [The Violent Entry of the Spiritual World into the Physical], G.A. 261, *Verlag der Rudolf Steiner Nachlassverwaltung, Dornach/Schweiz, 1. Auflage in dieser*

Zusammenstellung, Gesamtausgabe [Publishing House of the Administration of the Estate of Rudolf Steiner, Dornach/Switzerland, first edition in this form, Collected Edition] 1963, pp. 296-308. Translation by Violet E. Plincke. Typescript Translation Index No. S 33 Held in the Library of Rudolf Steiner House, London, pp. 1-17.

11. Sabarth, Erika, *The Pfeiffer Research Laboratory and Ehrenfried Pfeiffer.* Talk given by Erika Sabarth at a Coworkers' Meeting in 1980. Mercury Press, Spring Valley, NY, 1980. 7-page booklet.

12. Koepf, Herbert H., *Ehrenfried Pfeiffer: Pioneer in Agriculture and Natural Sciences,* with an Introduction by Heinz Grotzke, Bio-Dynamic Farming and Gardening Association, Inc., Kimberton, PS, 1991. See webpage: http://www.biodynamics.com/node/55.

13. Steiner, Rudolf, *What Is Biodynamics? A Way to Heal and Revitalize the Earth,* Seven Lectures with an Introduction by Hugh J. Courtney, edited by Marcia Merryman Means, Steinerbooks, Great Barrington, MA, 2005. See the Introduction: "So That the Earth May Be Healed: An Introduction to Biodynamic Agriculture" for mention of Pfeiffer's parting of the ways with the American Jewish playwright, editor, author and publisher Jerome Irving Rodale (1898-1971,) pp. 1-44.

14. Bird, Christopher and Peter Tompkins, *The Secret Life of Plants*. First published in the U.S.A. by Harper & Row, Inc., in 1973; Allen Lane, London, revised edition 1974; Penguin Books Ltd, Harmondsworth, UK. Paperback edition 1975. See Part 4, "Children of the Soil," pp. 195-260, and Part 5, "The Radiance of Life," pp. 261-319. In December, 1979 there was a documentary film released about *The Secret Life of Plants*. see webpage: http://www.psychobotany.com/projects/SLOP.htm. The entire film is on Google video at:
http://video.google.ca/videoplay?docid=4753736638977368381&q

=%22the+secret+life+of+plants%22&total=32&start=0&num=10 &so=0&type=search&plindex=.

15. Tompkins, Peter and Christopher Bird, *Secrets of the Soil*, Harper & Row, Publishers, New York, First Edtion 1989; Arkana, London, 1992; *Secrets of the Soil: New Solutions For Restoring Our Planet*, Earthpulse Press, Inc., Anchorage, Alaska. Revised First Earthpulse Printing, 1998. See Chapter 1, "Cornucopia," Chapter 2, "Pulse of Life," Chapter 3, "Moonshine," Chapter 4, "Golden Garbage," Chapter 7, "It Can Be Done," and Appendix D, "Steiner and Anthroposophy." See book review, "Secrets of the Soil: A Review Article," by Barbara Saunders-Davies, *Anthroposophy Today,* London, No. 19, Summer 1993, pp. 36-40.

Name Index

Adams, George [formerly Kaufmann, George Adams von] (1894-1963): 5, 240, 256, 257, 258, 262, 264
Ahrens, Lexie (b. 1927): 5, 7, 19, 22, 179, 199, 205
Aisenpreis, Ernst (1884-1949): 65, 76, 97, 99, 100
Aristotle (384 -322 BC): 186,188

Bach, Johann Sebastian (1685-1750): 52, 54
Baravalle, Hermann von (1898-1973): 106
Bauer, Michael (1871-1929): 41
Beethoven, Ludwig van (1770-1827): 52, 54
Bessenich, Frieda (1892-1969): 5
Binder, Theodor (d. 1947): 48, 49, 63, 106
Bockholt (-Kirchner), Margarethe (1894-1973): 185
Bölsche Wilhelm (1861-1939): 42
Bollinger (Electrician): 77
Bosch, Robert (1861-1942): 49, 51, 61

Christ, Jesus : 19, 43, 45, 80, 104, 105, 114, 130, 138, 139, 141, 158, 172, 178, 181, 187-190, 195, 217, 257
Clymer, R. Swinburne (1878-1966): 6 – 9, 193 – 198, 212 - 214, 241

Dunlop, D. N. (1868-1935): 5

Elias: 186, 187
Edson, James B.: 164, 165, 259
Emerson, Ralph Waldo (1803-1882): 197
Emmerich, Katharina von: 173
Englert, Curt (1899-1945): 198, 205

Felkin, Dr. Robert William (1853-1926) (Order of the Golden Dawn) Footnote 118: p. 192
Fichte, Johann Gottlieb (1762-1814): 42, 101, 114, 115
Fichter, Karl Friedrich (1869-1954): 88
Finckh, Helene (1883-1960): 222

Geyer, Christian (1862-1929): 44, 45, 48
Goethe, J. W. von (1749-1832): 34, 54, 56, 63, 64, 69, 70, 73, 81, 91, 101, 102, 133, 136, 194, 243, 249, 272
Groot, Georg (1899-1967): 113
Grunelius, Andreas von (1900-1987): 100

Haeckel, Ernst (1832-1919): 42, 101
Hamerling, Robert (1830-1889): 101
Hatshepsut (d. 1468 B.C.): 199
Hegel, Georg Wilhelm Friedrich (1770-1831): 42, 101
Herwarth, Lisa von (1914-): 4, 5, 6, 13, 18, 201
Hübbe-Schleiden, Wilhelm (1846-1916): 101
Howard, Sir Albert (1873-1947): 227ff., 270.

John the Baptist: 187, 188
John the Evangelist: 10, 179, 182, 187, 189, 190, 199

Keely, John Worrell (1837-1898): 2, 3, 5
Keyserlingk, Carl Graf von (1869-1929): 145
Kolisko, Eugen (1893-1939): 198

Lehrs, Ernst (1894-1979): 5, 107, 199, 205- 207
Leinhas, Emil (1878-1967): 106, 121
Lerchenfeld, Count Otto (1868-1938): 106, 196
Liebig, Justus von (1803-18730): 230
Lincoln, Abraham (1809-1865): 197
Linné, Carl (1707-1778): 40
Lymington, Lord [a.k.a Gerard Vernon Wallop 9th Earl of Portsmouth] (1898-1984): 231-232

Manes, also Mani (c. 210-c. 276): 193, 199
Maryon, Edith (1872-1924): 6, 94, 95, 99, 100, 101, 191, 192, 267, 276
McCarrison, Sir Robert (1878-1960): 231, 235, 236
Michelangelo Buonarotti (1475-1564): 84
Mitscher, Käthe (1892-1940): 80
Molay, Jacques de (c. 1244-1314): 80

Morgenstern, Christian (1871-1914): 60
Morse, Samuel Finley Breese (1791-1872): 48
Moses: 186, 197, 199

Nietzsche, Friedrich Wilhelm (1844-1900): 47, 244
Northbourne, Lord [a.k.a Walter Ernest Christopher James, 4th Baron Northbourne] (1896-1982):231

Oken, Lorenz (1779-1851): 101
Ormiston (-Briggs), Gwenda (1906-1997): 5, 11, 12, 18, 19, 20

Paijmans, Theo: 2, 239
Palm, Willi: 32, 42
Pfeiffer, Adelheid (1910-): 11
Pfeiffer (-Walter, Elsa, mother): 34, 36, 37, 38, 41, 42, 43, 48, 58, 59, 60, 61, 63, 66, 106
Pfeiffer [father): 35, 36, 48, 87
Piper, Kurt (1875-1952): 106
Plato (427-347 BC): 64, 186, 188
Poesnecker, G. E.: 9
Polzer-Hoditz, Ludwig (1869-1945): 5
Pracht, Edmund (1872-1938): 113
Prasâd, Râma Kasyapa, Pandit: 110, 272
Pyle, William Scott (1888-1938): 106

Ranzenberger, Hermann (1891-1967): 96
Riese, Erika (1893-1959): 5, 117, 118
Rittelmeyer, Friedrich (1872-1938): 43, 45, 48, 113
Roeschl (-Lehrs), Maria (1890-1969): 5, 106, 185, 199, 200, 205,207
Rosenkreutz, Christian: 8, 107, 109, 179, 189, 259, 273

Sabarth, Erika (1897-1991): 5, 116, 117, 271, 274
Scharff, Paul W. (b. 1930): 5, 7, 14,189, 211, 217, 219
Schelling, Joseph Friedrich Wilhelm (1757-1856):101
Schiller, Paul Eugen (1900-1992): 13, 241, 243
Schleutermann, Max: 92

Schmidt, Gerhard (1909-2003): 161
Selawry, Alla (1913-1992): 3, 5, 13, 239, 241
Seton, Ernest Thompson (1860-1946): 42
Steffen, Albert (1884-1963): 106, 108,110, 113
Stein, Walter Johannes (1891-1957): 5, 198, 212, 226
Steiner (-von Sivers), Marie (1867-1948): 4, 5, 75, 78, 79, 82, 83, 95, 106, 108, 113, 192, 197, 239, 251
Steinwand, Fercher von (1828-1902): 101
Stokowski, Leopold (1882-1977): 53
Stolle, Emma (1888-1956): 76
Stoß,Veit (c. 1438-1533): 44
Stracke, Viktor (1903-1952): 77

Toscanini, Arturo (1867-1957): 32, 52
Turgenieff, Assja (1890-1966):77

Unger, Carl (1878-1929): 59

Vacano, Harriet von (1862-1943):106
Vinci, Leonardo da (1452-1519): 84
Vreede, Elisabeth (1879-1943): 5, 108, 209, 210

Wachsmuth, Guenther (1893-1963): 2, 5, 100, 108, 110, 113, 118, 192, 257, 258
Wachsmuth, Wolfgang (1891-1954): 100, 106, 110
Wagner, Richard (1813-1883): 201
Walter, Babette [grandmother]: 30, 38, 41
Walter, Berta [aunt]: 30, 38, 41, 48
Walter, Emil [grandfather]: 39, 40, 41, 43, 47, 49, 53, 87
Washington, George (1732-1799): 197
Wegman, Ita Maria (1876-1943): 5, 6, 80, 100, 106, 108, 112, 113, 121, 185, 192, 197, 210, 217, 218, 239
Wirth [school teacher]: 47

Zbinden, Werner (1899-1977): 198
Zeylmans van Emmichoven, Johannes Emanuel (1926-2008): 2, 3, 222

"...I was one of the three to whom Rudolf Steiner gave the first agricultural indications in 1921. I felt obligated not only to accept them at face value, but also to investigate and to advance them further, without ever standing still. I wanted to remain open-minded and to substantiate these indications scientifically. This is what my conscience has been telling me to do, because I cannot hold any dogmatic views, but have to examine my findings critically.

It is the same with esoteric questions. I have followed the path of cognition for thirty years and can claim to have reached a few spiritual insights. I do not believe in speculation, only in clear understanding out of the consciousness soul. The laws of the spirit realm are as definite as those of nature. This is what we all have to understand. ..."

(extract from an undated letter
to Dr. Hans Heinze (1899-1997), engineer, farmer and journalist)